# THE
# COMPLETE
# BOOK
# OF MEXICAN
# COOKING

# ELISABETH LAMBERT ORTIZ

BALLANTINE BOOKS ● NEW YORK

Library of Congress Catalog Card Number: 67-18534

ISBN 0-345-32559-1

This edition published by arrangement with M. Evans and Company, Inc.

Printed in Canada

First Ballantine Books Edition: December 1985

# THE COMPLETE BOOK OF MEXICAN COOKING

# CONTENTS

# FOREWORD

The Mexican kitchen is an exciting one, but it is not easy to discover, even at firsthand. For the most part, the *señoras* I met socially didn't cook, and cooks don't write down their recipes. There is not a large literature available; and when I first went to Mexico soon after my marriage, my own situation was further complicated by my not knowing any Spanish. My husband, César Ortiz-Tinoco, who is Mexican, had been transferred from United Nations Headquarters in New York to the United Nations Information Center in Mexico City, and it was there that I began the voyage of discovery that ended with this book.

A decade ago Mexican women, not as liberated as they are now, were more dependent on servants; and no one took my attempts to learn the local cuisine seriously. The fact that I cooked at all was frowned on, until my cook-*cum*-maid reported to my mother-in-law that I was, after all, a respectable *ama de casa* (Spanish-elegant for housewife). She said I couldn't really cook; I only pretended to be able to; that I looked everything up in a book, and what real cook would do that?

My reputation as a non-cook restored, I took to the marketplace, where the selling women put up with my beginning Spanish and explained to me how to make some of the good things I had eaten in other people's houses and in restaurants.

1

It was a simple proceeding. I would look around for someone whose stall had some of the ingredients of the recipe I was after, choosing an older woman if possible, on the ground that she was probably an experienced cook. We would begin with the woman seated at her stall—usually in a long, full-skirted dress with a white apron, around her shoulders the inevitable *rebozo*, and nearly always with her hair in braids—selecting the ingredients from the neat little piles of chiles and herbs and tomatoes and onions and garlic in the order in which they were to be cooked. I'd be sent off to buy tortillas from the tortilla-sellers, avocadoes from the avocado woman, eggs from one of the little grocery stalls, or whatever else my stall didn't carry, for the market women in Mexico all specialize, as they have from time immemorial.

Then the cooking lesson would begin with an amused but pleased stall-owner achieving a miraculous kind of pidgin Spanish so that I would understand what she was talking about, while other market people, men and women, would call out from time to time, "*Qué va a llevar, marchanta?*" (What are you going to buy, customer?), as a way of drawing attention to their own stalls without impoliteness. I would understand from my teacher that I was to chop this and this and this, and fry them together; then add this and this and this, and simmer the lot; meanwhile grinding this to be added later; and so on. I would write down skimpy notes identifying the strange herbs and chiles as well as the new cooking method, and, for a modest number of *pesos*, carry off the dish to be cooked in my brightly striped shopping basket.

The system worked very well; and I made *Quesadillas de Flor de Calabaza* (tortillas stuffed with squash blossoms) right, to everyone's surprise, the very first time. My Spanish became rapid, fluent and grammatically a terror; and in no time at all I knew more about Mexican herbs, spices, fruits, and vegetables than did anyone but a market woman (or another such expert).

It didn't do me much good, however, as I got few chances to cook for more than my husband and myself. My fault, really. I stubbornly refused to adopt the Mexican custom of eating the main meal at midday, because this to me meant going back to the nursery and the ignominious years of childhood when my elder sister had been promoted to dinner at night and I hadn't. And my husband's family and friends were equally stubborn in refusing to give up their time-honored meal hours to please me. I did give a dinner party (at night) for some visiting American friends soon after my arrival, asking my mother-in-law to join us. On sitting down at the table she called my maid and said, *"Francisca, tráigame un pedazo de pan y un vaso de leche, nada más"* (Bring me a piece of bread and a glass of milk, nothing more), and then, pointing dramatically at the casserole I was bringing in, announced to my guests, "Don't eat that; it will make you sick." There is a profound superstition that eating at night in the high altitude is dangerous. Ah well, later on one compromised a little.

On our holidays I travelled all over the Republic eating, and making notes, and collecting recipes and strange, small, inaccurate cookbooks, in between visits to ruins, churches, museums, and markets. I found that Mexican food was even more varied and interesting than I had first believed, and that it was even harder to get good recipes than I had thought possible. I found, too, that the food wasn't necessarily coarse and fiery. Only the very, very poor put some taste in their tortillas by making them into pepper sandwiches with raw *serrano* chiles, seeds and all, for added fire.

Through my husband I discovered Spanish writers of the very early period of the Conquest, Bernal Díaz del Castillo, a captain with Hernán Cortes, and Father Bernardino de Sahagún, a Spanish priest who arrived in 1529 before the Conquest was consolidated. I wanted to know what *they* had to say about the food of the country. I tried to find descriptions of the marketplace, the kitchen, and the banquet hall, so that my husband could help me translate and fully understand them. He insisted, however, on going into the deeper matter of the books. It wasn't a lack of interest in food on his part. It was because he wanted me to have as full an understanding of pre-Columbian Mexico as possible, since the Mexican kitchen of today rests very solidly on its Aztec and Mayan foundations.

It amused me to find that I could actually cook from the descriptions of Father Sahagún. He tells about *Pipián de Camarones*, a sort of shrimp fricassee, with such fidelity that I have been able to include an interpretation of it in this book.

I became more and more determined to get to know the Mexican kitchen completely. Then, after four years, we were transferred to Bangkok, Thailand, where my husband was Chief of Information Services for the United Nations Economic Commission for Asia and the Far East (ECAFE). In spite of working as a foreign correspondent and as an editor on the Bangkok

*World*, the city's English-language morning newspaper, I found I had time, as well as opportunity, to cook Mexican style. Thai Government officials, members of the diplomatic corps as well as friends and colleagues, became wonderfully appreciative dinner guests.

Spain and Portugal were important presences in the Far East at about the same time as Christopher Columbus was discovering America, and as a result there was an enormous exchange of foods between Asia and Latin America, especially Mexico, in the early years after the Conquest. It meant that I could buy cornhusks for tamales in a Thai market because, though the Thai people don't make tamales, they do grow corn. And it sharpened my wits about Mexican food: knowing food origins, I could see what was indigenous in the cuisine and what was colonial. A later trip to Spain and Portugal rounded out my experience.

The stove in my Bangkok kitchen was a large tiled affair which burned charcoal and, though not so beautifully decorated, was exactly the same as the tiled stoves of the kitchens of colonial Mexico (only recently supplanted by modern gas and electric stoves). Since everyone in Bangkok eats at night, and because I had brought some essential Mexican foods as well as earthenware *cazuelas* (casseroles) with me, I was able to do a whole lot of Mexican cooking. I had the happy bonus of willing Thai helpers to do chores like onion-chopping and chile-grinding and operating the charcoal stove, which one does mostly by fanning and then stopping. Hot work in the tropics.

On subsequent visits to Mexico, sometimes quite long ones because of conferences my husband had to cover, I continued to collect material and to cook until I felt I knew enough to settle down to cooking all the recipes in this book. We were by then back in New York, and I found I could get everything I needed by shopping around a bit. But one thing bothered me. How to test a whole cookbook without wasting food? I did it by means of a list of willing victims who came to dinner, who accepted jars and pots of this and that, and who would sometimes even let me bring them dinner in a basket, the basket to be recovered later. I would like to put on record my gratitude to the New York friends who ate with me through eighteen months and approximately 340 recipes without losing their nerve.

These recipes are authentic. They are not adapted, as I feel that substituting for the original ingredients, except in rare instances, is to falsify the dish. I have left out those recipes requiring the few ingredients that aren't available; for instance, *pulque*, a fermented drink made from the agave (century plant). And I have taken advantage of the kind of modernization that makes cooking the traditional Mexican dishes a practical possibility in the servantless world of today. One can now do in minutes what used to take hours, and do it just as well.

I don't cook on a charcoal stove in New York and I don't grind my chiles in a *molcajete* (an Aztec mortar) while squatting on my heels. I use an electric blender as I was taught by a Mexican maid who was so modern she kept banker's hours, ten to four. She was disgusted with my cooking equipment. The well-turned-out kitchen has two blenders, she told me at a time when I had none. I am still not a two-blender woman, but perhaps the day will come when I measure up to Maria's exacting standards. Too, I make my tortillas with any one of the good brands of prepared tortilla flour, called *masa harina* (literally "dough flour"), which are available. And I use a tortilla press, which generations of women in Mexico have used even though the real expert can pat a tortilla paper thin by hand.

I would like to thank Mexican cooking authorities, such as Señora Josefina Velazquez de León, who has done great work in collecting traditional recipes which might otherwise have been lost, as well as in running a cookery school for both *señoras* and their maids; and Señora María A. de Carbia and Señora Esperanza Ramírez, who have also rescued some fine dishes from possible oblivion. I have found them, with others, helpful more than once in clarifying points for me.

I owe a debt of gratitude to José Wilson, longtime friend and colleague, who originally suggested I write this book. She was the most valiant of all the victims on my dinner list and her encouragement and enthusiasm never flagged. I would like to thank Nika Hazelton and the late Helen McCully for their most generous help and advice. And my special thanks to Herbert M. Katz, my editor-in-chief, for believing there was interest in authentic Mexican cooking, and in this book, and to James Beard, who has been such a good friend to me.

My husband, of course, has been invaluable. He doesn't cook, but he does have a very critical palate and he always knows whether a dish has the authentic flavor or not, as his knowledge of the Mexican kitchen is wide.

And finally I want to thank my mother-in-law and her cook

Catalina, as well as my own maid Enriqueta, who answered questions *ad nauseam*, dried herbs for me, and, above all, praised my cooking!

I have had a lot of fun doing this book and I hope anyone who uses these recipes will too.

*Elisabeth Lambert Ortiz*

# INTRODUCTION
# TO
# MEXICAN FOOD

The present-day Mexican kitchen in all its rich variety arose from a unique collision of cooking worlds—Aztec, Spanish, and, to a lesser extent, French. To the Spanish conquistadores the native cuisine of the Aztecs came as a delight and an astonishment. Bernal Días del Castillo, who accompanied Cortés, noted in his writing foods then unknown outside the Americas: chocolate, vanilla, corn, chiles, peanuts, tomatoes, avocadoes, squash, beans, both dried and green, sweet potatoes, pineapple, and papaya. To this list Spain added oil and wine, cinnamon and cloves, rice and wheat, peaches and apricots, and the cattle that provided beef, milk, and butter—all culinary contributions from Europe, Asia, and the Arab countries, since Spain was only just free of centuries of Arab domination. Later, during the brief reign of Maximilian and Carlotta (1864–67), sophisticated dishes of French, Austrian, and Italian origin were introduced.

Corn, chiles, tomatoes, and beans formed the basis of the indigenous kitchen and are still most important today. Corn was venerated by Aztecs and Mayas, and the deities of corn were part of their pre-Christian pantheon. When Fr. Sahagún, a Spanish priest who wrote about Mexico at the time of the Conquest, went wandering around the main market in Tenochtitlán, the ancient Aztec capital (now the site of modern Mexico

City), he described foods that can be found there today—
tortillas, *tamallis* (now spelled "tamales"), tacos, and *quesa-dillas*—very little changed in the intervening centuries except
for the addition of some introduced foods, such as chicken,
from Spain, which is used along with the native turkey for
fillings.

The corn dishes have all been grouped together under the
heading of "The Corn Kitchen," instead of being split up as
appetizers or luncheon or supper dishes, as they seem to make
better sense this way. The cooking technique involved, though
not hard to master, is the important thing. It differs quite a lot
from our own. Therefore it is explained for the reader in considerable detail, with the special hope that no one who loves
to cook will be frightened off by the unfamiliar.

If corn is vital to the Mexican kitchen, the chiles are no less
so; yet there is more misunderstanding about them than about
any other aspect of the cuisine. This misunderstanding began
when Columbus first encountered the fiery varieties in His-
paniola (now Santo Domingo–Haiti) and called them "peppers," thinking they were related to pepper (order Piperaceae,
genus *Piper*, of Oriental origin), which they aren't at all. Chiles,
botanically speaking, are capsicums, a genus of the order So-
lanaceae. There are an estimated sixty-one classified varieties
in Mexico alone, and they come sweet, pungent, and hot. Many
of the chiles used in India, Southeast Asia, and the Pacific
Islands today are of Mexican origin, though chiles are not
exclusively Mexican. Other species are native to tropical America and Asia.

Fortunately no cook needs all sixty-one varieties: nine will
do nicely and one can manage with fewer.

Those used most frequently in Mexican cooking are in two
groups: the red, used dried, and the green, used fresh. The ripe
red bell pepper and the sweet, heart-shaped red pimiento are
the exceptions. These are always used fresh, never dried. The
pimiento, which requires a hot climate, is not grown commercially in this country; it comes mainly from the Caribbean.
Because it is extremely perishable it is sold canned or in glass
jars.

Unfortunately, the names of these chiles vary from place to
place. In California a long, thin, black chile, probably a kind
of *pasilla*, is called *chili negro;* and there is a tendency to
confuse chile *ancho* with *mulato* and call it *pasilla*. New Mexico produces a very hot, large dried red chile marketed simply

as "New Mexico chili pods." In any event you can't trust chiles. They cross-fertilize by themselves so that there are a great many very slight variations within each species. Sometimes mild chiles will come up hot, and even the innocent bell pepper has been known to conceal a bite in its seeds and veins. Don't be discouraged. None of this is quite as confusing as it sounds. If the man in the shop tells you that a large, mild chile is not called *ancho* but something else, don't argue: take it. It could be that you are meeting a slight variation of the *ancho*—in fact it may be one of the sixty-one varieties without which you can manage very well. Quite often stores will sell a mixture of dried red chiles, calling them all *ancho*, or perhaps *pasilla*, and you will find when you get home that they are really a mixture of *ancho* and *mulato*. As they say in Mexico, "*no le hace*," don't worry—use them as they come.

You may even find an odd *guajillo* in the bag. This chile is long and narrow (four to five inches), smooth, and a light red in color. Don't throw it away. It is mild and gives a fine color to *pozole* and *mole de olla*. Simply remove the stem and seeds before adding it to the pot. *whah hē yah*

## THE DRIED RED CHILES

*Ancho*, the most used of the dried red chiles, is quite large (two to three inches long), broad, full flavored, and mild.

The *mulato* is darker in color, closer to brown than red, longer and more tapering than the *ancho*, and pungent in flavor.

The *pasilla* is long (seven inches or so), thin and very dark, less rich in flavor than either *ancho* or *mulato*, more pungent— "*picante*."

*Chipotle*, smaller than *mulato* and almost brick red, is available pickled as well as fresh. It has a very distinctive flavor and is extremely hot. (*jalepeno dried*)

*Morita*, smaller and darker than *chipotle*, but with an almost identical taste, is also available canned. It, with *chipotle*, is best used in this form, as the sublety of the flavor is enhanced by the pickling process.

All these chiles are wrinkled.

The tiny red chile *pequín*, sometimes called *tepín*, is hot, as is the rather larger, round *cascabel*.

# HOW TO PREPARE DRIED RED CHILES

The method is identical for dried *ancho, pasilla, mulato, chipotle* and *morita*. Canned *chipotle* and *morita* do not call for any preparation. The small dried red chiles are simply crumbled between the fingers.

Wash the chiles in cold water; remove veins, stems, and seeds; tear them roughly into pieces; place in a bowl and soak them in hot water, about one cup to six chiles, for about an hour. They are then ready to be pureed in the electric blender with other ingredients called for in the recipe. Always add the water in which they have been soaked. Don't try to blend too much at a time, or, from overlong blending, the mixture will lack character. If you do the pureeing in a food mill, always use the coarse disk and add the water in which the chiles have been soaked to the other ingredients in the casserole or saucepan. This is a lot easier than the old method, which was to grind the chiles in the *molcajete* with the *tejolote* (the large black-stone mortar and pestle of the Aztecs), a back-breaking job.

*cheh pō Hay*

# THE POWDERED CHILES

In some markets in the Southwest it is possible to buy chile *ancho*, chile *mulato*, and chile *pasilla* separately, in powdered form, without any added spices or herbs, as one buys Hungarian paprika. Chile in this form is popular in Mexico, where innumerable kinds are sold in the market, already ground. There is no discernible loss of flavor. The chile powder can be added to the other ingredients, moistened with a little stock.

*How to use powdered chiles*: One tablespoon is the equivalent of one prepared dried *ancho, mulato,* or *pasilla* chile. If, for example, a recipe calls for six *ancho* chiles, use six tablespoons of *ancho* powder. Cayenne pepper can be used instead of the small, dried, hot, red peppers, *pequín* or *tepín*, or *cascabel*. A hot red chile powder is sometimes marketed as Spanish paprika. One-eighth teaspoon of cayenne or Spanish paprika is about the equivalent of one chile *pequín*. Powdered *ancho, mulato,* or *pasilla* are very different from the chile powder, with added spices and herbs, which is commercially available. I would not recommend using the latter as a substitute for the powdered chiles.

Dried or powdered chiles keep well in a plastic bag in the refrigerator. Dried chiles lose their flavor and become too dry and brittle if they are kept where the air can get to them.

## THE GREEN CHILES

The green chiles, usually hotter than the red, are available fresh or pickled (*en escabeche*) in cans. They are also available canned in a variety of sauces, but these should not be used in cooking as they will alter the flavor of the finished dish.

*Serrano*, a small (one-and-one-half-inch long), tapering green chile, usually only available canned, but sometimes found fresh, is hot.

The larger *jalapeño*, available canned and, most of the time, fresh in California and the Southwest, is also hot; though there is a deseeded, pickled version labelled "Mild *Jalapeño*" that retains the flavor and eliminates most of the fire.

The long, thin, pale yellowish-green *largo* is available canned and is extremely hot, but has a most delicate flavor.

The small, lantern-shaped *habanero* chile of Yucatán is sold both fresh and bottled in its green, yellow, and red forms. *the hottest*

The dark green *poblano*, about the size of a bell pepper, available canned and fresh in California and the Southwest, has a very distinctive and pleasing flavor; though usually mild, it can sometimes be hot. To take the heat out of *poblanos*, or any fresh green chile, prepare as usual by removing the seeds, stem, and veins; then soak in cold, salted water or water with vinegar (about one tablespoon to two cups) for an hour, or longer if the chile is specially *picante*.

Bell peppers can be substituted for *poblano* chiles, although there is no use in pretending they are half as good. *Poblanos* and bell peppers should always be prepared as directed in *Chiles Rellenos* (Stuffed Peppers), page 214.

To prepare *serranos* and *jalapeños*, simply remove the seeds if you want a milder flavor and, if they are canned, rinse in cold water, since most of the heat is in the liquid. Canned chiles, once opened, will keep refrigerated, in a separate container with the liquid or sauce from the can, almost indefinitely.

*pasilla*
*jalapeños*
*guadjollo*

*Pronunce pasee ah
Hall a pane yo
whan hé yah*

## THE SWEET GREEN CHILES

There are two sweet green chiles, available fresh, both of which can be used in place of the hot green chiles when a milder version of a dish is preferred.

Chile *güero*, very pale yellowish green, medium size and tapering, is known as California green pepper or simply as sweet green pepper. The *güero* is sold canned from California.

The *valenciano*, a close relative, slightly deeper green and larger, is also known as sweet green pepper. It is found frequently in supermarkets. In fact, in all kinds of markets.

To prepare *güeros* and *valencianos*, remove the stems and seeds, and chop.

## HOT PEPPERS

Many markets carry fresh red or green chiles that are simply known as hot peppers. They vary in size from one to three inches, and can be used in place of chile *serrano*, to which they are closely related. They closely resemble the Mexican *chile de árbol*. As these peppers are sometimes very hot indeed, it is wise to remove the seeds unless you want a combination of flavor and fire.

These chiles can be found in Spanish, Mexican, and Puerto Rican grocery stores, packaged or loose, and in specialty shops loose as well as canned. The latter are often in a variety of sauces, which can add an extra flavor if the chiles are served on the side.

*Caution*

Always wash your hands with soap and warm water after handling chiles. Hot chile rubbed into the eyes can be devastatingly painful.

## THE MOLES

Chiles are an essential ingredient in the *mollis* that are among the most distinctive dishes in the Aztec kitchen. The Nahuatl word "*molli*" (Spanish "*mole*," pronounced "molay") means a sauce made with chile. Many people mistakenly think there is only one *mole*, the famous *Mole Poblano*, the chile sauce from Puebla that has bitter chocolate in it. On the contrary, endless variations are played on the *mole* theme. There are the green dishes using Mexican green tomatoes with sprigs of fresh coriander, green chiles, pumpkin seeds or nuts, and so on. The red dishes use the red tomato, with red chiles, herbs, spices, etc. The *pipianes*, similar dishes, also fit into this group.

The cooking technique of the *moles* is very different from any we use. It is closer to the method used for curries in India. The ingredients, chiles, tomatoes, nuts, herbs, spices, and seasonings, are all ground to a coarse paste or puree, and then cooked, while being stirred constantly, in hot lard for five minutes. Chicken, or pork, or whatever, is cooked separately in a small amount of stock or water, which is used to thin the chile mixture. Meat and sauce are then heated gently together just long enough to blend the flavors.

It is essential to cook the *mole* paste in fat, as otherwise the finished dish has a raw taste and the flavor of the chile never blends successfully with the other ingredients. The splash and hiss of the chile mixture when it hits the hot fat is a bit alarming. The trick is to lower the heat as soon as the mixture is in the skillet and to begin stirring it with a wooden spoon immediately. Depending on the juiciness of the tomatoes and the quality of the chiles, the paste or puree will vary in dryness. Either way, it makes no difference.

## THE TINGAS

During the colonial period cooks in the state of Puebla invented the *tingas*, which are a true wedding of Spain and Mexico, using a mixture of European and Mexican foods with a European cooking method. Onion and garlic are sautéed; tomatoes are added; then stock, herbs, and spices are put in; and the mixture is simmered to make a sauce. The precooked meat and, usually, *chorizo* sausage are then added, with canned *chipotle* chile. A *tinga* is really a stew, prepared in a special way. Chile, onions, garlic, and tomatoes are never ground and cooked in fat as they are in the *moles*.

chur ē zo

## TOMATOES, RED AND GREEN

The tomato turns up in Mexican dishes almost as often as chiles do, and is perhaps Mexico's best gift to the world of food. The red tomato, the *xictomatl* of the Aztecs, in Mexico *jitomate*, has spread everywhere and is available all year round. Canned Italian plum tomatoes are a good substitute if the available fresh tomatoes are not properly ripe. Fresh tomatoes should be peeled and seeded.

## HOW TO PEEL AND SEED TOMATOES

Drop the tomatoes, one at a time, into boiling water; remove and plunge them into cold water; then peel. The time that the tomato needs to be kept in boiling water will vary from ten seconds to two minutes, depending on its ripeness and the type of skin. A very ripe, thin-skinned tomato will almost peel by itself. It needs only ten seconds in boiling water. A thick-skinned tomato will usually peel easily after one minute in boiling water, but some specially tough-skinned ones may need up to two minutes.

To remove the seeds, cut the tomato in half and squeeze it very gently. The seeds come out readily.

The green tomato, the *miltomatl* of the Aztecs (in Mexico known variously as *tomate*, *tomate con cáscara*, *tomate verde*, *tomatito*, and *tomatillo*), small and green with a papery brown covering, is harder to get. It has a very delicate flavor which does not develop until it is cooked for two or three minutes. It can be bought canned in Spanish, Mexican, and Puerto Rican grocery stores and in many specialty food shops. In markets in the Southwest and California it can be bought fresh. To use fresh green tomatoes, remove the papery covering but not the skin or seeds, as there would be nothing left of the tomatoes if you did. Use the liquid that comes with canned green tomatoes, as it is full of flavor.

## BEANS

No Mexican meal is considered complete without beans, either cooked and served separately, or mashed and fried (*refritos*) and used as a garnish, especially with the dishes of the Corn Kitchen. They come in a wide range of size, color, and shape. The most popular are the black bean, *frijol negro*, the speckled bean, *frijol pinto*, the kidney bean and the California pink bean, both called *frijol rojo*, and a delicious pale yellow bean, *frijol canario*. Cooked beans are served in bowls separately after the meat course and before the sweets at the main meal of the day. They are rather soupy. Beans can be bought in almost any supermarket and in Spanish, Mexican, and Puerto Rican grocery stores.

## COOKING FATS

Lard is the principal cooking fat traditionally used in Mexico, with olive oil and salad oil tied for second place. A vegetable shortening, or salad oil, may be substituted for lard if preferred. Butter is seldom used.

## NUTS AS THICKENING AGENTS

For thickening sauces, finely ground nuts and seeds are used, rather than flour or egg yolks and cream. Peanuts, pecans and pumpkin seeds are indigenous to Mexico. The Spaniards introduced almonds, filberts (hazelnuts), walnuts, pine nuts (piñones, pignolias), and sesame seeds, all of which are widely used today and are available in any supermarket in the United States. *Masa harina* is sometimes used as a thickening agent, especially in Yucatán.

## HERBS AND SPICES IN MEXICAN COOKERY

Herbs and spices figure importantly in Mexican cooking. Almost all of the necessary ones can be found on the spice shelf of any supermarket. Anise, allspice, bay leaf, cinnamon, clove, cumin, coriander seeds, marjoram, oregano, sesame (used as a flavoring as well as a thickening agent), saffron, mint, and parsley are the most commonly used.

*cilantro = cē lan tro*

A few others are less readily available. One of the most important of these is fresh green coriander (as distinct from the seeds), known in Mexico as *cilantro* and in Puerto Rico as *culantro*. It is a very ancient herb which was introduced into Europe from Asia by way of Egypt in very remote times. A member of the same natural order as parsley (order Umbelliferae), it looks rather like a paler green Italian parsley, though its flavor is very much more pronounced. It is perhaps best known as Chinese parsley and is available in Chinese markets, stores which specialize in foods from India, and many Puerto Rican and Latin markets. Though easy to grow from seed, it unfortunately does not dry well. It is sold with its roots still on, and these should not be removed. It should be either wrapped in paper towels and put into a plastic bag or put into a glass jar, and then kept in the refrigerator. Do not rinse before storing, as it will rot very quickly. Because the roots are on it, it comes up very fresh and green when soaked in cold water five minutes or so before use. It can be frozen.

*Epazote, Chenopodium ambrosioides*, one of the anserinas, better known as wormseed, pigweed, or goosefoot, is indigenous to Mexico and is used in many of the tortilla dishes and in beans. It has spread quite widely in Europe, especially in Spain, where it is called *pazote* and is used mainly as a herbal tea. It dries excellently; and it is packaged in California as "Jerusalem oak Pazote." La Sevillana in Washington, D.C., and Casa Moneo in New York (see page 22), both carry it, as do many Puerto Rican markets. A European species is believed to have crossed the Atlantic and established itself in North America, which might account for the confusion in names. It is easy to grow from seeds which are available from J. A. Mako Horticultural Enterprises, Box 3482, Dallas, Texas 75234.

Annatto or annatta, in Mexico *achiote*, is the name given the seeds of a tree that grows in tropical America. It has a delicate flavor; and the red pulp surrounding the seeds colors food a deep, golden yellow. It is used in Yucatán as one would use saffron. Mexican, Puerto Rican, and Spanish groceries carry it, as do stores which specialize in Indian foods.

Most of the fruits and many of the vegetables from Mexico are available in markets here. Cheese presents rather more of a problem, as there are no exact equivalents and no export. Wherever *añejo* or Chihuahua cheese is called for Parmesan is an excellent substitute. Romano can also be used, and sometimes Gruyère. *Queso fresco*, fresh cheese, is the Spanish *queso blanco*, white cheese, and is soft and crumbly. Whey cheese, when available, is probably the closest substitute. Monterey Jack is a reasonable, though not wholly satisfactory one; and in a pinch mild cheddar can be used. It is worth searching for a crumbly fresh cheese in likely markets; otherwise one must regretfully make do. Anyway, in truth, the effect on the finished dish is usually minimal.

A few other unfamiliar foods may crop up. *Piloncillo*, for example, is Mexican brown sugar and comes in the form of little cone-shaped loaves. It is available in Spanish grocery stores. Dark brown sugar substitutes for it. *Chorizo*, Spanish hot sausage, can be bought imported from Spain in cans but is also made locally and sold in Mexican, Spanish, and Puerto Rican markets, as is the milder Spanish sausage, *longaniza*. *Garbanzos*, chick peas, are available cooked and canned or packaged dried in supermarkets. *Nopales* or *nopalitos*, are the young, fleshy paddles of the prickly pear cactus. They can be bought canned in Mexican, Spanish, and Puerto Rican grocery stores and in specialty food shops. The fruit, *tuna*, which is eaten raw, can be found in markets in the Southwest. Mexican chocolate can be bought in all Latin markets and in many specialty shops. Plantains (*plátano macho*), a type of banana which needs cooking to be edible, is sold in many markets; the ordinary banana can substitute for it. *Acitrón*, used in desserts, is often wrongly translated as citron peel—it is really *biznaga*, crystallized organ cactus. Citron peel can be used as a substitute.

## KITCHEN EQUIPMENT

Any ordinarily well-equipped kitchen, assuming it has an electric blender or a food mill, probably contains all the tools needed for making Mexican food, with the exception of the tortilla press and *comal*, explained in the Corn Kitchen section, and the *molinillo*, explained in the Drinks section.

Cooking in Mexico in the old days was in decorated earthenware casseroles (*cazuelas*) and pots (*ollas*) in a great variety of shapes and sizes; nowadays these share the kitchen with aluminum, enamelled iron, and stainless steel. The casseroles, which are handmade and can be bought in any shop carrying Mexican goods, are handsome enough to be brought directly from stove to table; and they have the added merit of keeping food hot far longer than do other types of serving ware. Users, however, should be careful to follow the instructions for seasoning them, as otherwise they are inclined to crack and can give food a clayey taste. They are lidless, but one can usually find saucepan lids of one's own to fit them. And, of course, your own casseroles will do just as well.

## SERVINGS

The recipes in this book, unless otherwise stated, are for six generous helpings in an American-style meal of three courses. The sort of menu I have found most popular for dinner consists of a main dish—such as a *mole*, *pipián*, or *tinga*—with rice, beans, guacamole, tortillas, and a side dish of chiles or one of the sauces, according to the main dish chosen, plus a dessert or fresh fruit. I have indicated in the Corn Kitchen which of the dishes make wonderful luncheons; the dry soups served with a salad and dessert also make good luncheons, or, with the addition of real soup, pleasant dinners. Any of the Mexican dishes will fit happily into the framework of American food and in fact the Mexican pattern would be hard to copy since meal hours in Mexico are rather confused.

## THE TRADITIONAL MEXICAN DAY

The old feudal hours, so well suited to an agricultural economy, are less well adapted to industrial society, and the strain is felt, particularly in Mexico City with its population of ten million. It is becoming impossible to go home for midday dinner and return to work three hours later: the distances to be travelled take up too much of the time.

The Mexican day begins with *desayuno*, breakfast, usually a selection of sweet breads with *Café con Leche* (milk coffee) and, sometimes, hot chocolate. In the country this is a first breakfast and is taken much earlier, perhaps at 5 a.m. It is followed at about 9 a.m. by *almuerzo*, a heartier second breakfast where fruit or fruit juice, *Huevos Rancheros* (Country-Style Eggs), beans, chile sauce, tortillas, and *Café con Leche* may be served. In the city *almuerzo* is a meal closer to our own luncheon; and it is taken at 11 or 11:30 by elegant young city gentlemen, who can be seen at Sanborn's having an early lunch (usually made up of the dishes in the Corn Kitchen section). They have probably had only a cup of coffee for *desayuno*. But people in Mexico despise eating early, so this meal is not called an early lunch: it is a late breakfast.

The *comida*, the main meal of the day, takes place anywhere from 2 to 5:30 p.m. One of Mexico's poets pointed out that if you only put off the *comida* long enough you could save a meal. Invited to *comida* in Mexico, it is hard to know at what time you will eat, as that has nothing to do with the time for which one is invited—and in any event half the guests will arrive hours late. It is wise to ask; and, if it is to be late and you usually breakfast only on a cup of coffee, to remember that *almuerzo* was invented for just such contingencies.

*Comida* is a heavy meal. It usually begins with a light soup, a consommé, for example, and is followed by that curiously named Mexican institution, the dry soup, *sopa seca*. Then comes the main course of meat or fish, a simple green salad or a green vegetable. After this come the beans. A chile sauce, usually *Salsa Cruda* or *Salsa Verde*, is always on the table. Tortillas and the very excellent rolls called *bolillos* are also served, usually fresh from the bakery, with wine or beer to drink. Fruit, fresh or stewed, is the usual dessert, though a more elaborate dessert is served on Sunday or when there are visitors.

Few people in Mexico dine at night. In the evening there is *merienda*, which may be eaten by the children at 6 or 7 p.m., or as late as 9 p.m. by the adults. It is a light meal, more like *desayuno* than anything else, except perhaps an old-fashioned English high tea. *Café con Leche*, *Leche en Chocolate* (cocoa made with milk), *atole* (corn gruel), a variety of sweet breads, jam, perhaps a little ham are usually all that is served.

*Cena* (dinner) is an occasion. It means guests, for example; a birthday to celebrate; a visit to a restaurant with friends; and so on. The meal is taken any time from 8 o'clock to midnight; usually the latter, which might explain the superstition that eating at night in the altitude (Mexico City is 7,600 feet) "*le hace daño*" (does one harm). Midnight feasts can upset anyone; and foreigners have been known to suggest eating at 7:30 p.m., but Mexico clings fiercely to the eating pattern of Spain, where everyone eats very late. It is a matter of national pride. After all, it was in the late seventeenth century that the English leisure class took to dining late to distinguish itself from the less cultivated persons who ate at noon.

## REGIONAL COOKING

Though each state in Mexico boasts special dishes, the regional pattern is dictated more by climate than anything else. Yucatán, with the distinctive cuisine of the Mayas, is the exception. However, since even this cooking depends on much the same raw material (corn, tomatoes, and chiles, for example), it bears the stamp of the Mexican kitchen of today.

The arid North is not really corn country; and it is here that the influence of Spain is strongest. Good food depends more on the excellence of the raw ingredients than on the delicacy or complexity of a sauce. Roast kid, accompanied by wheat and/or corn tortillas, beans, guacamole, and chile sauce, followed by *café de olla*, is magnificent if the kid is tender and of good quality.

The tropical coastal regions abound in fish and seafood and tropical fruits, but fundamentally there is little difference between the coastal kitchen and the kitchen of the high plateau. *Mole de Oaxaca* is darker and hotter than *Mole Poblano*; and in Oaxaca banana leaves are used for tamales, instead of corn husks as elsewhere in the Republic; but the dishes all fit into a basic pattern. There is an overall Mexican quality about Mexican food, no matter in which state it originates.

# NOTE ON THE AVAILABILITY OF FOODS NEEDED TO COOK MEXICAN STYLE:

In the Southwest United States (Texas, Arizona, New Mexico, and California) and in Florida, ingredients for Mexican cooking are readily available, partly because the principal ingredients are foods native to these regions and partly because these areas were once part of Spanish America and/or Mexico, and the food tradition persists. Here all the herbs, spices, chiles, and so on are available fresh and canned. Mojave Foods has an immense list of Mexican things that sell to independent markets all over the region. It is located at 5335 Valley Boulevard, Los Angeles, California 90032.

There are at present many Cubans in Florida; and, though the Cuban kitchen is different from the Mexican, many of the raw materials are the same. There is a large Mexican population in Texas and California, as there is in Chicago, where the Quaker Oats Company manufactures the *masa harina* that is needed for making tortillas and tamales. Other brands of *masa harina* are available from Texas. New York has many Puerto Ricans and Mexicans, and for this reason it is possible to buy everything needed with very little trouble. Ordinary small markets carry fresh as well as canned goods, herbs and spices.

In New York, for example, the upper Park Avenue (110th–116th Streets) market has all the tropical fruits and vegetables fresh, a lot of them coming from the West Indies. Joe's Grocery, at 71 East 79 Street, New York, N.Y. 10029, specializes in West Indian foods, which include many used in the Mexican kitchen, since the Spanish-speaking islands of the Caribbean have a food tradition that links them with Mexico. On the West Side, especially uptown, every other small grocery carries some of the needed foods; and downtown on the East Side are some of the best markets, especially on 14th Street, which is good from East to West. Fresh coriander (Chinese parsley) is always available in Chinatown.

The following stores sell, and will mail, foods needed for Mexican cooking:

LOS ANGELES: La Luz del Día, 624 North Main, Los Angeles, Calif., 90012, and 107 Paseo de la Plaza, Los Angeles, Calif., 90012.

NEW YORK: B. Altman & Co., Fifth Avenue and 34th Street, New York, N.Y. 10016, carries canned chiles, green tomatoes, cactus pieces and prepared foods, annatto (*achiote*), and *chile pequín*. Casa Moneo, 210 West 14th Street, New York, N.Y., 10011, carries a very wide range of Mexican foods: dried and canned chiles, bottled sauces, green tomatoes, dried corn husks, *ates*, Spanish *chorizo* and *longaniza* sausages, dried salt codfish (*bacalao*), cheeses, and dried *epazote* as well as *tortilla* presses, and *masa harina*.

CHICAGO: Casa Esteiro Spanish-Latin-American Products, 2719 West Division, Chicago, Ill., 60622, carries a wide range of Mexican foods.

DALLAS: J. A. Mako Horticultural Enterprises, P.O. Box 3482, Dallas, Texas, 75234, has authentic Mexican chile pepper seeds as well as *epazote* for those who want to grow their own. Mail order.

# THE CORN
# KITCHEN

Because of their antiquity, these dishes, which go back to Mexico's Aztec past, do not fit into the usual categories of a modern cookbook. However, they are extremely adaptable and can be used as appetizers or as luncheon or supper dishes.

They all depend on corn; and the cooking method is similar. All the tortilla dishes and the tamales are included here, with the exception of a few tortilla-based dry soups and the sweet tamales, which have been put into the Desserts section.

Fortunately, there are simpler ways of making these dishes today than in the past. The laborious process which required the boiling of dried corn with lime to make *nixtamal*, which was then ground on a *metate* (a three-legged, flat, oblong stone) with a *metlalpil* (a stone rolling pin) into flour to make the *masa* (dough) for tortillas and tamales has been modernized. Flour for the *masa* can be bought packaged as *masa harina* and is available in Spanish and Puerto Rican grocery stores.

Tortillas, which were the bread of ancient Mexico before the Spaniards introduced wheat, and which are the basis of many dishes, are easy to make. You need *masa harina*, a tortilla press, and a *comal*, which is a round iron or earthenware baking sheet. A griddle will do as a substitute. Traditionally, tortillas are made by patting a ball of *masa* between the palms of the hands until a thin, flat, round cake is formed. This is very difficult and very time consuming; and the tortilla press does the job just as well.

There were no appetizers in the old cuisine. However, a group of *bocadillos* (mouthfuls) that the Spaniards imaginatively called the *antojitos*—"little whims," "hankerings," or "fancies"—make admirable appetizers which far outshine the contrived bits and pieces that sometimes pass off as canapés in modern Mexico, or even modern America. Their bigger brothers, the *antojos*, full-sized whims, make excellent luncheon and supper dishes.

# Tortillas

2 cups *masa harina*              1 teaspoon salt
1⅓ cups warm water

Mix the ingredients to form a soft dough. Divide into balls the size of small eggs and flatten on the tortilla press between two sheets of plastic or waxed paper to thin pancakes about 4 inches across. If the tortillas stick, the dough is too moist. Scrape it off, add a little more *masa harina* to the dough and begin again. It does not hurt the dough to handle it.

Place ungreased *comal* over medium heat and cook tortillas, one at a time, about 1 minute on each side, or until the edges begin to lift and they are very slightly browned. Makes 1 dozen small tortillas.

*To keep warm*: Tortillas can be kept warm for several hours. Preheat oven to 150°F. Have ready a cloth napkin wrung out in hot water. As you make the tortillas, wrap them first in paper towels and then in the napkins, and put them in the oven. When there are a dozen stacked up, dampen the napkin again, wrap the lot in aluminum foil and keep in the oven until needed. Cold tortillas can be reheated over direct heat. They must be turned continually. If they have become dry, pat each one with damp hands.

*Large tortillas* (6 inches in diameter) are served, like bread, with meat dishes.

*Small tortillas* (4 inches in diameter) are used both as bread and in made-up dishes.

*Tiny tortillas* are used for appetizers.

A non-corn tortilla must be included here as the exception to prove the rule. These are the excellent. . . .

## *Tortillas de Harina del Norte*
### WHEAT TORTILLAS FROM THE NORTH

2 cups all-purpose flour     1 tablespoon lard
1 teaspoon salt     ¾ cup cold water, about
1 teaspoon baking powder

Thoroughly mix the dry ingredients. Cut in the lard and add enough water to make a stiff dough. Divide into balls as for corn tortillas and roll out on to a lightly floured board, making them as thin as possible. Bake about 2 minutes on each side on ungreased *comal* over medium heat. Makes about 1 dozen.

These wheat tortillas are excellent if freshly made, and can be used in place of corn tortillas. Though the practice is quite unorthodox, they are extraordinarily good spread with sweet butter and eaten hot.

## *Tacos*

Tacos are small (4-inch) tortillas stuffed with various mixtures, rolled, and fastened with a toothpick. They may be fried in lard and served with various sauces and chiles on the side, or left unfried so that they can be partly unrolled and have extras added, according to individual taste. In the United States, the taco is not rolled, but simply folded in half.

The taco has been called the Mexican sandwich; but in fact the *torta*, which is a split *bolillo* (a shuttle-shaped roll) with various fillings, is the real sandwich. For a party, set out bowls of various sauces, canned chiles, chopped lettuce, chopped, fried *chorizo* sausage, shredded chicken and pork, guacamole, *frijoles refritos*, and perhaps some of the madeup taco fillings. Serve with batches of hot tortillas to be filled and eaten unfried.

For variety, soaked and ground *ancho* or *pasilla* chiles (allow about 3 to ½ pound *masa harina*) may be added to the tortilla dough.

# Taco Fillings

1. *Tacos de Jamón*: Mix together 1 cup chopped boiled ham; 1 tablespoon finely chopped onion; 1 package (3-ounce size) softened cream cheese; 2 medium tomatoes, peeled, seeded, and chopped; and chopped canned *serrano* or *jalapeño* chile to taste. Stuff 12 small tortillas with the mixture and serve with *guacamole*, page 74.

2. *Tacos de Picadillo*: Make up the recipe for *Picadillo*, page 165, or *Picadillo de la Costa*, page 166, using 1 pound of chopped beef. Stuff the tacos in the usual way and serve with guacamole.

3. *Taco de Chorizo*: Skin, chop, and fry 3 *chorizo* sausages. Drain. Mix, in equal proportions, with small cubes of Monterey Jack or cheddar cheese. Stuff the tortillas, and serve with guacamole and chile *chipotle*.

4. *Tacos de Mole Poblano*: Stuff tortillas with leftover *Mole Poblano*, page 121, and serve with guacamole.

5. *Tacos de Adobo*: Stuff tortillas with leftover pork or chicken *Adobo*, and serve with guacamole.

6. *Tacos de Pollo*, or *de Cerdo*: Stuff tortillas with a mixture of shredded chicken or pork, a little finely chopped lettuce, freshly grated Parmesan cheese, and *Salsa de Chile Rojo*, page 79, or *Salsa Verde*, page 75.

7. *Tacos de Frijol*: Stuff tortillas with *frijoles refritos*, strips of *jalapeño* chile, and Monterey Jack, or similar cheese, and serve with guacamole.

# Tacos de Queso

### CHEESE TACOS

2 *poblano* chiles
3 medium tomatoes, peeled, seeded, and chopped
1 small onion, chopped
Salt
Freshly ground pepper

Pinch of sugar
2 tablespoons oil
¼ pound Monterey Jack or similar cheese
12 small tortillas
Sour cream

Prepare the chiles, as described in the Introduction.
   Combine the prepared chiles with the tomatoes and onion

in the electric blender, and blend to a smooth puree. Add salt, pepper, and sugar to taste. Heat the oil in a skillet and cook the puree, over a moderate heat, for 5 minutes, stirring constantly. Keep the filling warm while making the tacos.

Place a strip of cheese with a spoonful of the chile puree on each tortilla, and garnish with a little sour cream. Serve at once.

# Tostadas

*Tostadas* are tortillas that have been fried until golden brown and crisp in hot lard or oil, then covered with various combinations of meats, poultry, fish, sauces, chiles, etc. For a luncheon dish, use the small, 4-inch tortillas. For appetizers, use the tiny, 2-inch tortillas. Radishes and green olives are a favorite garnish.

## Tostadas Tapatías

### GUADALAJARA-STYLE *TOSTADAS*

3 *chorizo* sausages
2 cups *frijoles refritos*
12 small or 24 cocktail tostadas
Shredded lettuce

1 onion, minced
2 cups guacamole
3 tablespoons freshly grated Parmesan cheese

Skin, chop fine, and fry the *chorizos*. Heat up the beans. Spread the beans on the *tostados*; follow with a layer of the sausage, a layer of lettuce, a little onion, a layer of guacamole, and a sprinkling of grated cheese.

*Note*: Some cooks dress the lettuce with oil and vinegar, seasoned with salt and pepper.

# Totopos de Michoacán

## MICHOACÁN *TOTOPOS*

| | |
|---|---|
| 2 *ancho* or *pasilla* chiles | Lard or salad oil |
| 1½ cups *masa harina* | Guacamole |
| ½ cup cooked red kidney beans, mashed | Parmesan cheese |
| ½ teaspoon salt | Any filling |

Prepare the chiles, as described in the Introduction; then blend in the electric blender. Mix the *masa harina*, beans, and the prepared chiles with salt to taste and, if necessary, a little warm water to make a fairly stiff dough. Shape into half-size (2-inch) tortillas, using a piece of dough about the size of a walnut, and making them somewhat thicker than usual. Bake on the *comal*. Then fry in hot lard on both sides until golden. Drain on paper towels; spread with *guacamole*, page 74; and sprinkle with freshly grated Parmesan cheese. You may use, instead, any of the *taco* fillings, page 28. Makes 12.

# Tostadas de Sardinas

## SARDINE *TOSTADAS*

| | |
|---|---|
| 1 tablespoon salad oil or butter | Salt |
| 1 onion, finely chopped | Freshly ground pepper |
| 1 large tomato, peeled, seeded, and chopped | 12 small or 24 cocktail *tostadas* |
| 1 large potato, freshly boiled and finely diced | 3 tablespoons freshly grated Parmesan cheese |
| 1 can (3¾-ounce size) boned sardines in oil, mashed | Finely chopped lettuce |
| | Oil and Vinegar Dressing |
| | *Chipotle* or tomato sauce |

Heat the oil or butter in a skillet, and sauté the onion until limp. Add the tomato and cook until thick; then add the potato and cook for a minute or two, stirring. Add the sardines, remove from the heat, and season with salt and pepper.

Cover the *tostadas* with some of the above mixture, followed by grated cheese and a layer of lettuce sprinkled with the Oil and Vinegar Dressing. Serve with *chipotle* or tomato sauce.

# Tostadas de Frijol

### BEAN *TOSTADAS*

3 cups Mexican black
  beans, cooked very
  thick
1 package (8-ounce size)
  cream cheese, cut into
  cubes
12 small or 24 cocktail
  *tostadas*

1 large onion, minced
1 large avocado, cut in
  strips
1 canned *chipotle* chile,
  cut in strips

Heat the beans with the cream cheese, but do not allow the
mixture to boil, as the cheese and beans should remain separated. Spread a layer of the mixture on the *tostadas*, followed
by a layer of onions, strips of avocado, and strips of *chipotle*
chile.

# Tostadas Compuestas

### MIXED *TOSTADAS*

12 small or 24 cocktail
  *tostadas*
1 cup red kidney beans,
  mashed
1 head of lettuce
2 freshly cooked potatoes,
  diced
Oil and Vinegar Dressing

2 cooked chicken breasts,
  shredded
1 cup guacamole
Freshly grated Parmesan
  cheese
Canned *chipotle* chiles, cut
  in strips

Cover the *tostadas* with a thin layer of the beans. Toss the
lettuce leaves and the potatoes lightly in a little of the dressing.
Place a layer over the beans. Add a layer of chicken slivers,
a layer of guacamole, and a sprinkling of grated cheese. Place
strips of the *chipotle* chiles on the *tostadas*; or serve the chiles
on the side, since they are very hot.

# Tostadas de Camarón

## SHRIMP TOSTADAS

1 tablespoon salad oil or
  butter
1 onion, finely chopped
1 large tomato, peeled,
  seeded, and chopped
1 pound shrimp, cooked
  and chopped
Salt
Freshly ground pepper

12 small or 24 cocktail
  *tostadas*
3 tablespoons freshly
  grated Parmesan cheese
Finely chopped lettuce
Oil and Vinegar Dressing
*Chile Verde* or bottled
  *jalapeño* sauce

Heat the oil or butter in a skillet and sauté the onion until transparent. Add the tomato and cook until thick. Add the shrimp; then stir in salt and pepper to taste, and remove from the heat. Cover the *tostadas* with some of the shrimp mixture, cheese, and a layer of lettuce sprinkled with the dressing; and serve with either *Chile Verde* or bottled *jalapeño* sauce.

# Quesadillas

These are turnovers made by stuffing unbaked tortillas with a variety of fillings, pinching the edges together, and frying them golden in lard or oil. For a first course, use the small (4-inch) tortilla; for cocktails, the half-sized one. There are a variety of *quesadilla* doughs that are somewhat easier to handle than the plain *mesa*. Amounts given are for 12 small or 24 cocktail *quesadillas*. *Quesadillas* may also be baked in the same way as *tortillas*.

# Quesadilla Dough

2 cups *masa harina*
2 tablespoons all-purpose
  flour
½ teaspoon baking
  powder

½ teaspoon salt
2 tablespoons melted butter
1 egg
½ cup milk, about

Mix the dry ingredients together thoroughly; add the melted butter, egg, and enough milk to form a fairly stiff dough. Form into tortillas; stuff; fold over; seal the edges; and fry in hot lard or oil. Drain on paper towels and serve hot.

# Masa de Quesadilla con Chile Ancho

### DOUGH WITH *ANCHO* CHILE

2 *ancho* chiles            ½ teaspoon salt
2 cups *masa harina*

Prepare the chiles, as described in the Introduction.

Mix the *masa harina* with salt; add the chiles and enough warm water to form a fairly stiff dough.

# Masa de Quesadilla con Tuétano

### DOUGH WITH BONE MARROW

1 pound beef marrow      ¼ cup all-purpose flour
     bones                   ½ teaspoon salt
1¾ cups *masa harina*     1 egg
½ teaspoon baking         ½ to ¾ cup milk
     powder

Place the bones in a preheated 350°F. oven for 15 minutes. Scrape out the marrow.

Mix the marrow with the other ingredients into a fairly stiff dough and use for *quesadillas*.

# Masa de Quesadilla con Queso

## DOUGH WITH CHEESE

2 cups *masa harina*
¼ cup freshly grated
 Parmesan cheese
2 tablespoons all-purpose
 flour

½ teaspoon baking
 powder
½ teaspoon salt
1 tablespoon melted butter
½ cup light cream

Mix all the dry ingredients thoroughly; add the butter, cream, and enough *warm* water to make a fairly stiff dough.

# Fillings for Quesadillas

*Relleno de sesos* (Brain Filling). Sauté one finely chopped onion in three tablespoons of butter until transparent. Add 1 pair of cooked and chopped calf's brains and cook until golden. Stir in a sprig or *epazote* or a pinch of nutmeg and a little chopped *serrano* or *jalapeño* chile. Season to taste with salt and pepper; and cook 2 to 3 minutes. The mixture should be quite dry at this point.

*Picadillo, Mole Poblano, Adobo*, beans, sardines, etc., may all be used to stuff *quesadillas*, as well as the following fillings.

*Chorizo sausage*. Sauté, in a little lard or oil, some finely chopped onion, skinned and finely chopped *chorizo* sausage, cooked and diced potatoes, peeled and chopped tomato, a few slices of either *serrano, jalapeño*, or *chipotle* chile, salt, and freshly ground pepper. When the mixture is fairly dry use it to stuff the *quesadillas*.

*Queso y rajas* (cheese and *poblano* chile). Prepare *poblano* chiles (page 11) and cut into small strips. Cut Monterey Jack or a similar cheese into strips. Mix the cheese and the chiles together; moisten them with a little sour cream; and season with salt and freshly ground pepper. Use to stuff *quesadillas*.

Two of the most popular Mexican fillings are *huitlacoche*, a mushroom-like fungus growth on the ears of corn, and *flor de calabaza*, squash blossoms, not usually available in the United States. In any event, here are the recipes:

*Huitlacoche*. Sauté, in a little lard or oil, finely chopped onion and garlic, chopped *huitlacoche* fungus, a little chopped *serrano* chile, and salt and freshly ground pepper to taste. Cook until the onion is tender.

*Flor de calabaza*. Sauté finely chopped onion, garlic, strips of chile *poblano*, some *epazote*, and chopped squash blossoms in a little oil. Season to taste with salt, and sprinkle with grated cheese.

## Panuchos

These are from Yucatán, where the distinctive Maya kitchen is prevalent. They are not as tricky to make as you might think. Hearty as an appetizer or a first course, they also make a good light luncheon.

12 4-inch tortillas
½ recipe (1 cup) *frijoles* made with black beans
3 hard-cooked eggs, sliced
Lard or salad oil

2 cooked chicken breasts, boned and shredded
1 recipe *Cebolla Escabechada*

Make the tortillas a little thicker than usual. To fill, lift up the top layer of each tortilla and carefully spread a thin layer of beans inside the little pocket, placing a slice of the egg on top of the beans.

Heat the lard in a skillet and fry the tortillas, bottom side down. Drain. To serve, top with shredded chicken and a spoonful of *Cebolla Escabechada*, page 37.

*Variation*: In place of the *Cebolla Escabechada*, top the chicken with shredded lettuce, a little Tomato Sauce, and a sprinkling of freshly grated Parmesan cheese.

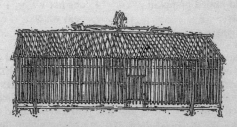

# Papatzules

## STUFFED TORTILLAS IN
## PUMPKIN-SEED SAUCE

This Yucatán dish, usually served as an appetizer, makes a very good
luncheon followed by a simple dessert or fruit.

*Salsa de Tomate* (Tomato
   Sauce)
*Salsa de Pepitas*
   (Pumpkin-seed Sauce)

24 4-inch tortillas, kept
   warm
12 hard-cooked eggs,
   finely chopped

### SALSA DE TOMATE

1 large onion, finely
   chopped
4 to 6 tablespoons lard or
   salad oil
2 pounds (about 6
   medium) tomatoes,
   peeled and chopped

Salt
Pinch of sugar
1 whole, fresh, hot green
   pepper, preferably
   *habanero*, stem left on

Heat the oil in a heavy skillet and sauté the onion until it is
soft but not browned. Add the tomatoes, salt, sugar, and the
whole chile pepper and simmer the mixture over moderate heat,
until it is thick, about 10 minutes. Remove and discard the
pepper. Keep warm.

### SALSA DE PEPITAS

1 pound hulled pumpkin
   seeds
2 or 3 leaves *epazote*

4 cups hot water, 1 cup
   cold water
Salt

Toast the pumpkin seeds lightly in a heavy skillet, cool slightly,
then pulverize them in a blender. Transfer to a bowl. Simmer
the *epazote* leaves in the cup of water for 10 minutes. Strain
and discard the leaves. Bring the flavored water almost to a
boil then gradually stir it into the pumpkin seeds to make a
fairly dry paste. If *epazote* leaves are not available, use plain

hot water. Knead the paste until the green pumpkin seed oil begins to ooze out. Carefully spoon the oil into a dish and reserve it. There will be about 6 tablespoons. Transfer the paste to a heavy saucepan and over very low heat gradually stir in the hot water and cook just long enough to heat the sauce through. Do not let it boil. It will be the consistency of very heavy cream. Season with salt to taste.

To assemble the dish, dip each tortilla in the pumpkin-seed sauce, fill with some of the egg, and roll it up. Arrange the tortillas on a platter or plates. Pour any remaining sauce over the tortillas, then pour over all the tomato sauce. Sprinkle with the reserved pumpkin-seed oil. The dish is served at room temperature.

## Cebolla Escabechada

### SOUSED ONIONS

| | |
|---|---|
| 1 onion, sliced very thin | 1 bay leaf |
| Salt | Pinch of cumin |
| 3 *serrano* chiles | 1 clove garlic |
| Pinch of oregano | ½ cup white vinegar |

Soak the sliced onion in salted water for 5 minutes. Drain and place it in a saucepan with all the remaining ingredients, plus *½ cup of water*. Bring up to a boil; remove from the heat, and cool.

## Chilaquiles

| | |
|---|---|
| Lard | 3 sprigs of fresh green coriander |
| 18 4-inch, day-old tortillas, cut into ¼- to ½-inch strips | 1 cup grated cheese, Monterey Jack or cheddar |
| 1 can, 10-ounce size, Mexican green tomatoes | ½ cup meat stock (or use canned broth) |
| 1 small white onion, chopped | Salt |
| 3 *serrano* chiles | Freshly ground pepper |
| Sprig of *epazote* | |

Heat 2 to 3 tablespoons of lard in a skillet and fry the tortillas, a few strips at a time, on both sides, without browning. Drain on paper towels. Add more lard as it is needed while frying the tortillas.

Drain the tomatoes, reserving their liquid. Place the tomatoes, with a little of the liquid from the can, the onion, chiles, *epazote*, and coriander in the electric blender and blend until smooth. It may be necessary to puree it bit by bit. Cook the puree in the fat remaining in the skillet (adding, if necessary, a bit more) for 2 to 3 minutes, stirring constantly. Take the skillet off the heat, and stir in the remainder of the tomato liquid. Taste for seasoning.

Grease an earthenware casserole; add a layer of the tomato sauce, followed by a layer of tortillas and a sprinkling of cheese. Continue making layers in the same order until you have used up all ingredients, *except the cheese*, of which enough should remain to sprinkle on at the end. Pour any remaining sauce, along with the meat stock, over the top, and sprinkle with the remaining cheese. Bake in a preheated 350°F. oven for about 30 minutes, or until the cheese has melted and the casserole is hot throughout. Serves 6.

## *Chilaquiles con Pechuga de Pollo*

### *CHILAQUILES* WITH CHICKEN BREASTS

Lard
18 4-inch, day-old tortillas, cut into ¼- to ½-inch strips
1 can (10-ounce size) Mexican green tomatoes
1 small white onion, chopped
3 or more sprigs of fresh coriander

3 or 4 *serrano* chiles, or to taste
Salt
Freshly ground pepper
1 cup heavy cream
3 cooked chicken breasts, boned and shredded
½ cup freshly grated Parmesan cheese

Heat 2 to 3 tablespoons of lard in a skillet and fry the tortillas, a few strips at a time, on both sides, without browning. Drain on paper towels. Add more fat as it is needed and continue frying the tortillas until all are cooked. Drain the tomatoes, reserving the liquid. Combine the tomatoes, onion, coriander, and chiles in the electric blender and blend to a smooth puree. Add a little lard to the skillet, if necessary, and cook the puree for 2 to 3 minutes, over moderate heat, stirring constantly. Take the skillet off the heat and stir in the liquid from the tomatoes. Taste for seasoning.

Grease an ovenproof casserole; add a layer of the sauce, a layer of tortillas, some of the cream, and a layer of chicken. Repeat the layers until all the ingredients are used, finishing with a layer of tortillas topped by cream. Sprinkle with all of the grated cheese; and bake in a preheated 350°F. oven for 30 minutes, or until the cheese has melted and the dish is hot throughout. Serves 6.

## *Chilaquiles Rojos con Pechuga de Pollo*

### RED *CHILAQUILES* WITH CHICKEN BREASTS

4 *ancho* chiles
Lard
18 4-inch, day-old
    *tortillas*, cut into
    ¼- to ½-inch strips
1 large onion, chopped
1 sprig of *epazote*
Chicken stock or canned
    condensed broth
1 pound (about 3 medium)
    tomatoes, peeled,
    seeded, and chopped

Salt
Freshly ground pepper
Pinch of sugar
1 cup heavy cream
3 cooked chicken breasts,
    boned and shredded
½ cup grated cheese,
    Monterey Jack or
    cheddar

Prepare the chiles, as described in the Introduction.

Heat 2 or 3 tablespoons of lard in a heavy skillet and fry the tortillas, a few strips at a time, on both sides without browning. Drain on paper towels. Add more fat as it is needed and continue cooking the tortilla strips until all are fried. Combine the prepared chiles, onion, and the *epazote* with a little stock in the electric blender and reduce to a smooth puree. In the lard remaining in the skillet (if necessary, add enough to bring the amount up to about 2 tablespoons), cook the puree for 5 minutes, over moderate heat, stirring constantly. Add the tomatoes, salt and pepper and sugar to taste. Simmer gently until the sauce is smooth and well blended.

Grease an ovenproof casserole; add a layer of the sauce, a layer of tortillas, some of the cream, and a layer of chicken. Repeat the layers until all the ingredients are used, finishing with a layer of tortilla and some cream. If the tomatoes did not supply sufficient juice, add ½ to 1 cup of chicken stock. Sprinkle the cheese over the top; and bake in a preheated 350°F. oven for 30 minutes, or until the cheese has melted and the dish is heated through. Serves 6.

# Pambacitos

## MINIATURE STUFFED ROLLS

*Pambacitos*, made from tiny bread rolls having nothing to do with corn whatever, are further proof that Mexican cooks are inventive. Having them in the Corn Kitchen is proof that Mexican cooks are also rule-breakers. Still, the fact is that here is where *Pambacitos* belong.

Lard or vegetable
  shortening
3 *chorizo* sausages,
  skinned and chopped
2 medium potatoes, freshly
  cooked and diced
1 onion, finely chopped
Salt
Freshly ground pepper
1 egg, lightly beaten

12 small rolls
Finely shredded lettuce
Oil and Vinegar Dressing
1 cup *frijoles refritos*
*Salsa verde* or *Salsa de
  Jitomate*
Freshly grated Parmesan
  cheese
Radishes, thinly sliced

Heat 1 tablespoon of lard in a skillet. Add the sausages, potatoes, and onion, and sauté until the onion is tender. Season with salt and pepper to taste. Stir in the beaten egg and cook until the egg has set.

Cut the tops off the rolls and set them aside; pull out the crumbs from the bottom; then fry both parts in hot lard. Toss the lettuce in the dressing to coat lightly; place a layer in the bottom of each roll; add a layer of beans, a layer of the sausage mixture, a little of the sauce, a sprinkling of cheese, and 1 or 2 slices of radish. Replace the top and eat immediately, while hot.

# Enchiladas Rojas

### RED ENCHILADAS

Enchiladas make an excellent luncheon dish. Allow 3 or 4 tortillas per person, according to appetite; and serve garnished with chopped lettuce, radishes, and olives.

| | |
|---|---|
| 6 *ancho* or *mulato* chiles | Freshly ground pepper |
| 1 pound (about 3 medium) tomatoes, peeled, seeded, and chopped | Pinch of sugar |
| | 1 cup heavy cream |
| | 2 eggs, lightly beaten |
| 2 onions, finely chopped | 6 *chorizo* sausages, |
| 1 clove garlic, chopped | skinned and chopped |
| Sprig of *epazote* | ½ cup freshly grated |
| Lard or salad oil | Parmesan cheese |
| Salt | 24 small tortillas |

Prepare the chiles as described in the Introduction.

Combine the prepared chiles, the tomatoes, *half the chopped onion*, the garlic, and *epazote* in the electric blender, and blend, a small amount at a time, to a smooth puree. Heat *2 tablespoons of lard* in a skillet and add the puree. Cook over a moderate heat, stirring constantly, for 5 minutes. Season to taste with salt, pepper, and sugar. Stir in the eggs and cream; then remove from the heat. Set the sauce aside.

Heat 1 tablespoon of lard or oil in a skillet, add the sausage, and cook until lightly browned. Drain. Mix the sausages with a little of the sauce mixture and *⅓ of the grated cheese*.

Heat 3 tablespoons of lard in a skillet. Dip the tortillas, one by one, in the chile sauce, and fry on both sides in the hot lard until limp—a matter of seconds. Place a little of the sausage mixture on each tortilla; then roll them up and place them in a dish that can go into the oven. When all the tortillas are filled and rolled, sprinkle with the remaining cheese and chopped onion. Heat the sauce and pour over the whole business. Place in a preheated 350°F. oven until hot throughout.

# Enchiladas Verdes

## GREEN ENCHILADAS

6 *poblano* chiles, fresh or
canned, or 6 bell
peppers
1 can (10-ounce size)
Mexican green tomatoes
3 sprigs of coriander
1 cup heavy cream
1 egg, lightly beaten
Salt
Freshly ground pepper

3 tablespoons lard or salad
oil
24 4-inch tortillas
6 small, cooked chicken
breasts, shredded
1 package (3-ounce size)
cream cheese
1 onion, finely chopped
¼ cup freshly grated
Parmesan cheese

Prepare the chiles as described in the Introduction; cook in boiling salted water for 5 minutes; then drain.

Combine the prepared chiles in the electric blender with the green tomatoes, coriander, and enough of the liquid from the tomatoes to blend to a thick puree. Mix the cream with the eggs, add to the puree, and season to taste with salt and pepper.

Heat the lard in a skillet. Dip the tortillas, one by one, into the puree and fry in the hot fat on both sides until limp. Mix together the shredded chicken breasts, the cream cheese softened at room temperature, and the onion. After each tortilla is fried, spread with some of the chicken mixture, roll up, and place in a fireproof baking dish. Keep warm in the oven. When all the tortillas are filled, warm the remainder of the sauce and pour over them. Sprinkle with grated cheese. Serve hot, garnished with lettuce, radishes, and chopped onion. Serves 6.

# Enchiladas Suizas

## SWISS ENCHILADAS

Make the enchiladas as for *Enchiladas Rojas* or *Verdes* but *do not add beaten egg and cream to the chile sauce*. Dip the tortillas in the plain sauce, fry in hot lard until limp, fill, and arrange in an ovenproof dish. Warm the remaining sauce; pour over the enchiladas; then add 1 cup of heavy cream. Place the dish, uncovered, in a preheated 350°F. oven for 15 to 20 minutes or until hot throughout.

# Enchiladas de Mole

## ENCHILADAS WITH *MOLE* SAUCE

*Mole Poblano*\* makes excellent enchiladas. Warm the sauce, dip the tortillas into it, fill them with warmed-up shredded chicken or turkey mixed with a little sauce, and keep hot in the oven. When all the enchiladas are made, place three or four on a plate, and decorate with a little finely chopped onion and lettuce. Just before serving, pour a little extra warm sauce over the enchiladas and sprinkle with sesame seeds. Serve with guacamole.

# Budín de Tortilla y Mole Poblano

## TORTILLA PUDDING WITH *MOLE POBLANO* SAUCE

3 tablespoons lard or salad
    oil
12 day-old, 4-inch tortillas
2 cups *Mole Poblano*
    Sauce\*
2 cooked chicken breasts,
    boned and thinly sliced

½ cup heavy cream
Salt
Freshly ground pepper

Grease an ovenproof casserole well. Heat the lard in a skillet and fry the tortillas on both sides, without allowing them to become crisp or brown. Place a layer of the sauce in the bottom of the casserole; follow with a layer of tortillas; then a layer of chicken. Continue until all ingredients are used, ending with tortillas. Pour the cream over all, and bake for 30 minutes in a preheated 350°F. oven or until heated throughout. Serves 6.

# Tamales

Tamales, which are made from a more elaborate dough than are tortillas, and steamed with or without a filling in dried cornhusks (or, in Oaxaca, in banana leaves), are mainly eaten

\*Use the recipe for Mole Poblano de Guajolote (121–22) omitting the turkey.

as meals themselves. *Tamales Blancos*, the unfilled ones, are eaten as bread with certain dishes such as *Mole Poblano*; sweet tamales are eaten as a dessert; and half-sized ones can be eaten as appetizers.

Tamales may be filled with a variety of meats and sauces. *Mole Poblano* made with either turkey or chicken and *Adobo Rojo* made with pork or chicken are among the most popular fillings. *Picadillo* also makes an excellent filling. Meat and poultry for tamales should always be boneless and either shredded or cut into small pieces.

## *Plain Tamales*

2 dozen dried cornhusks
⅓ cup lard
2 cups *masa harina*
1½ teaspoons salt

1½ teaspoons baking
   powder
1½ cups warm stock,
   about

Soak the cornhusks in hot water until softened. Cream the lard until it is very light and fluffy. Mix the *masa harina* with the salt and baking powder, and beat it into the lard, bit by bit. Gradually beat in enough stock to make a rather mushy dough. Shake the excess water from the softened cornhusks. Spread 2 tablespoons of the dough on the center part of each husk, leaving room to fold over the ends at top and bottom. Fold the husk over at the sides so that the dough is completely encased, then fold the ends of the husks over at the top and bottom so that they overlap in the middle. Tie with kitchen string or with a thin strip from the corn husk, to hold the folded-down portions in place. Put the tamales in a steamer, with the bottom ends of the cornhusks down, and steam for about 2 hours, or until the dough comes away from the husks. Sheets of kitchen parchment, about 8 inches by 4 inches, can be substituted for cornhusks. For filled tamales, spread a tablespoon of dough in the center part of each husk, top it with a tablespoon of filling, and fold over so that the filling is completely covered by the dough; tie up and steam as for plain "blind" tamales.

*Note*: If using an *adobo* filling, add 1 *ancho* or *mulato* chile, prepared in the usual way, as described in the Introduction, and pureed in the electric blender, to the dough with ¼ teaspoon each of cumin and oregano.

# Tamal de Cazuela con Pollo

## TAMAL PIE WITH CHICKEN

*Filling*:
6 *ancho* chiles
1 3½- to 4-pound chicken
1 large onion, chopped
2 cloves garlic, chopped
3 large tomatoes, peeled, seeded, and chopped
¼ cup blanched almonds
½ cup raisins
2 tablespoons lard or salad oil
Salt
Freshly ground pepper

Prepare the chiles as described in the Introduction.

Place the chicken in a heavy kettle that has a lid, and barely cover with cold water. Bring to a boil; cover; then simmer until tender when pierced with a fork. Lift out of the liquid and, when cool enough to handle, strip the meat off the bones. Discard skin, bones, and fat. Cut the meat into fairly large pieces. Set aside.

Combine the onion, garlic, tomatoes, almonds, raisins, and the prepared chiles in the electric blender; and blend, a small quantity at a time, to a coarse puree. Heat the lard in a skillet; add the puree; and cook, stirring constantly, over a moderate heat, for 5 minutes. Season to taste.

*Dough*:
½ cup lard
3 cups *masa harina*
1 teaspoon baking powder
Pinch salt
½ cup light cream
½ cup chicken broth, or canned condensed broth

Cream the lard until it is very light and fluffy. Mix the dry ingredients together, and add to lard. Add the chicken broth and cream, and beat until the dough is so light a little ball will float on the top of a glass of water.

Grease a 2-quart casserole, and line the sides and bottom with a layer of the dough. Arrange the chicken pieces in the center, add half the sauce, and cover with the remaining dough. Place in a preheated 350°F. oven and bake for 1 hour. Serve with the remaining sauce, heated.

# Tamal de Cazuela, Estilo Yucateco

## TAMAL PIE, YUCATÁN STYLE

1 3½- to 4-pound
   chicken
1 large onion, finely
   chopped
2 cloves garlic, chopped
1 pound (about 3 medium)
   tomatoes, peeled,
   seeded, and chopped
6 *pequín* chiles, crumbled
1 tablespoon annatto,
   ground

½ teaspoon oregano
¼ teaspoon cumin
Sprig of *epazote*
Chicken stock, or canned
   condensed broth
Tomato juice
Salt
Freshly ground pepper

Place the chicken with all the remaining ingredients in a large heavy casserole, with a cover, and add enough stock barely to cover. Bring to a boil; reduce heat; then simmer, covered, until chicken is tender when pierced with a fork—about 1 hour. Cool the chicken in the broth.

When chicken is cold enough to handle, strip the meat off the bones in fairly large pieces. Discard skin, fat, and bones. Skim as much fat as possible off the broth; then strain through a sieve lined with dampened cheesecloth, pressing to release all the juices from the vegetables. Measure. If there are not 3 cups of broth, add enough chicken stock and tomato juice (half and half) to make up the quantity. Taste for seasoning. Set aside for the moment.

*To make the dough*: Cream ½ cup of lard and work into 3 cups of *masa harina*, adding enough chicken broth to make a soft dough.

Grease an ovenproof casserole, and line the bottom and sides with the dough. Moisten the pieces of chicken in the broth; then lay them on top of the dough in the casserole. When all the chicken is in, cover with a layer of the dough. Cover casserole and place in a preheated 350°F. oven and bake for 1 hour.

Serve with the remaining broth heated, as a sauce. If a thicker sauce is desired, add a little *masa harina*. Serves 6.

# Tamal de Cazuela con Puerco

## TAMAL PIE WITH PORK

3 *ancho* chiles
2½ pounds pork for
    stew, cut into 2-inch
    cubes
1 onion, chopped
1 clove garlic, chopped
1 pound (about 3 medium)
    tomatoes, peeled,
    seeded, and chopped
½ teaspoon ground
    coriander seeds

1 teaspoon dried oregano
1 bay leaf
2 tablespoons lard or
    salad oil
Salt
Freshly ground pepper
Pinch of sugar

Prepare the chiles as described in the Introduction.

Place the pork in a heavy saucepan with a lid; add salt and enough water almost to cover. Bring to a boil; then reduce heat and simmer until the meat is tender when pierced with a fork—about 1½ hours. Skim off any scum that rises to the surface. Drain, reserving the stock.

Combine the prepared chiles, onion, garlic, tomatoes, coriander seed, oregano, and bay leaf in the electric blender, and reduce to a thick puree. If the blender won't accommodate all the ingredients, blend part at a time. Heat the lard in a skillet; add the puree; and cook, over a moderate heat, 5 minutes, stirring constantly. Season to taste with salt, pepper, and a little sugar.

*To make the dough*: Follow directions on page 45, using 1 cup (about) stock from the pork in place of the chicken broth.

Grease an ovenproof casserole, with a cover, and line the sides and bottom with the dough. Moisten the pieces of pork with the chile puree; then arrange in the casserole. When all the pork has been arranged, cover with the remaining dough so the pork is completely enclosed. Place in a preheated 350°F. oven, and bake for 1 hour. Heat the remaining chile sauce and serve with the pie.

# SOPAS

## SOUPS

Mexican men take soup seriously. They tend to feel deprived if a soupless meal is served at midday. Consequently, Mexican cooks take the stock pot seriously, too; and cookbooks in Mexico start the soup section with *"Manera de hacer un buen caldo"*—"How to make a good stock." You may, of course, substitute canned bouillon or chicken consommé, as many people do today; but here are the traditional recipes for meat and chicken stock. Either may be served as a soup in its own right, with the addition of *garbanzos* (chick peas) or rice.

The Aztecs and Mayas, so far as I have been able to determine, were not particularly soupy people; as indeed, their cooking methods suggest, since so often meals would have stew following soup. This is probably a Spanish aspect of the cuisine.

# How to Clarify Stock

5 cups stock                              2 egg whites

Skim and discard all the fat from the stock. The simplest way to do this is to put the stock in the refrigerator until the fat sets hard and can be lifted off. Strain the stock and measure.

Beat the egg whites. Add the egg whites to the cold stock, place over very low heat, and beat constantly with a wire whisk until the stock comes to a simmer. Let it stand for 15 minutes. Line a colander with several layers of damp cheesecloth and stand it above a 3-quart bowl. All of it must be over the bowl. Pour the stock very gently into the colander and allow the clarified stock to drain. Remove the colander. Makes 1 quart.

Stock freezes well. It is a good idea to freeze it in pint jars, since stock takes a considerable time to thaw and it is a nuisance to have to thaw quarts just to obtain a single pint or less.

# Caldo Sencillo

## MEAT STOCK

2 pounds beef shank
2 pounds short ribs of beef
1 large marrow bone
4 quarts water
2 carrots, scraped and
   sliced
1 turnip, scraped and
   sliced
1 onion, sliced

1 clove garlic
1 parsnip, scraped and
   sliced
1 leek, split in two
1 celery rib
Few sprigs of parsley
Bay leaf
6 whole peppercorns
Salt

Combine the meat and bone in cold water; cover and simmer about an hour, or until the meat is half cooked. (For a browner stock, first sear the meat in hot fat or oil.) Add the remaining ingredients; cover and simmer over a very low heat for another 3 or 4 hours. Cool and refrigerate. Remove fat; strain and use stock as the basis of any soup calling for a meat stock. Can be frozen successfully. Makes 3 quarts.

# Caldo de Pollo

## CHICKEN STOCK

| | |
|---|---|
| 1 large stewing fowl, disjointed | 1 carrot, scraped and chopped |
| 4 quarts water | 1 celery rib |
| 1 onion, sliced | Few sprigs of parsley |
| 1 clove garlic | 6 whole peppercorns |
| 1 leek, split in two | Salt |

Place the chicken in a heavy pan with the cold water. When it comes to a boil, add all the other ingredients, cover, and simmer gently for 3 hours. Cool and refrigerate. Remove fat; strain and use the stock as the basis for any soup calling for chicken stock. Makes about 3 quarts. Can be frozen successfully.

# Sopa de Albóndigas

## MEAT-BALL SOUP

Make the *albóndigas* according to recipe on page 189 for *albondiguítas*; then cook in the following soup.

| | |
|---|---|
| 2 tablespoons oil | 2 quarts meat stock or canned beef broth |
| 1 small white onion, finely chopped | Salt |
| 1 clove garlic, crushed | Freshly ground pepper |
| 1 cup tomato puree | 1 recipe *albondiguítas* |

Heat the oil, and sauté the onion until tender, without allowing it to brown. Add along with the garlic and tomato puree to the meat stock. Taste for seasoning. Bring to a boil; add the meat balls; cover and simmer gently until meat balls are cooked—about three-quarters of an hour. Serves 6.

# Sopa de Elote

## CORN SOUP

1 onion, finely chopped
2 tablespoons (¼ stick)
  butter
2½ cups cooked corn
3 tomatoes, peeled and
  seeded

4 cups meat stock or
  canned broth
1 cup heavy cream
Salt
Freshly ground pepper

Sauté the onion in the butter until tender but not browned. Put
2 cups of the corn, reserving ½ cup for garnish, into the
electric blender with the onion and tomatoes and a small amount
of stock, and blend to a smooth puree. Combine remaining
stock and the puree in a saucepan; season to taste with salt and
pepper; and cook gently for 5 minutes. Whisk cream into soup
without allowing soup to come to a boil. Serve garnished with
reserved corn. Serves 6.

# Caldo Tlalpeño

## SOUP *TLALPEÑO* STYLE

6 cups meat stock or
  canned broth
2 chicken breasts, cooked
  and cut into large strips

1 whole canned chile *largo*
1 large avocado cut into
  strips

Heat the stock; add the chicken pieces and chile *largo*. Simmer,
covered, very gently for 5 minutes so that chicken is heated
through and flavor of chile *largo* is released into soup. Remove
chile and discard. Pour into soup bowls, distributing the pieces
of chicken. Garnish with avocado strips. Serves 6.

# *Sopa de Fideos*

## VERMICELLI SOUP

| | |
|---|---|
| 2 tablespoons olive oil | Salt |
| 2 ounces fine noodles or vermicelli | Freshly ground pepper |
| | Pinch of sugar |
| 1 onion, chopped | 1 tablespoon chopped parsley |
| 1 clove garlic, chopped | |
| 4 medium tomatoes, peeled, seeded, and chopped | ¼ cup dry sherry, if liked |
| 2 quarts beef stock | ¼ cup grated Parmesan cheese |

Heat the oil, and sauté the noodles or vermicelli until golden brown, taking care not to let them burn. Drain and set aside, reserving the oil.

Combine onion, garlic, and tomatoes in the electric blender, and reduce to a puree. Cook the vegetable mixture in the reserved oil, adding a little more if necessary, for 5 minutes, stirring constantly. Place noodles, tomato puree, and the stock in a large saucepan. Season to taste with salt, pepper, and a pinch of sugar. Cover, and simmer gently until noodles are tender. Add the parsley and sherry. Serve immediately with grated cheese on the side. Serves 6.

# *Sopa de Aguacate*

## AVOCADO SOUP

| | |
|---|---|
| 3 large, ripe avocadoes | 6 cups rich chicken stock or canned chicken broth |
| Salt | |
| Freshly ground pepper | ¼ cup dry sherry |
| 1 cup heavy cream | Paprika (optional) |

Peel and mash the avocadoes; then push them through a sieve. Season to taste with salt and pepper; beat in the cream. Place in a heated soup tureen. Heat the stock; add the sherry; check the seasoning; and, when very hot pour over the avocadoes in the tureen, mixing well. If liked, garnish with a sprinkling of paprika.

If the soup is not hot enough it can be heated in a double boiler, taking care not to cook the avocado. This soup cannot be made ahead of time, as it turns brown. It can be accompanied by tortillas, quartered and fried crisp in lard or oil. The soup is also delicious served chilled. Serves 6.

## Sopa de Avellanas y Esparragos

### FILBERT AND ASPARAGUS SOUP

½ cup filberts
1 tablespoon butter
1 onion, chopped
2 ounces boiled ham
5 cups rich chicken stock
   or canned chicken broth
¼ cup dry sherry

Salt
Freshly ground pepper
½ cup heavy cream
1 10-ounce can asparagus
   tips, cut into 1-inch
   pieces

Cover the filberts with boiling water and let stand for 6 minutes. Drain and remove the skins. Dry thoroughly. Sauté until golden in the butter. Lift out of the butter with a slotted spoon and set aside. Sauté the onion in remaining butter, adding a little more if necessary, until limp but not brown. Combine the nuts, onion, and ham in the electric blender with a little stock, and blend to a smooth paste. Heat the remaining stock, add the sherry and the nut mixture, stirring to blend well. Taste for seasoning; and simmer for 10 to 15 minutes. Remove from the heat and beat in the cream. Add the asparagus tips. Reheat soup without allowing it to come to a boil. Serves 6.

## Sopa de Flor de Calabaza

### SQUASH-BLOSSOM SOUP

Dishes made with squash or pumpkin flowers are as popular in Mexico today as they were in Aztec times. The fresh blossoms are available in all the markets. You may find them in Mexican markets in the United States, but, if not, you can always start your own pumpkin patch.

1 pound squash blossoms
4 tablespoons (½ stick)
   butter
1 small white onion, finely
   chopped

2 quarts chicken stock or
   canned chicken broth
Sprig of *epazote*
Salt
Freshly ground pepper

Remove the stems from the squash blossoms and chop the blossoms roughly. Heat the butter and sauté the onion until limp; add the squash blossoms and sauté for a few minutes longer. Heat the chicken stock with the *epazote*; add the squash blossoms and the onion; taste for seasoning; cover; and simmer gently for 5 minutes. Remove *epazote* and serve. Serves 6.

## *Sopa de Pechuga de Pollo y Almendras*

### CHICKEN BREAST AND ALMOND SOUP

½ cup blanched
  almonds
2 tablespoons (¼ stick)
  butter
1 onion, chopped
2 cooked chicken breasts
2 quarts chicken stock or
  canned chicken broth

Salt
Freshly ground pepper
Pinch of nutmeg
¼ cup dry sherry
1 tablespoon chopped
  parsley

Sauté the almonds in the butter until golden. Place almonds, onion, and *one of the chicken breasts* in the electric blender with a little stock, and reduce to a puree. Add the mixture to the remaining stock, with the nutmeg and the second chicken breast, cut into small pieces. Taste for seasoning.

Heat gently, stirring from time to time. Stir in the sherry, and serve with some of the pieces of chicken in each soup plate. Sprinkle with parsley. Serves 6.

# Sopa de Media Hora

## HALF-HOUR SOUP

6 zucchini
1 large onion
6 young carrots
2 large, ripe tomatoes,
　peeled, seeded, and
　chopped
Bay leaf

2 quarts chicken stock or
　canned chicken broth
Salt
Freshly ground pepper
1 large avocado, cut into
　strips

Slice zucchini lengthwise; then cut into half-inch slices. Chop the onion; scrape and slice the carrots; peel, seed, and chop the tomatoes. Add all the vegetables and the bay leaf to the stock, and taste for seasoning. Cover, and simmer until vegetables are tender and tomato has completely disintegrated— about 30 minutes if vegetables are young. Remove the bay leaf and serve with a garnish of avocado slices. Serves 6.

# Sopa a la Mexicana

## SOUP MEXICAN STYLE

3 chicken breasts (½
　breast per person),
　skinned and boned
2 quarts very rich chicken
　stock
2 small zucchini, thinly
　sliced
3 young carrots, scraped
　and thinly sliced

1 cup green peas
3 large tomatoes, peeled,
　seeded, and sieved
1 large avocado, sliced
Salt
Freshly ground pepper
Pickled *jalapeño* or
　*serrano* chiles

Cut the chicken breasts in half and poach very gently in the chicken stock with the zucchini, carrots, and peas for 10 minutes. Add the sieved tomatoes and cook until tender, a matter of minutes. Adjust the seasoning. Serve so that each plate has a few slices of carrot, zucchini, some peas, and half of a chicken breast. Garnish with the avocado. Serve with either pickled *jalapeño* or *serrano* chiles on the side. Serves 6.

# Sopa de Bolitas de Tortilla

## TORTILLA-BALL SOUP

| | |
|---|---|
| 12 stale 4-inch tortillas | 1 egg, lightly beaten |
| 1 cup milk | 2 egg yolks |
| 1 small white onion, chopped | Salt |
| 1 clove garlic, chopped | Freshly ground pepper |
| ¼ cup grated Parmesan cheese | Oil or lard |
| Sprig of *epazote*, chopped | 2 quarts meat stock or canned beef broth |
| | ½ cup tomato puree |

Soak the tortillas in the milk. When they are soft, place in the electric blender with the onion and garlic and blend until smooth. Combine with the cheese, *epazote*, egg and yolks, and salt and pepper to taste. Shape into small balls; fry in hot lard or oil until lightly brown. Set aside and keep warm.

Heat meat stock and tomato puree together. When thoroughly hot, add the tortilla balls and serve.

If preferred, do not fry the tortilla balls but poach them in the hot stock and tomato puree for about 10 minutes. Serves 6.

# Sopa de Jericalla

## SOUP WITH CUSTARD GARNISH

| *Soup*: | *Jericalla*: |
|---|---|
| 6 cups chicken stock or canned chicken broth | 4 eggs |
| ½ cup dry sherry | 1 cup chicken stock |
| | Pinch of nutmeg |
| | Salt |
| | White pepper |

Heat the chicken stock; add the sherry; taste for seasoning; and keep warm.

Beat the eggs lightly and place in the top of a double boiler over hot water. Gradually add 1 cup of chicken stock. Season with a pinch of nutmeg, salt, and pepper. Cover and cook until custard sets. Remove from heat; cool; cut into squares or strips and serve as a garnish with the soup. Serves 6.

# Sopa de Elote con Pimientos

## CORN SOUP WITH SWEET RED PEPPERS

1 onion, chopped
2 tablespoons butter
  (¼ stick)
2 cups cooked corn
3 canned pimientos
4 cups meat stock or
  canned broth

Salt
Freshly ground pepper
¾ cup heavy cream
Paprika

Sauté the onion in the butter until tender but not browned. Combine with the corn and peppers in the electric blender with a small quantity of the stock, and blend to a smooth puree. Pour the remaining stock and puree into a saucepan; season to taste with salt and pepper; and cook gently for 5 minutes. Whisk cream into soup without allowing the soup to come to a boil. Serve sprinkled with a little paprika. Serves 6.

# Caldo Miche

## CATFISH SOUP

2 quarts water
1 onion, finely chopped
1 pound (about 3 medium)
  tomatoes, peeled,
  seeded, and chopped
6 canned *largo* chiles
1 clove crushed garlic
Bay leaf

½ teaspoon oregano
2 pound catfish, or other
  similar fish, whole
Salt
Freshly ground pepper
2 or 3 sprigs coriander,
  chopped

In a large kettle combine the water, onion, tomatoes, chiles, garlic, bay leaf, and oregano. Cook over a moderate heat until the onion is tender and the tomatoes have disintegrated. Add the fish and simmer, covered, very gently for 10 to 15 minutes, or until the fish flakes easily when tested with a fork. Lift the fish out of the broth carefully, and remove the head, skin, and bones. Return the fish in large pieces to the broth; season to taste with salt and pepper. Simmer gently for another 5 minutes. Just before serving, sprinkle with the fresh coriander. Serves 6.

# Sopa de Frijol

## BLACK-BEAN SOUP

1 cup dry black beans
2 quarts cold water
4 tablespoons lard or oil
1 medium onion, chopped
1 clove garlic, chopped
½ teaspoon chile
    *pequín*, crumbled

1 tomato, peeled, seeded,
    and chopped
¼ teaspoon oregano
Salt
Freshly ground pepper
⅓ cup dry sherry

Wash the beans but do not soak them. Place in a large saucepan with the water; cover and cook gently until *almost tender*. Heat the oil or lard in a skillet; add the onion, garlic, and chile. When the onion is tender but not browned, stir in the tomato. Combine this mixture with the beans, oregano, and salt and pepper to taste. Simmer, covered, until the beans are very tender. Push the beans through a sieve or puree them in an electric blender. Return to the saucepan; simmer a few minutes longer; stir in the sherry and serve.

    Soup may be accompanied by tortillas cut into fourths and fried crisp, crumbled fresh cheese, or a slice of lime. Serves 6.


# Sopa de Calabaza

## ZUCCHINI OR SUMMER SQUASH SOUP

1 large onion, finely
    chopped
1 pound zucchini or
    summer squash, roughly
    chopped
6 cups meat stock or
    canned broth

1 egg yolk
½ cup cream
Salt
Freshly ground pepper

Cook the onion and zucchini in the stock until tender. Push the vegetables through a sieve; return the puree to the broth; and taste for seasoning. Keep warm. Beat egg yolk and cream together. Add a little of the hot soup to the egg mixture; then whisk mixture into soup and heat through. Do not allow it to boil, or it will curdle. Serves 6.

# Sopa de Tortilla

## TORTILLA SOUP

6 stale 4-inch tortillas
½ cup salad oil
2 quarts chicken, meat
   stock or canned broth
1 onion, finely chopped

½ cup tomato puree
1 tablespoon chopped
   coriander leaves
Grated cheese

Cut the tortillas into strips about ¼ inch wide, and fry in hot oil on both sides until they are crisp and lightly browned. Drain on paper towels and keep warm.

Heat the stock with the onion, simmering gently until onion is tender. Add the tomato puree and simmer for 5 minutes longer. Add the coriander.

Place the tortillas at the bottom of a large heated soup tureen, or in individual soup bowls, and pour the hot broth over them. Serve with grated cheese. Serves 6.

# Sopas Secas

## DRY SOUPS

No one quite knows why these dishes are called dry soups in Mexico. It is probable that when the Spaniards introduced rice and the pastas a certain amount of confusion arose as to just where they fitted into a meal. The interesting thing is the speed with which the Aztecs embraced rice (which originated in Asia) and the pastas (which Marco Polo had brought to Italy as a result of his thirteenth-century journeys to China), compared with the slow acceptance of corn by Europeans.

Since the Spaniards put both rice and pasta into soup, perhaps the Aztecs concluded that these were the operative parts of the new dishes, hence "wet soup" and "dry soup." Still, who knows—and who knows if we will ever know? After the soup (wet) at the traditional Mexican late midday meal comes the "dry soup," served as a separate course in the way the Italians serve fettucine or a risotto. In this country, we would probably serve dry soup as a luncheon dish or as an accompaniment to broiled chops or other meats.

# *Arroz Gualdo*

## GOLDEN RICE

¼ cup salad oil                          Salt
2 tablespoons annatto seeds      4 cups water
2 cups rice
1 small white onion, finely
    chopped (optional)

Heat the oil in a skillet. Add the annatto seeds and fry over a
very low heat until the seeds are brown and the oil is a deep
orange-red. Lift the seeds from the oil with a slotted spoon and
discard. Add the rice and the onion. Fry until the rice has
absorbed all the oil, taking care to see that it does not burn.
Transfer it to a saucepan; add salt and the water; cover and
bring to a boil. Reduce heat to very low, and cook until the
rice is tender and has absorbed all the water. Rice will be quite
a deep golden color. Serves 6.

# *Arroz a la Mexicana*

## RICE MEXICAN STYLE

2 cups rice                                    ¼ cup olive or salad oil
1 large onion, chopped               Salt
2 cloves garlic, crushed             Freshly ground pepper
4 cups stock, or canned            ½ cup cooked green
    broth                                             peas
1½ cups tomato,                         Fresh hot, red peppers, cut
    peeled, seeded, and                    into flowers*
    chopped, or 1½ cups             Fresh coriander sprigs
    canned Italian plum              1 large avocado, peeled
    tomatoes                                    and sliced

Cover the rice with hot water and allow to stand for 15 minutes.
Drain and rinse in cold water until the water runs clear. Drain
again and dry thoroughly.
    Place the onion and garlic in the electric blender with ½
*cup of the stock*, and blend to a smooth puree. Remove from

*Slice the peppers from the tip to the stem end into 4 or 5 sections, which will
then curl back forming "flowers."

the blender and set aside. Place the tomatoes, either fresh or canned, in the blender, and reduce to a puree. Heat the oil in a skillet and sauté the rice until golden. Transfer to a saucepan; add the onion puree, tomato puree, stock, and salt and pepper to taste. Bring to a boil; lower the heat; cover and cook until *almost* all the liquid has been absorbed. Mix in the peas and continue cooking until all the liquid has been absorbed.

Serve garnished with peppers, sprigs of coriander, and slices of avocado. Serves 6 to 8.

## *Arroz Verde*

### GREEN RICE

4 *poblano* chiles or bell peppers
2 cups rice
Good handful of parsley sprigs
1 large onion, chopped

1 clove garlic, crushed
4 cups stock
¼ cup olive or salad oil
Salt
Freshly ground pepper

Prepare the chiles as described in the Introduction.

Cover the rice with hot water and allow it to stand for 15 minutes. Drain and rinse in cold water until the water runs clear. Drain again and dry thoroughly. Place the chiles in the electric blender with the parsley, onion, garlic, and a little stock. Blend until smooth. Heat the oil in a large saucepan and sauté the rice until golden. Add the puree and cook for a few minutes longer. Add the remaining stock and season to taste with salt and pepper. Cover; bring to a boil; then reduce heat and cook until the rice is tender and all the liquid has absorbed. Serves 6.

# Sopa Seca de Fideos con Chorizo

## DRY SOUP OF VERMICELLI WITH SPANISH SAUSAGE

1 *ancho* chile
2 tablespoons lard or oil
2 *chorizo* sausages, skinned and chopped
½ pound (1 8-ounce package) thin noodles or vermicelli
1 onion, chopped
1 clove garlic, chopped
1 pound (about 3 medium) tomatoes, peeled, seeded, and chopped

½ teaspoon oregano
Salt
Freshly ground pepper
Pinch sugar
1½ cups stock
¼ cup grated Parmesan cheese
1 canned *chipotle* chile, chopped

Prepare the chile as described in the Introduction.

Heat the lard or oil in skillet, and fry the sausages. Drain on paper towels and set aside. In the same fat sauté the noodles until golden, stirring constantly to prevent them from burning. Drain the noodles and place in a greased, flameproof casserole.

Combine the chile, onion, garlic, and tomatoes in the electric blender, and blend to a smooth puree. Heat the fat remaining in the skillet (adding, if necessary, enough to bring the quantity up to 2 tablespoons), and cook the puree for 5 minutes, stirring constantly. Mix in the oregano, salt and pepper to taste, a pinch of sugar, and the stock. Pour over the noodles. Arrange the sausages in a layer on top and cook, uncovered, over a low heat until the noodles are tender and all the liquid has absorbed. Or cook in a preheated 350°F. oven for about 30 minutes. To serve, sprinkle with the cheese and decorate with the chopped *chipotle* chile. Serve more cheese separately. Serves 6.

## *Arroz Amarillo*

### YELLOW RICE

Although this rice cooks to a rosy red, not a yellow, for some curious reason it is always called *Arroz Amarillo*.

| | |
|---|---|
| 2 cups rice | 1½ cups tomato, |
| 1 large onion, chopped | peeled, seeded, and |
| 2 cloves garlic, crushed | pureed |
| 4 cups stock | Salt |
| ¼ cup olive or salad oil | Freshly ground pepper |

Cover the rice with hot water and allow it to stand for 15 minutes. Drain and rinse in cold water until the water runs clear. Drain again and dry thoroughly.

Place the onion and garlic with a little stock or water in the electric blender and blend until smooth. Heat the oil in a skillet or casserole—use one which has a cover—add the rice and onion puree, and sauté until rice is golden. Add the tomato, remaining stock, salt and pepper to taste. Bring to a boil; cover; lower heat and cook until the rice is tender and all liquid has been absorbed. Serves 6.

## *Sopa Seca de Tortilla con Crema y Queso*

### DRY SOUP OF TORTILLAS WITH CREAM AND CHEESE

| | |
|---|---|
| ½ cup salad oil or lard | Freshly ground pepper |
| 1 onion, finely chopped | Pinch of sugar |
| 1 clove garlic, chopped | 18 small, day-old tortillas, |
| 1 pound (about 3 medium) | cut in ½-inch strips |
| tomatoes, peeled, | 1 cup (½ pint) heavy |
| seeded, and mashed | cream |
| ½ teaspoon oregano | 1 cup (about ¼ pound) |
| Salt | grated Parmesan cheese |

Heat *two tablespoons of the oil or lard* in a heavy skillet, and sauté the onions and garlic until tender, but not brown. Add the tomatoes, oregano, salt, pepper, a pinch of sugar, and cook, stirring, until sauce is smooth and the flavors are well blended. Set aside.

Heat the remaining fat in a skillet, and fry the tortillas without browning them. Drain on paper towels. Pour a layer of the sauce into a greased, ovenproof casserole; follow this with a layer of the tortillas, a layer of cream, a layer of sauce, and

a layer of grated cheese, ending with cheese. Place in a pre-heated 350°F. oven until heated through—15 minutes or more. Serves 6.

## Sopa Seca de Tortilla con Chile Poblano

### DRY SOUP OF TORTILLAS WITH POBLANO CHILE

6 canned *poblano* chiles,
  or 6 bell peppers,
  coarsely chopped
½ cup salad oil or lard
1 onion, finely chopped
1 clove garlic, chopped
Salt
Freshly ground pepper

Pinch of sugar
18 small, day-old tortillas,
  cut in ½-inch strips
1 cup (about ¼ pound)
  grated Parmesan cheese
1 cup (½ pint) heavy
  cream
Butter

Rinse the *poblano* chiles, removing the seeds, if any. If using bell peppers, prepare as described in the Introduction, then simmer for about ten minutes.

Heat the oil in a heavy skillet, and sauté the onion and garlic until tender but not brown. Add the *poblanos* or bell peppers, and sauté until they are quite soft. Lift out of the fat, drain on paper towels, season to taste with salt, pepper and sugar and set aside. In the remaining fat, fry the tortillas but do not allow them to become crisp or brown. Drain on paper towels.

Grease a shallow, ovenproof casserole, and arrange a layer of tortillas topped with some cream, a layer of the chile mixture, a layer of cheese, until all the ingredients are used up, finishing with a layer of cheese. Dot with butter, and place in a pre-heated 350°F. oven until hot throughout—about 30 minutes. Serves 6.

# *Sopa Seca de Fideos*

## DRY SOUP OF VERMICELLI

2 tablespoons lard or oil
½ pound (1 8-ounce package) thin noodles or vermicelli*
1 onion, minced
1 clove garlic, minced
1 pound (about 3 medium) tomatoes, peeled, seeded, and mashed

Salt
Freshly ground pepper
Pinch of sugar
½ teaspoon oregano
1½ cups meat stock
¼ cup grated Parmesan cheese

Heat the oil or lard in a large, heavy skillet, and fry the noodles until golden brown, stirring constantly to prevent their burning. Drain and pour into a flameproof casserole.

Fry the onion, garlic, and tomato in the fat remaining in the skillet for about 5 minutes, stirring constantly. Season to taste with salt, pepper, a pinch of sugar, and the oregano. Mix stock in well and pour over the noodles in the casserole. Cook over a low heat, uncovered, for about half an hour, stirring from time to time. Or cook in a preheated 350°F. oven for 30 minutes. The dish is ready when the noodles are tender and all the liquid has been absorbed. Before serving, sprinkle with the grated cheese, serving some extra cheese on the side. You may slide the casserole under the broiler to melt cheese. Serves 6.

*Spaghetti, tagliatelle (fettucine), wide egg noodles, or macaroni may all be used for this dish.

# Sopa Seca de Tortilla con Chorizo

### DRY SOUP OF TORTILLAS WITH
### SPANISH SAUSAGE

| | |
|---|---|
| Salad oil or lard | Freshly ground pepper |
| 3 *chorizo* sausages, | Pinch of sugar |
| skinned and chopped | ½ teaspoon oregano |
| 1 onion, finely chopped | 18 small, day-old *tortillas*, |
| 1 clove garlic, chopped | cut into ½-inch |
| 1 pound (about 3 medium) | strips |
| tomatoes, seeded, | ½ cup heavy cream |
| peeled, and mashed | ½ cup (about 2 ounces) |
| Salt | grated Parmesan cheese |

Heat a little oil or lard in a heavy skillet, and fry the sausages. The amount of fat to use depends on the sausages, which are sometimes dry, but which more often give off a quantity of fat. When done, lift out the sausages, drain on paper towels, and set aside. Fry the onion and garlic in 2 tablespoons of fat until limp but not brown; add the tomatoes and continue cooking, stirring from time to time, until the sauce is smooth. Add salt and pepper to taste, a pinch of sugar, and the oregano. Set aside.

Heat more oil or lard in the skillet, and fry the tortilla strips without letting them become crisp and brown. Drain on paper towels. Grease a shallow, ovenproof casserole; add a layer of tomato sauce on the bottom; then a layer of tortillas; a layer of sausage, until all the ingredients are used up, finishing with a layer of tortillas. Cover with the cream, and sprinkle with the cheese. Place in a preheated 350°F. oven until hot through-out—about 30 minutes. Serves 6.

# Sopa Seca de Sesos

### DRY SOUP MADE WITH BRAINS

"Calf's brains form the most wholesome and reparative diet for all those who are debilitated by excessive head-work; and the same remark applies to the brains of the ox and the sheep," wrote Escoffier in *A Guide to Modern Cookery*.

After giving his admirable recipe for cooking brains, M. Escoffier went on to point out a peculiarity of this organ meat, which is this: although brains take only 30 minutes to cook "until done," they may cook for as long as 2 hours, as the process only tends to make them firmer—which may be desirable.

2 pairs calf's brains
Salt
1 tablespoon vinegar
Salad oil or lard
1 large onion, finely
  chopped
1 clove garlic, chopped
1 pound (about 3 medium)
  tomatoes, peeled,
  seeded, and mashed

4 canned *serrano* chiles,
  chopped
Freshly ground pepper
Pinch of salt
4 sprigs of *epazote*
18 4-inch day-old tortillas
1 cup heavy cream
Grated Parmesan cheese

Carefully remove the membrane enveloping the brains and put them to soak in cold water for an hour. Drain; place in a saucepan with enough boiling salted water to cover them well. Add the vinegar; bring to the boiling point; and simmer, skimming as necessary, for 30 minutes. Drain and chop coarsely. Set aside.

Heat 3 tablespoons of oil in a large skillet, and fry the onion and garlic until the onion is tender. Add the tomatoes, chiles, salt, pepper, sugar, and *epazote*; and cook until the sauce is smooth and well blended. Set aside ¼ of the sauce. Mix the brains gently into the remaining sauce. Keep warm.

With kitchen shears cut the tortillas into strips about ½- to 1-inch wide. Heat 6 tablespoons of oil in a skillet, and fry the tortillas on both sides for a few minutes, without browning. Drain on paper towels. Grease an ovenproof casserole and cover the bottom with a thin layer of the sauce. Follow this with a layer of tortillas topped with some cream, and a layer of the brains mixed with the sauce. Continue in this way until all the ingredients are used, ending with tortillas and cream. Pour the reserved sauce over the dish, and sprinkle it with cheese. Place in a preheated 350°F. oven until heated through—about 20 minutes or more. Serves 6.

*Note*: Day-old tortillas are preferred because fresh tortillas absorb too much liquid. However, fresh tortillas, dried in a moderate oven for 5 to 10 minutes, can be used.

# SALSAS
## SAUCES

Sauces were an integral part of the pre-Columbian Mexican kitchen. The importance of their role can be seen from a look at the ingredients used today, the principal ones being the indigenous tomatoes, chiles, and avocadoes. When combined with herbs and other seasonings, they produce a fascinating variety, ranging from the mild through pungent and hot to very hot. Even now little use is made of European foods such as flour, cream, butter, and eggs.

In addition to the sauces that are part and parcel of individual dishes, there are what might be called the "on-the-table-sauces," without which no Mexican meal is complete. A bowl of *Salsa Cruda* (Uncooked Tomato Sauce), or *Salsa Verde* (Green Sauce), freshly made, is as important to the table setting as salt and pepper.

Mexican sauces are often added to soups, are used to enliven any of the dry soups, and are eaten with plain meat or fish. A spoonful in a tortilla, which, rolled up, becomes a taco, is customary. The very good rolls called *bolillos* are used to mop up the sauce on one's plate as the French use their excellent bread to mop up sauce or gravy. *Guacamole*, which is served whenever avocadoes are in season, is eaten both as a sauce and a salad.

All the sauces in this chapter can be used with the dishes from the Corn Kitchen.

The most popular of the table sauces are: *Salsa Verde, Salsa de Chile Güero, Salsa Cruda, Salsa de Jitomate, Salsa de Chipotle, Salsa Ranchera, Salsa de Chile Rojo*, and *Salsa de Chile Pasilla*.

In addition there are the bottled sauces, which closely resemble American Tabasco. Most of them can be bought in Spanish-American markets. All the bottled chile sauces are hot. One is even called *Esta Sí Pica*, which can be translated as "This One Really Stings." It is made from small, hot, red chiles, and sting, indeed, it does. There are others made from different species of hot, red chiles from both the North and from Yucatán; and there are the sauces made from green *serrano* and *jalapeño* chiles.

There are no set rules for serving bottled sauces—a dash on tacos or *tostadas* adds a piquant touch without too much heat. The adventurous cook is encouraged to experiment, for, although the sauces all have heat in common, their flavors differ subtly.

# *Guacamole*

## AVOCADO SAUCE

2 large, very ripe avocadoes

1 medium tomato, peeled, seeded, and chopped

½ small white onion, minced

2 or more canned *serrano* chiles, chopped

Several sprigs of fresh coriander, finely chopped

Salt

Freshly ground pepper

Pinch of sugar

Peel and mash the avocadoes. Mix well with all the other ingredients and pile into a serving dish with an avocado pit in the center. This is supposed to keep the guacamole from turning dark.

If you are not using the guacamole immediately, cover tightly with aluminum foil or plastic wrap to exclude the air (possibly a more reliable formula than the retention of the avocado pit), and refrigerate.

Use either as a sauce or a salad. It also makes an excellent dip with fried tortilla triangles, along with a cocktail. Makes about 4 cups.

# Guacamole del Norte

## AVOCADO SAUCE, NORTHERN STYLE

2 large, very ripe
  avocadoes
½ can (10-ounce size),
  or about 6, Mexican
  green tomatoes, drained
½ small white onion,
  minced

Few sprigs of fresh
  coriander, finely
  chopped
2 or more canned *serrano*
  chiles, chopped
Salt
Freshly ground pepper

Peel and mash the avocadoes. Mix well with all the other ingredients and pile into a serving dish with an avocado pit in the center. If not using immediately, it's best to cover the dish securely with aluminum foil or plastic wrap and refrigerate, although the addition of the green tomatoes does seem to help to prevent the guacamole from turning dark.

Use as a sauce, salad, or dip with fried tortilla triangles. Makes about 4 cups.

# Salsa Verde I

## GREEN SAUCE

1 10-ounce can Mexican
  green tomatoes, drained
1 small white onion, finely
  chopped
2 or more canned *serrano*
  chiles, chopped

1 clove garlic, chopped
6 sprigs fresh coriander,
  chopped
Salt
Freshly ground pepper

Combine all the ingredients in the electric blender, blend for a second or two, or mix and mash thoroughly. Taste for seasoning. Makes about 1½ cups.

## Salsa Verde II
### GREEN SAUCE

Make the sauce as above, omitting the onion and garlic and doubling the amount of coriander leaves—use up to a good handful. Blend until smooth in the electric blender. Makes about 1 cup.

## Salsa de Chile Güero
### GREEN CHILE SAUCE

This mild and delicate sauce is made from the medium-sized, tapering, pale-green *güero* chiles, always available canned, and at certain times of the year fresh, in supermarkets and in some markets specializing in fresh fruits and vegetables. In this country, they are known as California peppers or, more usually, as sweet green peppers. In spite of this vague nomenclature, they are quite unmistakable. They are not hot, and still they could never be confused with the green bell pepper—it is so much darker in color, so different in shape, so different in flavor.

This sauce, excellent scrambled into eggs, can also be served hot or cold, as an accompaniment to any delicate white fish, or with chicken.

4 sweet (California) green peppers (*güero* chiles)
1 large tomato, peeled, seeded, and chopped (or ½ can Mexican green tomatoes, drained)
6 sprigs of parsley, chopped (or 6 sprigs of fresh coriander)
1 small white onion, chopped
1 clove garlic, crushed
1 canned *serrano* chile, chopped
Salt
Freshly ground pepper
Pinch of sugar
3 tablespoons salad oil

Simmer the *güero* chiles in boiling water for 5 minutes. Drain, and remove the stems and seeds. Place in the electric blender with the tomato, onion, garlic, parsley, chile, salt and pepper to taste, and a pinch of sugar. Blend for 2 or 3 seconds.

Heat the oil in a skillet and cook the mixture, stirring constantly, for 2 or 3 minutes. Makes about 1½ cups.

# *Salsa de Jitomate*

## TOMATO SAUCE

2 tablespoons salad oil
1 onion, finely chopped
1 clove garlic, finely
 chopped
2 large tomatoes, peeled,
 seeded, and chopped
½ teaspoon sugar

2 or more *serrano* chiles,
 chopped
Salt
Freshly ground pepper
1 tablespoon fresh
 coriander, chopped

Heat the oil and fry the onion and garlic until limp. Add all the other ingredients, *except the coriander*, and cook gently for 15 minutes. Taste for seasoning. Add the coriander and cook for a minute or two longer. Serve either hot or cold. Makes about 2 cups.

# *Salsa Cruda*

## UNCOOKED TOMATO SAUCE

This sauce appears on Mexican tables almost as often as salt and pepper. It is used with cooked meats, poultry, fish, and eggs, and with tacos and *tostadas*.

2 very ripe large tomatoes,
 peeled and chopped fine
2 or more canned *serrano*
 chiles, chopped
1 small onion, finely
 chopped

1 tablespoon fresh
 coriander, chopped
Salt
Freshly ground pepper
Pinch of sugar

Mix all ingredients, taste for seasoning, and serve cold. Makes about 2½ cups.

# Salsa de Almendra Verde

## GREEN ALMOND SAUCE

3 tablespoons olive oil
1 slice white bread
¾ cup blanched
   almonds
1 10-ounce can Mexican
   green tomatoes
1 clove garlic, chopped

6 sprigs of green coriander
Canned green *serrano*
   chiles, rinsed
1 cup chicken stock, or
   canned chicken broth
Salt
Freshly ground pepper

Heat 2 *tablespoons of the oil* in a skillet, and fry the bread
until it is golden brown on both sides. Drain on paper towels,
and chop coarsely. Add the remaining oil to the skillet, and
sauté the almonds until they are golden. Drain. Combine the
bread, almonds, green tomatoes with ½ cup of their liquid,
garlic, coriander, and chile in the electric blender, and blend
until smooth. Pour into a saucepan; add the stock; taste for
seasoning; and simmer gently for 5 minutes. Makes about 2
cups. Will keep about 1 week refrigerated.

# Salsa Ranchera

## COUNTRY-STYLE SAUCE

2 tablespoons salad oil
2 large tomatoes, peeled,
   seeded, and mashed
Salt
Freshly ground pepper

Pinch of sugar
1 12-ounce can *jalapeño*
   chiles, rinsed and
   chopped
1 tablespoon vinegar

Heat the oil in a skillet, add the tomatoes, and cook down to
a thick puree. Season to taste with salt, pepper, and a pinch
of sugar. Remove from heat, add the chiles and vinegar, and
mix well. Makes about 1½ cups.

# Salsa de Almendra Roja

## RED ALMOND SAUCE

The versatile almond sauces are excellent over hot, drained green vegetables such as peas and green beans, and very good over any hot, cooked

fish or meat, *except beef*. However, other dishes on the menu should be plain, since the sauces are quite rich.

| | |
|---|---|
| 3 tablespoons olive oil | ¼ teaspoon oregano |
| 1 slice white bread | 1 small tomato, peeled, |
| 1 small white onion, finely | seeded, and chopped |
| chopped | 1½ cups chicken stock, |
| 1 clove garlic, chopped | or canned chicken broth |
| ½ cup blanched | Salt |
| almonds | Freshly ground pepper |
| ½ teaspoon crumbled, | Pinch of sugar |
| chile *pequín* | |

Heat *2 tablespoons of the oil* in a skillet, and fry the bread until it is golden brown on both sides. Drain on paper towels; then chop coarsely. Add the remaining oil to the skillet, and sauté the onion, garlic, almonds, and crumbled chile until the almonds are golden and the onion is transparent. Do not brown. Combine with the bread, oregano, and the tomato in the electric blender with *½ cup of the stock*, and blend until smooth. Pour into a saucepan, add the remaining stock, and taste for seasoning. Simmer gently for 10 to 15 minutes. Makes about 2 cups. Will keep about 1 week refrigerated.

## *Salsa de Chile Rojo*

### RED CHILE SAUCE

This is the classic Mexican Red Chile Sauce. It is mild. For a touch of fire, add 6 crumbled *pequín* chiles.

| | |
|---|---|
| 4 *ancho* chiles | 1 tablespoon salad oil |
| 2 large tomatoes, peeled, | Salt |
| seeded, and chopped | Freshly ground pepper |
| 1 large onion, chopped | ½ teaspoon sugar |
| 1 clove garlic, chopped | 3 tablespoons olive oil |
| 5 or 6 sprigs of parsley, | 1 tablespoon wine vinegar |
| chopped | |

Prepare the chiles as described in the Introduction.

Combine the chiles, tomatoes, onion, and garlic in the electric blender, and blend to a puree. Heat the oil in a skillet, add the puree, and cook for 5 minutes, stirring constantly. Add the parsley, salt and pepper to taste, and the sugar. Cool. Stir in the olive oil and vinegar well.

If using the hot *pequín* chiles, add them to the blender with the tomatoes and other ingredients. Makes about 2 cups.

## *Salsa de Chile Pasilla*

### PASILLA CHILE SAUCE

| | |
|---|---|
| 4 *pasilla* chiles | 1 tablespoon salad oil |
| 1 teaspoon dried oregano | 3 tablespoons olive oil |
| Salt | 1 tablespoon wine vinegar |
| Freshly ground pepper | |

Prepare the chiles as described in the Introduction, and place in the electric blender. Reduce to a smooth puree. Add the oregano and salt and pepper to taste, and mix well. Heat the *1 tablespoon salad oil* in a skillet and cook the puree for 5 minutes, stirring constantly. Cool; then stir in the olive oil and vinegar. Serve cold. Makes about 1½ cups.

## *Salsa de Chile Chipotle*

### CHIPOTLE CHILE SAUCE

| | |
|---|---|
| 1 onion, finely chopped | Salt |
| 1 clove garlic, chopped | Freshly ground pepper |
| 2 tablespoons salad oil | ½ teaspoon sugar |
| 2 large tomatoes, peeled, seeded, and chopped | Canned *chipotle* chiles to taste, chopped |
| ½ teaspoon oregano | |

Sauté the onion and garlic in hot oil until tender but not brown. Add all the other ingredients and cook gently for about 15 minutes. Taste for seasoning. Makes about 2 cups.

# HUEVOS

## EGGS

Though the Aztecs had quail, duck, turkey, pigeon, and other eggs, it was the Spaniards who introduced the domestic hen and their own egg dishes, which Mexico has adopted, adapted, and added to its own repertoire.

Almost all the Mexican egg dishes are hearty enough to make a satisfying luncheon, especially if served with a green salad, fruit, and cheese.

The classical Mexican egg dish, *Huevos Rancheros* (Country-Style Eggs) appears on just about every hotel and restaurant menu in the country. Before industrialization changed the old patterns, these egg dishes were popular at *almuerzo*, the second and heartier breakfast that followed the coffee and rolls of the dawn hours on ranches and farms. They are ideal for a late, lazy breakfast or brunch. Travelers in Mexico will find that they provide an excellent source of energy for a long morning of sight-seeing.

# Huevos Rancheros

## COUNTRY-STYLE EGGS

1 recipe *Salsa de Jitomate**
3 tablespoons lard or salad
    oil
12 small (4-inch) tortillas
12 eggs (2 per person)

Butter
½ recipe *Frijoles
    Negros Refritos* (Fried
    Beans)
Canned *serrano* chiles

Heat the lard in a skillet, and fry the tortillas on both sides until limp. Drain on paper towels. Place two tortillas, side by side, on each person's plate, and keep warm.

Fry the eggs in butter until the whites are set. Slide an egg onto each tortilla, spoon some hot sauce over each egg, and serve with a couple of tablespoons of hot beans. Serve remaining *Salsa de Jitomate* and a dish of *serrano* chiles on the side. Serves 6.

*Note*: Some people prefer to have their tortillas fried until crisp.

# Huevos Motuleños

## EGGS YUCATÁN STYLE

4 tablespoons lard
6 large (6-inch) tortillas
½ recipe *Frijoles
    Negros Refritos*
½ recipe (1 cup) *Salsa
    de Jitomate*
6 eggs

Bottled hot chile sauce
    from Yucatán or
    Tabasco
1 cup cooked green peas
2 tablespoons grated
    Parmesan cheese

Heat the lard in a skillet, and fry the tortillas on both sides until crisp. Spread 3 of the tortillas with a layer of the heated beans and keep hot.

Fry the eggs and place 1 egg on each of the tortillas. Gently lay a second tortilla on top of each egg and top it with a second fried egg. Spoon the tomato sauce over the eggs, and add a good sprinkle of the bottled chile sauce. Arrange a garland of green peas around each serving. Sprinkle with grated cheese. Serves 3.

*Fresh coriander may be omitted from the recipe.

# Huevos con Cecina

## EGGS WITH DRIED BEEF

1 2½-ounce package
  dried beef
1 tablespoon butter
2 canned *serrano* chiles,
  chopped, or ½
  teaspoon chile *pequín*,
  crumbled

1 onion, finely chopped
Salt
Freshly ground pepper
4 eggs
2 tablespoons heavy cream

Pour boiling water over the dried beef; drain and chop coarsely. Heat the butter in a skillet, and sauté the onion until limp. Add the beef and the chiles, and cook gently for 2 or 3 minutes. Beat the eggs with the cream and scramble them into the beef mixture over moderately low heat. Stir, with a wooden spoon, slowly and constantly, to reach the entire surface of the pan, until the eggs are set—about 3 or 4 minutes. Serve immediately. Serves 2.

# Huevos a la Mexicana

## EGGS MEXICAN STYLE

¼ recipe (½ cup)
  *Salsa de Jitomate*\*
12 eggs, beaten lightly

Salt
Freshly ground pepper

Heat the sauce in a large skillet. Scramble the eggs into the sauce, over a moderately low heat, for 3 or 4 minutes, stirring slowly and constantly with a wooden spoon to reach the entire surface of the pan. Serve immediately, once the eggs are set. Serves 6.

Hot tortillas and beans, either plain or *refritos* (fried), and a dish of *serrano* chiles traditionally accompany these eggs.

\*Fresh coriander may be omitted from the recipe.

# *Huevos con Nopalitos*

## EGGS WITH CACTUS PIECES

1 8-ounce can *nopalitos*  Salt
3 tablespoons butter  Freshly ground white
2 tablespoons heavy cream   pepper
6 eggs, lightly beaten

Drain the liquid from the cactus pieces. Rinse thoroughly in cold water, and drain well in a colander.

Heat the butter in a skillet and sauté the cactus pieces lightly. Beat the heavy cream into the eggs; season with salt and pepper to taste. Scramble the eggs into the cactus pieces, over moderately low heat, stirring slowly and constantly with a wooden spoon to reach the entire surface of the pan. The eggs will set to a creamy consistency in 3 to 4 minutes. Serve immediately. Serves 3.

# *Huevos Revueltos*

## SCRAMBLED EGGS

4 tablespoons butter  3 tablespoons chopped
1 onion, finely chopped   parsley
3 tablespoons sour cream  Salt
6 eggs, lightly beaten  Freshly ground pepper

Heat the butter in a skillet. Sauté the onion until tender but not brown. Remove from the heat, and set aside. Beat the sour cream into the eggs with a whisk. Mix in the parsley; then season to taste with salt and pepper. Reheat the onion and butter mixture over moderately low heat. Add the eggs and scramble, stirring slowly and constantly with a wooden spoon, to reach the entire surface of the pan, for 3 to 4 minutes. Serve immediately. Serves 3.

## *Huevos a la Malagueña*

### EGGS MALAGA STYLE

2 tablespoons butter
2 boiled ham steaks, about
   3 ounces each
1 8-ounce can green
   asparagus
2 thick slices tomato

1 4-ounce can baby peas
12 small button mushroom
   caps, sautéed in butter
4 eggs
1 canned pimiento, cut into
   strips

Melt the butter in a large, flat, ovenproof dish. Arrange 1 ham
steak with half the asparagus, 1 slice of tomato, and 6 of the
mushroom caps on each end of the dish. Divide the dish in
two with a little wall of the peas. Break 2 of the eggs directly
onto the dish at each end next to the garnish and inside the
wall of peas. Garnish with the strips of pimiento. Place in a
preheated 350°F. oven until the eggs are set—about 10 to 15
minutes. Serves 2.

## *Huevos Revueltos con Ejotes*

### EGGS SCRAMBLED WITH GREEN BEANS

1 10-ounce package frozen
   cut green beans, thawed
½ cup chicken broth
2 tablespoons butter

Salt
Freshly ground pepper
6 eggs, lightly beaten

Cook the beans in the hot chicken broth for 8 minutes. Drain
and set aside. Heat the butter in a skillet, and sauté the onion
until limp, but not brown. Add the beans; season to taste with
salt and pepper; and sauté for 2 minutes. Scramble the eggs
into the vegetable mixture over a moderately low heat, and
cook, stirring slowly and constantly with a wooden spoon to
reach the entire surface of the pan. The eggs will set to a creamy
consistency in 3 to 4 minutes. Serve immediately. Serves 3.

*Note*: This makes an interesting vegetable dish, especially with
broiled meat, but it also makes a hearty breakfast or light
luncheon. It can be served with ham and *Salsa Verde*.

# Huevos con Camarones

## EGGS WITH SHRIMP

2 tablespoons oil
2 tablespoons butter
1 large onion, finely
    chopped
1 clove garlic, chopped
½ pound (about 2
    small) tomatoes, peeled,
    seeded, and chopped
3 canned *jalapeño* chiles,
    deseeded, rinsed, and
    cut into strips

½ pound raw shrimp,
    peeled, deveined, and
    coarsely chopped
Salt
Freshly ground pepper
6 eggs
Lemon wedges

Heat the oil and butter in a heavy skillet. Sauté the onion and garlic until the onion is tender, but not brown. Add the tomatoes and cook, stirring from time to time, for about 5 minutes. Add the chiles and shrimp to the skillet; season to taste with salt and pepper. Remove from the heat.

Beat the eggs until well blended. Scramble the eggs into the shrimp mixture, and cook over a moderately low heat, stirring slowly and constantly with a wooden spoon to reach the entire surface of the pan. The eggs will set to a creamy consistency in 3 to 4 minutes. Cook for 1 minute longer. Because this is to be cut and served pie fashion, it must be cooked this extra time, without stirring. Serve with lemon wedges. Serves 3.

# Huevos con Chorizo

## EGGS WITH SPANISH HOT SAUSAGE

1 tablespoon butter
1 onion, finely chopped
1 clove garlic, chopped
2 *chorizo* sausages,
    skinned and chopped
1 pound (about 3 medium)
    tomatoes, peeled,
    seeded, and chopped

Salt
Freshly ground pepper
Pinch of sugar
2 canned *largo* chiles,
    chopped
6 eggs, lightly beaten

Heat the butter in a skillet, and sauté the onion until limp. Add the garlic and sausages, and sauté for about 5 minutes. Add the tomatoes, salt and pepper to taste, sugar, and the chiles. Cook gently for another 5 minutes. Stir the eggs into the mixture and cook, over moderately low heat, stirring slowly and constantly with a wooden spoon to reach the entire surface of the pan. The eggs will set to a creamy consistency in 3 to 4 minutes. Serve immediately. Serves 3.

## *Tortilla Española a la Mexicana*

### SPANISH POTATO OMELET, MEXICAN STYLE

Spaniards are immensely fond of their *Tortilla de Patatas a la Española*. So are the Mexicans. But the Mexicans have substracted half the potatoes and added a wicked little touch of chile *pequín*.

| | |
|---|---|
| ¼ cup heavy olive oil | ½ teaspoon chile |
| 2 medium-sized potatoes, peeled and cut into small dice | *pequín*, crumbled |
| | 4 eggs |
| | Salt |
| 1 medium onion, finely chopped | Freshly ground pepper |

Heat the oil in an omelet pan, and sauté the potatoes, onion, and chile over a low heat until the potatoes and onion are cooked.

Beat the eggs with *2 teaspoons of cold water* and salt and pepper to taste. Pour over the vegetables; stir with the back of a fork until the eggs form a custard. Cook for a minute or so longer, without stirring, until the eggs are set. This type of omelet is not rolled, but is served flat. Some cooks brown the top very quickly in a preheated broiler. Serves 2.

## *Tortilla a la Mexicana*

### MEXICAN OMELET

| | |
|---|---|
| 1 chicken breast, boned | 3 tablespoons butter |
| Chicken stock | 6 eggs |
| 2 *ancho* chiles | Salt |
| 1 large tomato, peeled, seeded, and chopped | Freshly ground pepper |

Poach the chicken breast in stock for 10 minutes. Cool; then cut into cubes. Set aside.

Prepare the chiles as described in the Introduction. Place with the tomato in the electric blender, and blend to a smooth puree. Heat *1 tablespoon of the butter* in a skillet; add the puree; and cook, stirring constantly, for about 5 minutes. Add the cubes of chicken. Season to taste with salt and pepper, and keep warm.

Beat the eggs with salt and pepper, until just blended. Heat the remaining butter in an omelet pan over high heat until it foams. Pour in the beaten eggs and stir them rapidly with the back of a fork for 3 to 4 seconds. Add the chicken mixture, tilt the pan, and roll the omelet over the filling. Slide it out of the pan onto a warm serving platter. Serves 3.

## *Huevos Adobados*

### EGGS IN *ADOBO* SAUCE

6 *ancho* chiles
2 large onions, chopped
1 clove garlic, chopped
1 large tomato, peeled, seeded, and chopped
⅛ teaspoon ground cloves
¼ teaspoon cinnamon
2 or 3 sprigs of fresh coriander

Chicken stock
Salt
Freshly ground pepper
1 teaspoon sugar
2 tablespoons lard or salad oil
1 tablespoon vinegar
12 eggs

Prepare the chiles as described in the Introduction.

Combine the chiles, onion, garlic, tomato, cloves, cinnamon, coriander, ¼ *cup of the stock*, salt and pepper to taste, and sugar in the electric blender, and blend to a coarse puree.

Heat the lard in a skillet; add the puree and cook for 5 minutes, stirring constantly. Then add the vinegar. If the mixture is too thick to pour, add a little more stock—about ¼ cup. Pour into a flameproof casserole and set aside.

Fill a large saucepan with water and bring to a boil. Add the eggs; remove from heat and leave for 8 minutes. Drain and cover the eggs with cold water, allowing them to stand for 2 minutes. Shell the eggs carefully and add them to the prepared sauce. Heat gently until the eggs and sauce are both thoroughly hot.

Serve on a bed of plain white rice with *Guacamole del Norte*, page 75. Serves 6.

*Note*: It is worth going to the trouble to prepare the eggs as described (actually they are *Oeufs Mollet*), so they will be delicate and tender. After being heated in the sauce, the eggs will be firm—but still tender.

## Huevos en Rabo de Mestiza

### EGGS "EN RABO DE MESTIZA"

In Mexican cookbooks, *Rabo de Mestiza* is always put in quotation marks—no one seems to know what it means. Actually, it is a Spanish phrase dating back to the early days of the Conquest which means, literally, "in the rags and tatters of the daughter of a Spaniard and an Indian." It must be remembered that sixteenth-century Spaniards were rather inclined to give bizarre names to food. *Ropa Vieja*, an honorable Spanish dish, means "Old Clothes," and the famous *Olla Podrida*, an excellent stew, means "Rotten Pot"! Whatever one calls them, Eggs "*en Rabo de Mestiza*" taste fine.

2 fresh *poblano* chiles\* or 2 bell peppers
4 tablespoons olive oil
1 onion, finely chopped
1½ pounds tomatoes (about 4 to 5 medium), peeled, seeded, and chopped
Salt
Freshly ground pepper
Pinch of sugar
6 slices Monterey Jack, cheddar, or similar cheese
6 eggs

Prepare the chiles as described in the Introduction, and cut into strips. Heat the oil in a skillet which has a cover, and sauté the chiles, being careful not to allow them to brown. Add the onion, and continue cooking until the onion is tender. Add the tomatoes, salt and pepper to taste, and the sugar. When the tomatoes have cooked down and the mixture is as thick as heavy cream, lay the slices of cheese on top and continue cooking for a few minutes. The cheese will partially melt.

Break the eggs into a saucer, one by one, and slide carefully on top of the cheese. Cover and cook for about 3 minutes. Then turn off the heat and allow the eggs to stand until the whites have set. Serves 3.

\*If canned *poblano* chiles are used for this dish, it is not necessary to prepare them. They need only to be rinsed.

# Huevos Revueltos en Salsa Verde

## EGGS SCRAMBLED WITH GREEN SAUCE

1 small white onion,
    chopped
Heart of a romaine lettuce
Handful of fresh coriander
3 canned *jalapeño* chiles,
    deseeded and chopped
½ 10-ounce can Mexican
    green tomatoes

2 tablespoons salad oil
    or lard
Salt
Freshly ground pepper
8 eggs, lightly beaten

Place the onion, lettuce, coriander, chiles, and green tomatoes with half their liquid in the electric blender, and blend to a smooth puree. Heat the oil in a skillet, and cook the puree, stirring constantly, for 2 or 3 minutes or until it reaches the consistency of heavy cream. Season to taste with salt and pepper.

Scramble the eggs into the sauce over a moderately low heat, stirring slowly and constantly with a wooden spoon to reach the entire surface of the pan. In 3 to 4 minutes the eggs will have set. Serves 4.

# Pisto

## SCRAMBLED EGGS WITH VEGETABLES

3 tablespoons oil
1 onion, finely chopped
4 cooked new potatoes,
    peeled and cut in cubes
2 small chopped zucchini
    or summer squash,
    cooked and coarsely
    chopped
¼ pound boiled ham,
    chopped
1 pimiento, chopped
3 or 4 sprigs of parsley,
    chopped

1 teaspoon crushed, dried
    chile *pequín*
2 medium tomatoes,
    peeled, seeded, and
    chopped
1 cup cooked green peas
Salt
Freshly ground pepper
6 eggs, lightly beaten with
    1 tablespoon cold water

Heat the oil in a large, heavy skillet, and sauté the onion until tender but not brown. Add the potatoes, zucchini, ham, pimiento, parsley, and chile. Sauté over moderate heat for about 5 minutes, stirring so that the mixture does not burn, and taking care not to break up the vegetables. Add the tomatoes and continue cooking for a few more minutes. Add the peas. Season to taste with salt and pepper. Fold the eggs into the vegetable mixture gently, and cook until the eggs have set. Serves 3 to 4.

*Note*: Like omelets, egg dishes of this nature are best made in small servings.

# PESCADOS

## FISH

Mexico's coastline, bordering the Pacific, the Gulf of Mexico, and the Caribbean, is enormously long. As a result, there is a great abundance of fish and seafood, many varieties of which are also to be found in the United States. Snapper and red snapper, pompano, flounder, perch, bluefish, mackerel, black bass and striped bass, tuna, albacore, and brill (Pacific sole) are among the common fish in the markets. Mexican oysters and shrimp and the moro crabs of Yucatán are famous. Squid, octopus, clams, abalone, conch, turtle, mussels, frogs' legs, crayfish, and prawns, as well as lesser known mollusks such as *percebes*, are all available. Perhaps the best known fish dish is *Huachinango a la Veracruzana* (Red Snapper Veracruz Style). *Seviche* and the *Escabeches* are popular, but there are also many lesser known dishes of great subtlety using saffron, coriander, and various nuts. And, of course, there are the Mexican versions of some of the dried cod dishes of Spain.

Many Mexican fish recipes depend upon the *Court Bouillon* that follows.

# Court Bouillon with White Wine for Poaching Fish

Fish trimmings (head, tail, fins, bones)
2 cups dry white wine
2 quarts water
1 onion stuck with 1 clove
1 carrot, thinly sliced

1 bay leaf
3 sprigs of parsley
1 pinch of thyme
1 clove
10 peppercorns, bruised
1 teaspoon salt

Place all the ingredients in a fairly large kettle. Bring to a boil slowly over moderate heat. Reduce heat to simmer, and cook, uncovered, skimming regularly, for 30 minutes. Taste for seasoning. Strain through a fine sieve or several layers of cheesecloth. Makes about 1½ quarts. Can be frozen successfully.

# Pescado en Salsa de Avellanas

## FISH IN FILBERT SAUCE

2 cups court bouillon
3 pounds fillets of any non-fat white fish
3 tablespoons olive oil
1 thin slice white bread
1 clove garlic, chopped
½ cup filberts

Small handful of parsley sprigs
1 teaspoon powdered saffron
Salt
Freshly ground pepper

Bring the court bouillon to a boil; add the fillets; reduce heat to simmer and poach until fish flakes easily with a fork—a matter of minutes. Keep warm on a serving platter.

Heat the olive oil in a skillet and fry the bread with the garlic, taking care not to let the garlic burn, or it will taste bitter. In the electric blender, combine the bread, coarsely chopped, garlic, filberts, parsley, saffron, and the liquid in which the fish was poached; and blend to a smooth puree. Adjust seasoning. Pour into a saucepan and heat through. Cover the fish with the hot sauce and serve immediately. Serves 6.

# Pescado en Almendrada Verde

## FISH IN ALMOND AND CORIANDER SAUCE

2 cups court bouillon
3 pounds fillets of any
   non-fat white fish
3 tablespoons olive oil
1 clove garlic
1 thin slice white bread
½ cup blanched
   almonds

3 canned green *serrano*
   chiles
A good handful of fresh
   green coriander
Salt
Freshly ground pepper

Bring the court bouillon to a boil; add the fish fillets; reduce
the heat to simmer and poach until the fish flakes easily with
a fork—a matter of minutes. Arrange on a warm platter and
keep warm. Heat the oil with the garlic in a skillet, and fry
the bread on both sides; discard the garlic, and chop the bread
coarsely.

   In the electric blender, combine the bread, almonds, chiles,
coriander, and the court bouillon in which the fish was poached;
and blend to a smooth puree. Bring the sauce to a simmer,
taste for seasoning, and pour over the fish. Serve immediately.
Serves 6.

# Pescado en Salsa de Azafrán y Nuez

## FISH IN SAFFRON AND PECAN SAUCE

2 cups court bouillon
3 pounds fillets of any
   non-fat white fish
1 onion, chopped
1 clove garlic, chopped
¾ cup pecans
Good handful of parsley
   sprigs

½ teaspoon saffron
   powder
Salt
Freshly ground pepper
Lemon juice

Bring the court bouillon to a boil; add the fillets; reduce heat
to simmer and poach the fish until it flakes easily with a fork—
a matter of minutes. Lift the fish out of the broth carefully and

keep warm in a shallow serving dish. Strain the broth.

Place the onion, garlic, pecans, parsley, saffron, and the liquid from the poached fish in an electric blender; and blend to a smooth puree. Heat the puree in a saucepan but do not let it boil, add a good squeeze of lemon juice, and taste for seasoning. Spoon the hot sauce over the fish and serve at once. Serves 6.

# Pescado en Salsa de Almendra y Nuez

## FISH IN ALMOND AND WALNUT SAUCE

1 cup dry white wine
1 10-ounce can Mexican green tomatoes
2 onions, chopped
1 clove garlic, crushed
Salt
Freshly ground pepper
3 pounds fish fillets (halibut, flounder, or sole)

½ cup blanched almonds
½ cup walnuts
1 tablespoon sesame seeds
6 canned *serrano* chiles
3 or 4 sprigs of fresh coriander
Lemon juice

Make a court bouillon with the white wine, *1 cup of the liquid from the green tomatoes*, onions, garlic, and salt and pepper. Simmer for 15 minutes. Add the fish, and poach until the fillets flake easily with a fork. Transfer the fillets to a shallow, flameproof serving platter and keep warm.

Place the almonds, walnuts, sesame seeds, chiles, drained green tomatoes, coriander, and all the court bouillon, including the onion and garlic, in an electric blender, and blend until smooth. This may have to be done piecemeal, since the blender probably will not accommodate all the ingredients at one time. Heat the sauce but do not let it boil, pour over the fillets and serve at once. Serves 6.

# Pescado con Perejil

## FISH IN PARSLEY SAUCE

1 10-ounce can Mexican
green tomatoes
1 onion, finely chopped
1 clove garlic, chopped
2 good handfuls of parsley,
finely chopped
Salt

Freshly ground pepper
6 fillets of any white, non-
fat fish
Canned *serrano* chiles
Pimiento-stuffed green
olives

Drain the green tomatoes, reserving the liquid; then mash. Mix thoroughly with the onion, garlic, parsley, and salt and pepper to taste. Grease an ovenproof dish. Add a layer of the tomato mixture. Arrange the fish fillets on top, and spoon the remaining tomato mixture over the fish. Bake in a preheated 400°F. oven for 15 to 20 minutes, or until the fish flakes easily with a fork. If the fish seems dry, add a little of the reserved liquid from the tomatoes.

Garnish with the *serrano* chiles and olives. Serves 6.

# Tapado de Robalo

## SMOTHERED SEA BASS

½ cup olive oil
3 pounds sea bass (or
striped bass) fillets
Flour
Salt
Freshly ground pepper
1 onion, finely chopped
1 clove garlic, chopped
Good handful of parsley
sprigs, finely chopped

3 medium tomatoes,
peeled, seeded, and
chopped
1 10-ounce can Mexican
green tomatoes
1 bay leaf
3 canned *serrano* chiles,
chopped

Heat the oil in a skillet. Dust the fillets with flour which has been seasoned with salt and pepper, and fry the fish on both sides until golden, or until it flakes easily with a fork. Arrange on a warm serving platter and keep warm.

In the oil left in the skillet, fry the onion and garlic. Add the parsley, tomatoes, both red and green, with the liquid from the green tomatoes, and all the remaining ingredients. Taste for seasoning. Cook over a moderate heat, stirring from time to time, until the sauce is well blended and has the consistency of heavy cream. Pour over the fish, and serve. Serves 6.

## *Pescado en Vino Blanco*

### FISH IN WHITE WINE

1 whole 4-pound sea bass
    or similar fish
Salt
Freshly ground pepper
Flour
½ stick butter
1 large onion, finely
    chopped

⅛ teaspoon nutmeg
2 cups dry white wine
2 or 3 sprigs of fresh
    coriander, chopped
Lemon juice

Dust the fish in flour which has been seasoned with salt and pepper. Heat the butter in a large skillet, and sauté the fish on both sides until golden. Transfer the fish to a buttered flame-proof casserole with a cover.

Sauté the onion in the butter remaining in the skillet until limp. Add the onion to the casserole. Mix the nutmeg, wine, coriander, and salt and pepper to taste, and pour over the fish. Cover, and simmer very gently over a very low heat until the fish flakes easily when tested with a fork—about 25 minutes. Just before serving, finish with a generous sprinkling of lemon juice. Serves 6.

# *Pescado Yucateco*

## FISH YUCATÁN STYLE

1 whole 5- to 6-pound
   pompano or red snapper
Juice of 1 lemon
Salt
Freshly ground pepper
¼ cup olive oil
1 onion, finely chopped
½ cup green olives
1 4-ounce can pimientos,
   chopped, with the liquid

1 teaspoon annatto, ground
Scant handful of fresh
   green coriander or
   parsley sprigs, chopped
Juice of 1 orange
2 hard-cooked eggs,
   chopped

Sprinkle the fish with the lemon juice and salt and pepper.
Arrange in a generously buttered flameproof casserole. Set
aside.

   Heat the oil in a skillet, and sauté the onion until limp. Add
the olives, pimientos and their juice, annatto, and coriander.
Cook over a moderate heat for 3 to 4 minutes; then add the
orange juice. Taste for seasoning. Pour the hot sauce over the
fish in the casserole, and cook in a preheated 400°F. oven for
30 minutes, or until the fish flakes easily with a fork. Garnish
with the hard-cooked eggs. Serves 6.

# *Pescado en Chile Pasilla*

## FISH IN *PASILLA* CHILE SAUCE

6 *pasilla* chiles
2 cups court bouillon
3 pounds mackerel or
   bluefish fillets
3 tablespoons olive oil
1 slice white bread
1 medium onion, chopped

1 clove garlic, chopped
¼ teaspoon powdered
   cumin
Salt
Freshly ground pepper
Lemon juice

Prepare the chiles as described in the Introduction.

   Bring the court bouillon to a boil; add the fish; reduce heat
to simmer and poach until the fillets flake easily with a fork—

a matter of minutes. Transfer to a serving platter and keep warm.

Heat the olive oil in a skillet, and fry the bread with the garlic clove, taking care not to burn the garlic. Discard the garlic. Chop the bread coarsely. Place the prepared chiles, bread, onion, cumin, and all the court bouillon from the fish in an electric blender, and blend until smooth. Taste for seasoning. Bring the sauce to a boil, and simmer for 10 minutes to blend the flavors. Stir in the lemon juice and pour over the fish. Serves 6.

## *Pescado Naranjado*

### FISH IN ORANGE JUICE

| | |
|---|---|
| 6 individual cod or halibut steaks | 3 cloves garlic, crushed |
| Flour | ¼ cup olive oil |
| Salt | Lemon juice |
| Freshly ground pepper | Juice of 4 medium oranges, strained |
| Good handful of parsley sprigs, finely chopped | |

Dust the fish steaks with flour which has been seasoned with salt and pepper. Mix the parsley, garlic, and olive oil together. Add a good squeeze of lemon juice. Spread the mixture over both sides of the fish steaks, and arrange fish in a greased ovenproof casserole large enough for the steaks to lie flat. Pour the orange juice over all; cover; and bake for 20 minutes in a preheated 450°F. oven, or until the fish flakes easily with a fork. Serves 6.

*Note*: *Arroz Verde* (Green Rice) is a pleasant accompaniment.

## Bacalao con Crema

### DRIED COD IN CREAM

| | |
|---|---|
| 2 pounds dried cod fillets | 1 cup stock from fish |
| Flour | 1 cup heavy cream |
| Salt | ¼ teaspoon dried |
| Freshly ground pepper | *epazote* or sprig of |
| ½ cup olive oil | fresh, chopped *epazote* |
| 2 onions, finely chopped | Scant handful of parsley |
| 6 medium potatoes, freshly | sprigs, chopped |
| boiled and peeled | |

Soak the cod for several hours in cold water, or overnight, depending on the hardness and saltiness of the fish, changing the water several times. Drain. Cover with fresh cold water; bring to a simmer and cook gently until the fish is tender or flakes easily with a fork—about 15 minutes. Drain the fish, reserving the stock, and dry on paper towels. Cut into slices and dust with flour which has been seasoned with salt and pepper. Heat the oil in a skillet, and fry the fish until lightly brown on both sides. Drain on paper towels, and arrange in a greased ovenproof dish with a cover.

In the remaining oil, sauté the onions and add to the fish. Slice the potatoes and fry them in the oil, adding more if necessary. Add them to the fish. Steep the dried *epazote* in a cup of the fish stock for a few minutes; combine with the cream and pour over the cod. For fresh *epazote*, just add to cream. Sprinkle with chopped parsley, cover, and cook for 30 minutes in a preheated 300°F. oven. Serves 6.

# Huachinango a la Veracruzana
## RED SNAPPER VERACRUZ STYLE

6 large red snapper fillets
Flour
Salt
Freshly ground pepper
½ cup olive oil
1 onion, finely chopped
1 clove garlic, minced
2 cups tomato puree
⅛ teaspoon cinnamon
⅛ teaspoon ground
    cloves
3 canned *jalapeño* chiles,
    seeded and cut into
    strips

Juice of ½ lemon
½ teaspoon sugar
12 small new potatoes,
    cooked and peeled
3 slices white bread, cut
    into triangles
Butter
½ cup pimiento-stuffed
    green olives, cut in half

Dust the fillets lightly with flour that has been seasoned with salt and pepper. Heat *half the oil* in a large skillet, and sauté the fish, on both sides, until golden and easily flaked with a fork. Set aside and keep warm. Add the remainder of the oil, the onion, and the garlic to the skillet, and fry until the onion is transparent but not brown. Add the tomato puree, cinnamon, and cloves, and cook, stirring, for about 5 minutes; add the chiles, lemon juice, sugar, and salt and pepper to taste, and bring to a boil. Reduce the heat; add the potatoes and fish fillets and heat through. Do not cook further.

Meanwhile, melt some butter in a frying pan. When hot, fry the bread triangles until light brown.

To serve, arrange the fish on a hot serving platter covered with the sauce, surrounded with the potatoes and garnished with the olives and fried bread. Serves 6.

# Pescado en Adobo

## FISH IN *ADOBO* SAUCE

6 *ancho* chiles
1 whole 5-pound striped
  bass, sea bass, snapper,
  or sea trout
Flour
Salt
Freshly ground pepper
½ cup olive oil
1 onion, chopped
1 clove garlic, chopped
⅛ teaspoon ground
  cloves

¼ teaspoon cinnamon
¼ teaspoon oregano
¼ teaspoon cumin
½ teaspoon thyme
1 teaspoon sugar
3 large tomatoes, peeled,
  seeded, and chopped
Lemon juice
½ cup grated Parmesan
  cheese
Butter

Prepare the chiles as described in the Introduction.

Dust the fish with flour which has been seasoned with salt and pepper. Heat the olive oil in a large skillet, and sauté the fish on both sides until golden. Place in a large, greased, fireproof casserole and keep warm.

Combine the prepared chiles, onion, garlic, cloves, cinnamon, oregano, cumin, thyme, sugar, tomatoes, and salt and pepper to taste, and blend in the electric blender to a coarse puree. Heat the oil remaining in the fish skillet, and cook the puree for 5 minutes, stirring constantly. Add a generous squeeze or two of lemon juice.

Pour the sauce over the fish in the casserole. Sprinkle with the grated cheese, dot with butter, and bake in a preheated 400°F. oven for 45 minutes, or until the fish flakes easily with a fork. Serves 6.

Noodles, rice, or boiled potatoes make good accompaniments for this robust dish; it should be served with well-chilled beer.

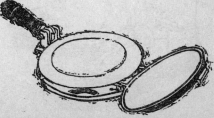

# *Arroz con Jaibas Yucateco*

### RICE WITH CRAB IN THE YUCATÁN STYLE

2 cups rice
½ cup olive oil
1 large onion, chopped
1 or 2 cloves garlic,
  chopped
1 pound (about 3 medium)
  tomatoes, peeled,
  seeded, and chopped
1 teaspoon annatto, ground
5 cups chicken stock,
  about

Salt
Freshly ground pepper
1½ pounds lump
  crabmeat,* broken up
4 pimientos, cut in strips
1 bay leaf
1 cup young raw peas
½ cup dry sherry

Soak the rice in hot water for 15 minutes, rinse in cold water, drain well and dry thoroughly; heat the olive oil in a heavy ovenproof casserole, and sauté the rice until golden; place the onion, garlic, tomatoes, annatto, and *½ cup of the stock* in the electric blender. Blend, a small amount at a time, until smooth. Measure; then add enough stock to make 6 cups. Pour over the rice; add salt and pepper to taste, the crabmeat, pimientos, bay leaf, and peas.

Cover the casserole and cook in a preheated 350°F. oven for 30 minutes, or until all the liquid has been absorbed. At this point, stir the sherry in gently so as not to break up the crabmeat, and just heat through. Serves 6 to 8

*Or shrimp or lobster in the same amount.

# Bacalao a la Vizcaína

## DRIED COD IN THE STYLE OF VIZCAYA

2 pounds dried cod fillets
1 small onion, sliced
¼ cup olive oil
1 onion, chopped
2 cloves garlic, chopped
1 pound (about 3 medium)
   tomatoes, peeled,
   seeded, and chopped
1 7-ounce can pimientos
Salt

Freshly ground pepper
12 small new potatoes,
   freshly cooked and
   peeled
½ cup dry sherry
3 slices white bread, cut in
   triangles
Handful of parsley sprigs,
   chopped
Stuffed green olives

Soak the cod for several hours in cold water, or overnight, depending on the hardness and saltiness of the fish, changing the water several times. Drain; cover with fresh cold water; add *the sliced onion*; bring to a simmer, and cook gently about 15 minutes, or until the fish flakes easily with a fork. Drain well; cut into large slices.

Heat the oil, and fry the cod lightly on both sides. Drain on paper towels, arrange in a shallow, fireproof casserole, and keep warm. Reserve the oil. Place the *chopped onion*, garlic, tomatoes, and *half of the pimientos*, chopped, in an electric blender, and blend to a puree. Heat the reserved oil; add the puree and cook for 5 minutes, stirring constantly. Season to taste with salt and pepper, and pour over the cod. Add the remaining pimientos, cut into strips, and the potatoes. Finally, add the sherry and heat for about 5 minutes, or until the fish and potatoes are hot through. Meanwhile, fry the bread in the reserved olive oil until lightly brown on both sides.

Garnish the cod with chopped parsley, olives, and fried bread, and serve at once. Serves 6.

# Pipián de Camarones

## SHRIMP FRICASSEE

Father Sahagún, the Spanish priest, who arrived shortly after the Conquest (1519–21) and wrote extensively of Aztec Mexico, describes this dish in such detail (and with such relish) that I have been able to work out this version of it. The Aztecs would have used honey where I have used sugar, and certainly a different type of onion, as the modern variety was introduced by Columbus to the New World. But the basic outline is the same. Sahagún's descriptions of Mexican foods are of especial interest, since he tells us a good deal about the cuisine before the foods of Europe and Asia were introduced by the Spaniards.

2 pounds raw jumbo
  shrimp
1 cup Mexican *pepitas*
  (pumpkin seeds)
1 small onion, chopped
2 cloves garlic, chopped
6 sprigs fresh green
  coriander
½ pound tomatoes
  (about 1 large or 2
  small), peeled, seeded,
  and chopped

6 *pequín* chiles, crumbled
3 whole pimientos,
  chopped
½ tablespoon ground
  coriander seeds
Salt
Freshly ground pepper
½ teaspoon sugar
3 tablespoons salad oil
1 tablespoon lemon juice

Cook the shrimp for 5 minutes in boiling water to cover. Cool and peel. Set aside. Reserve the liquid. Place the *pepitas* in an electric blender, and blend as fine as possible. Set aside. Combine the onion, garlic, fresh coriander, tomatoes, *pequín* chiles, and pimientos in the electric blender, and blend to a smooth puree. Stir in the ground coriander, salt and pepper to taste, the sugar, and the *pepitas*.

Heat the oil in a skillet, and cook the mixture for 5 minutes, stirring constantly. Add about 1 cup of the reserved shrimp water to bring the sauce to a consistency of heavy cream. Add the shrimp, and heat, stirring, without allowing the mixture to boil. Just before serving, stir in the lemon juice. Serves 6.

## Bacalao en Chile y Almendra

### DRIED COD WITH CHILE AND ALMOND SAUCE

3 *ancho* chiles
2 pounds dried cod fillets
¼ cup blanched
  almonds
1 onion, chopped
1 tomato, peeled, seeded,
  and chopped

½ teaspoon oregano
3 tablespoons salad oil
Salt
Freshly ground pepper
Pinch of sugar

Prepare the chiles as described in the Introduction.

Soak the fillets for several hours in cold water, or overnight, depending on the hardness and saltiness of the fish, changing the water several times. Drain; then cover with fresh, cold water; bring to a simmer and cook gently about 15 minutes, or until the fish flakes easily with a fork. Place the prepared chiles, almonds, onion, tomato, and oregano in the electric blender, and blend to a coarse puree.

Heat the oil in a heavy skillet, and cook the chile mixture for 5 minutes, stirring constantly, until the sauce is of the consistency of heavy cream. Season to taste with salt and pepper and a pinch of sugar. Add the cod to the sauce and heat thoroughly.

Here, white rice is definitely called for. Serves 6.

## *Arroz Verde con Jaibas*

### GREEN RICE WITH CRAB

2 cups rice
½ cup olive oil
2 10-ounce cans Mexican
  green tomatoes
1 onion, chopped
1 clove garlic, chopped
Good handful of fresh
  coriander

Salt
Freshly ground pepper
1½ pounds lump
  crabmeat,* broken up
4 cups chicken stock,
  about

Soak the rice in hot water for 15 minutes; rinse in cold water; drain well and dry thoroughly. In a heavy, lidded casserole heat the oil, and sauté the rice until golden. Place the green tomatoes, half of their liquid, the onion, garlic, and coriander in an electric blender, and blend to a smooth puree. Measure. You need 6 cups. If it does not reach 6 cups, add the remainder of the tomato liquid and sufficient stock to make up the quantity. Season to taste with salt and pepper and pour over the rice. Add the crabmeat. Cover the casserole and cook, in a preheated 350°F. oven, for 30 minutes, or until the rice has absorbed all the liquid. Serves 6 to 8.

*Shrimp or lobster may be substituted in the same amount.

# Seviche

*Seviche*, or *ceviche*, as it is often spelled, comes originally from Polynesia. Like all migratory dishes, it has undergone changes that make this version authentically Mexican.

Mexicans prefer to use such fat fish as mackerel or pompano for *seviche*. I have always liked a delicate white fish, such as sole. Limes are preferred, although lemons may be used, since both contain the citric acid that "cooks" the fish.

I think it is only fair to point out that Mexican cookbooks—and cooks—always specify lemons. This is because they insist on calling their small juicy limes "lemons" (*limones*), which they are not. It is little use arguing that a lemon is a lemon and a lime is a lime, at the same time pointing out that lemons are exceedingly rare in Mexico. "No, es *limón*" ("No, it's a lemon") is the answer you will get when you point to a lime and call it by its name, *lima*. The better part of valor is to give up the unequal linguistic struggle and read "lime" for "lemon" in all Mexican recipes.

1 pound mackerel or
    pompano fillets, cut into
    small squares of
    julienne
Juice of 6 limes
1 large or 2 small
    tomatoes, peeled,
    seeded, and chopped
1 small onion, chopped
    very fine
2 or more canned *jalapeño*
    chiles, seeded and cut
    into strips

¼ cup olive oil
1 tablespoon white vinegar
Small handful of parsley
    sprigs, finely chopped
¼ teaspoon oregano
Salt
Freshly ground pepper
Green olives

Arrange the fish in a deep dish, and cover with the lime juice. Refrigerate for about 6 hours, turning once, about halfway through the process. At the end of the marinating period, drain, and reserve the juice.

Combine the tomatoes, onion, chiles, oil, vinegar, parsley, oregano, and salt and pepper to taste, and add the reserved lime juice. Pour the sauce over the fish, toss gently, and refrigerate until ready to serve. Garnish with green olives. Serves 6.

This is an excellent appetizer, especially in hot weather.

# Escabeche Estilo Yucatán

## SOUSED MACKEREL FROM YUCATÁN

1 pound mackerel fillets
Salt
Freshly ground pepper
Juice of 2 limes or 1
    lemon
Flour
⅓ cup salad oil
2 cloves garlic, crushed
2 bay leaves
½ teaspoon powdered
    cumin

½ teaspoon nutmeg
1 tablespoon paprika
1 cup vinegar
1 large onion, sliced very
    thin
6 *pequín* chiles, crumbled
Romaine lettuce
Stuffed green olives
Radishes

Cut the fillets in half, and soak in a quart of cold water mixed with *1 tablespoon of salt* and the lime juice for 30 minutes. Drain; dry thoroughly; dust lightly with flour which has been seasoned with salt and pepper; and fry in a skillet in *2 tablespoons of the oil*, heated. Drain, and place in a deep serving dish. Combine the garlic, bay leaves, cumin, nutmeg, paprika, vinegar, onion, and salt and pepper to taste, in a saucepan. Bring to a boil very slowly; then simmer gently until the onion has wilted. Pour over the fish. Add the chiles and the remaining oil. Cool; then refrigerate for 24 hours.

Serve as a first course, garnished with lettuce, olives, and radishes. Serves 6.

# *Pescado en Salsa de Jitomate y Cilantro*

### FISH IN TOMATO AND CORIANDER SAUCE

¼ cup olive oil
1 3-pound halibut steak or similar firm fish steak
2 large tomatoes, peeled, seeded, and chopped
1 large onion, chopped
1 clove garlic, chopped
Heart of a romaine lettuce, chopped
Handful of fresh green coriander, chopped

1 4-ounce can pimientos and the liquid
1 cup court bouillon or bottled clam juice
Salt
Freshly ground pepper
Pinch of sugar
1 avocado, peeled and sliced

Heat the oil in a skillet, and brown the fish lightly on both sides. Remove to a flameproof casserole and keep warm. Place the tomatoes, onion, garlic, lettuce, coriander, the pimientos and bouillon or juice in an electric blender, and blend until smooth. Season to taste with salt, pepper, and a pinch of sugar.

Heat the oil in which the fish was browned; add the sauce and cook for 3 or 4 minutes, stirring constantly. Pour the sauce over the fish, and simmer gently over very low heat until the fish flakes easily with a fork. Lift the fish out of the sauce carefully with two spatulas and place on a warm serving dish. Pour the sauce over all, and garnish with the sliced avocado. Serves 6.

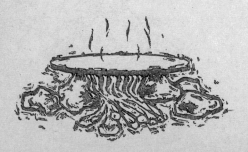

# Pescado en Escabeche

## SOUSED FISH

It is strange that both "soused" and "pickled" (the other name for this dish) are slang words for anyone a few sheets to the wind, since no liquor at all is used in this recipe.

1 pound fillets of sole or any similar white fish
Juice of 2 limes or 1 lemon
Flour
Salt
Freshly ground pepper
¼ cup salad oil
1 onion, thinly sliced
2 canned *jalapeño* chiles, rinsed, deseeded, and cut into strips
3 cloves garlic, chopped
1 teaspoon oregano
2 bay leaves
½ teaspoon ground cumin
1 cup vinegar
Lettuce
Green olives

Pour the lime juice over the fish, and allow it to stand for 15 minutes. Dip the fillets in flour which has been seasoned with salt and pepper. Heat the oil in a skillet, and sauté the fish gently on both sides until it is golden brown. Arrange in a shallow dish and set aside.

Fry the onion in the oil remaining in the pan until it is limp but not brown. Add all the other ingredients, and bring almost to the boiling point. Pour over the fish, cover, and refrigerate for 24 hours.

Serve as a first course, garnished with lettuce and olives, with bread and sweet butter. Serves 6.

# Pescado Borracho

## DRUNKEN FISH

6 *ancho* chiles
1 5- to 6-pound whole
  snapper or similar fish
Flour
Salt
Freshly ground pepper
¼ cup olive oil
1 onion, firmly chopped
1 clove garlic, chopped
Good handful of parsley
  sprigs, finely chopped

3 medium tomatoes,
  peeled, seeded, and
  chopped
¼ teaspoon ground
  cumin
½ teaspoon oregano
1 cup pimiento-stuffed
  green olives, cut in two
2 tablespoons capers,
  drained
2 cups dry red wine

Prepare the chiles as described in the Introduction. Place in an electric blender, and blend to a coarse puree.

Dust the fish with flour which has been seasoned with salt and pepper. Heat the oil in a frying pan, and brown the fish lightly on both sides in the hot oil. Then place it in a large, ovenproof casserole and set aside.

Sauté the onion and garlic in the oil remaining in the fish skillet; add the pureed chile, the parsley, tomatoes, cumin, oregano, and salt and pepper to taste. Cook, over a moderate heat, stirring for 5 minutes. Add the olives, capers, and red wine, and mix well.

Pour over the fish; cover; and cook in a preheated 400°F. oven for about 30 minutes, or until the fish flakes easily with a fork. Serves 6.

# AVES

## POULTRY

The number of poultry dishes in Mexico is almost endless. For the most part they derive from the Aztec *mollis* (literally, a sauce made with any of the chiles), though ingredients introduced by the Spaniards are freely used. The *tinga*, a type of stew, is an exception. Here the cooking method is European, though the ingredients are a mixture of indigenous and introduced foods.

It is curious that there are so few recipes for duckling. The Aztecs had domesticated ducks, but today they are not either very good or very readily obtainable. Pheasant, a great favorite in pre-Columbian days, is not now always available. At the same time, there is so great a variety of other birds it would be churlish to dwell upon these few cooking casualties of the Spanish Conquest.

# Pollo en Mole Verde

## CHICKEN IN GREEN CHILE SAUCE

8 *poblano* chiles*
2 2½-pound broiler-
  fryers, cut into serving
  pieces
2 cups chicken stock, or
  canned condensed broth
1 cup *pepitas*
½ cup walnuts
½ cup almonds

1 large onion, chopped
1 clove garlic, chopped
2 10-ounce cans Mexican
  green tomatoes
Handful of fresh coriander
Salt
Freshly ground pepper
2 tablespoons lard or salad
  oil

Prepare the chiles as described in the Introduction.

Place the chicken pieces in a flameproof casserole which has a lid, and add the stock. Bring to a boil, reduce heat, cover and simmer until almost tender—about 45 minutes. Drain; reserve the stock and keep the chicken warm. Pulverize the *pepitas* in the electric blender as finely as possible. For the best results, do ½ cup at a time. Set aside.

Combine the walnuts, almonds, onion, garlic, green tomatoes and the liquid from the can, coriander, and the prepared chiles, and reduce in the electric blender, bit by bit, to a coarse puree. Stir in the *pepitas*. Season to taste with salt and pepper.

Heat the lard in a large skillet and cook in the sauce for 2 or 3 minutes, stirring constantly. Thin to the consistency of heavy cream with the reserved chicken stock. Pour the sauce over the chicken in the casserole; cover; and cook over the lowest possible heat until the chicken is tender when pierced with a fork, without allowing the sauce to boil—about 15 minutes. Serves 6.

*Note: Mole Verde* can also be made with turkey, or with boneless loin of pork cut into 2-inch chunks; and pecans may be substituted for walnuts.

*If using canned *poblanos*, it is not necessary to prepare them.

# Mole Poblano de Guajolote

## TURKEY MOLE PUEBLA STYLE

Without doubt the most famous of all the *mollis* is the *Mole Poblano*, turkey or chicken in a chile sauce containing bitter chocolate. Legend has it that the nuns of the Convent of Santa Rosa invented the dish in early colonial times to honor a visiting viceroy and archbishop. Nothing could be more unlikely, especially after a glance at the complex list of ingredients. Although one can only speculate, what may have happened is that, on hearing the guests were a viceroy, equated with the king, and an archbishop, equated with the high priest, the Indian girls at the Convent gave the nuns what is clearly a royal recipe. There would have been no reason for the girls to have mentioned the dish before, since among the Aztecs chocolate was forbidden to women, and among men was reserved for royalty, the military nobility, and the higher ranks of the clergy. Though not inventors, the good nuns are to be thanked for having saved the dish from possible oblivion. They must also be credited with introducing their own refinements, the cloves and cinnamon, for example, though I am inclined to feel they might have done better with the original herbs and spices.

This *mole* can be made with chicken or pork.

6 *ancho* chiles*
4 *pasilla* chiles*
4 *mulato* chiles*
1 8-pound turkey, ready to cook, cut into serving pieces
4 tablespoons lard
2 onions, chopped
4 cloves garlic, chopped
1 cup blanched almonds
½ cup raisins
½ teaspoon ground cloves
½ teaspoon cinnamon
½ teaspoon coriander seeds, ground
½ teaspoon anise
4 tablespoons sesame seeds
2 to 3 sprigs fresh coriander
1 tortilla or 1 slice of toast, cut up
1 pound (about 3 medium) tomatoes, peeled, seeded, and chopped
1½ 1-ounce squares unsweetened chocolate
Salt
½ teaspoon ground cumin

Prepare all three chiles as described in the Introduction.

Cover the turkey pieces with salted water; bring to a boil and simmer 1 hour. Drain, reserving 2 cups of the stock. Dry the pieces of turkey thoroughly with paper towels. Heat the

*If the three types of chile are not available, probably the best thing to do is to use all *ancho* chiles.

lard in a skillet; then brown the turkey pieces in the hot fat, a few pieces at a time. Transfer to a large, flameproof casserole, reserving the lard.

Combine the onions, garlic, almonds, raisins, cloves, cinnamon, coriander seeds, anise, 2 *tablespoons of the sesame seeds*, fresh coriander, tortilla or toast, prepared chiles, and the tomatoes. Blend, a small amount at a time, in the electric blender to make a coarse puree. Heat the lard remaining in the skillet, adding, if necessary, enough fat to make about 3 tablespoons. Cook the puree in the hot fat for 5 minutes, stirring constantly. Add the 2 cups of turkey broth, the chocolate, salt and pepper to taste, and cook, stirring, over low heat until the chocolate has melted. The sauce should be quite thick—somewhat thicker than heavy cream. Pour the sauce over the turkey in the casserole, and cook, covered, over the lowest possible heat for 30 minutes. Just before serving, sprinkle with the remaining sesame seeds. Serves 8 to 10.

This makes a splendid party dish served with hot tortillas, guacamole, *frijoles* (beans) and white rice.

## *Mole Poblano Picante*

### HOT *MOLE* PUEBLA STYLE

8 *mulato* chiles
4 *ancho* chiles
4 *pasilla* chiles
1 8-pound, ready-to-cook turkey, cut into serving pieces
4 tablespoons lard
4 tablespoons sesame seeds
1 large onion, chopped
2 cloves garlic, chopped
1 tortilla, or slice of toast, cut up
1 cup blanched almonds
⅛ teaspoon ground cloves
⅛ teaspoon cinnamon
½ teaspoon ground coriander seed
¼ teaspoon anise
½ cup raisins
3 large tomatoes, peeled, seeded, and chopped
4 canned *chipotle* chiles
2 1-ounce squares unsweetened chocolate
Salt
Freshly ground pepper
1 teaspoon sugar

Prepare the *mulato, ancho*, and *pasilla* chiles as described in the Introduction.

Place the turkey pieces in a flameproof casserole with a lid, and poach, covered, in salted water to barely cover for 1 hour. Drain, reserving the stock. Dry the turkey pieces thoroughly with paper towels. Heat the lard in a skillet, and brown the turkey pieces, a few at a time. Arrange the turkey pieces in the casserole and keep warm. Combine 2 *tablespoons of the sesame seeds*, the onion, garlic, tortilla, almonds, cloves, cinnamon, coriander seed, anise, raisins, tomatoes, prepared chiles, and *chipotle* chiles, and reduce, bit by bit, to a coarse puree in the electric blender.

Heat the remaining lard in a skillet, adding, if necessary, a little more lard to bring it up to 3 tablespoons. Cook the puree, stirring constantly, for about 5 minutes. Add 2 cups of the turkey stock, chocolate, salt and pepper to taste, and the sugar, and cook, over very low heat, until the chocolate has melted. Pour the sauce over the turkey; cover; and cook over the lowest possible heat for 1 hour, stirring occasionally. The sauce should be rather thicker than the consistency of heavy cream. If it seems too thick, thin with turkey stock. Sprinkle with remaining sesame seeds just before serving. Serves 8 to 10.

*Note:* Chipotle chile and its close relative *morita* chile have the most exotic flavor of any of the Mexican chiles. They are also exceedingly *picante* and can really lift your head off. If you do not care for hot food, experiment with the *chipotle*, for even in a small quantity its flavor will survive. Begin with a half chile, tasting and adding more to your *mole* with caution until you find the amount that suits your taste.

## *Pollo en Salsa de Chile Ancho*

### CHICKEN IN MILD RED CHILE SAUCE

| | |
|---|---|
| 6 *ancho* chiles | 2 cloves garlic, chopped |
| 4 tablespoons lard or salad oil | 2 cups chicken stock |
| | Salt |
| 2 2½-pound broiler-fryers, cut into serving pieces | Freshly ground pepper |
| 2 onions, finely chopped | |

Prepare the chiles as described in the Introduction.

Heat the lard or salad oil in a skillet, and sauté the chicken pieces until golden. Lift out of the fat, and place in a flameproof casserole that has a cover. Sauté the onion and garlic in the remaining fat until limp. Add to the chicken. Puree the prepared *ancho* chiles in the electric blender. Heat the remaining fat in the skillet (add more, if necessary, to make about 2 tablespoons), and cook the *ancho* puree for about 5 minutes, stirring constantly. Stir into the chicken stock; taste for seasoning; then pour the sauce over the chicken in the casserole. Cover and simmer, over very low heat, until the chicken is tender, about 45 minutes.

Serve with a green salad, radishes, and avocado slices dressed with oil and vinegar. Serves 6.

## Pipián Verde de Ajonjolí

### GREEN CHICKEN FRICASSEE WITH
### SESAME SEEDS

| | |
|---|---|
| 1 3½- to 4-pound chicken, cut into serving pieces | 2 10-ounce cans Mexican green tomatoes |
| 2 cups chicken stock | 6 canned *serrano* chiles, rinsed |
| 1 cup sesame seeds | 2 tablespoons lard |
| 1 large onion, chopped | Salt |
| 1 clove garlic, chopped | Freshly ground pepper |
| Handful of fresh coriander | |

Place the chicken pieces in a flameproof casserole; add the stock; cover and poach for 45 minutes or until almost tender. Drain; reserve the stock and keep the chicken warm. Pulverize the sesame seeds in the electric blender as finely as possible and set aside. Combine the onion, garlic, coriander, drained tomatoes (reserving the liquid), and the *serrano* chiles in the electric blender, and blend to a coarse puree. If necessary, blend in two lots.

Heat the lard in a skillet; add the puree and the sesame seeds, and cook for 2 or 3 minutes, stirring constantly. Add the liquid from the canned tomatoes and, if necessary, a little of the reserved stock to bring the sauce to medium-thick consistency. Taste for seasoning. Pour the sauce over the chicken in the casserole; cover; and cook over very low heat until the chicken is tender, another 15 minutes. Serves 6. Serve with *Arroz Amarillo* (Yellow Rice), page 66, or plain white rice.

# *Pipián Rojo de Ajonjolí*

## RED CHICKEN FRICASSEE WITH SESAME SEEDS

This dish has probably changed very little in the centuries since Fr. Sahagún sampled a version of it from one of the big earthenware *ollas* (pots) in the main marketplace of Tenochtitlán, the Aztec capital of Mexico and the site of modern Mexico City. From his writings one gathers he found it good indeed.

The *pipián* recipes in this section illustrate the Mexican delight in playing variations on a kitchen theme. There are the red and green *pipiánes* using sesame seeds and the red and green *pipiánes* using pumpkin seeds (*pepitas*). The recipes may look similar to the casual eye, but the finished dishes have a vastly dissimilar taste.

6 *ancho* chiles
1 3½- to 4-pound chicken, cut into serving pieces
2 cups chicken stock or canned condensed broth
1 cup sesame seeds
1 large onion, chopped
1 or 2 cloves garlic, chopped
1 sprig of *epazote*

4 medium tomatoes, peeled, seeded, and chopped
⅛ teaspoon ground cloves
⅛ teaspoon cinnamon
2 tablespoons lard or salad oil
Salt
Freshly ground pepper
Pinch of sugar

Prepare the chiles as described in the Introduction.

Place the chicken pieces in a flameproof, covered casserole; add the stock; cover and poach for 45 minutes. Drain; reserve the stock and keep the chicken warm. Pulverize the sesame seeds in the electric blender as finely as possible and set aside. Place the prepared chiles, onion, garlic, *epazote*, tomatoes, cloves, and cinnamon in the electric blender, and blend to a coarse puree. Because of the quantity involved, puree in two lots.

Heat the lard in a skillet, add the sesame seeds, and cook, stirring, for a minute or two; then add the puree and continue to cook, stirring constantly, for 5 minutes. Add a sufficient amount of the reserved stock to bring the sauce to a medium-thick consistency—like heavy cream. Add salt and pepper to taste and a pinch of sugar. Pour over the chicken pieces in the casserole, and cook over low heat for 15 minutes, or until the chicken is tender when pierced with a fork. Serves 6. White rice is good with this.

# *Mole Poblano de Dos Chiles*

## TURKEY *MOLE* PUEBLA STYLE WITH
## TWO CHILES

6 *mulato* chiles
6 *pasilla* chiles
1 8-pound, ready-to-cook
turkey, cut into serving
pieces
1 pound boneless pork
loin, cut in 2-inch
chunks
4 tablespoons lard
½ cup almonds
½ cup peanuts
1 tortilla or slice of toast,
coarsely chopped

4 tablespoons sesame seeds
⅛ teaspoon ground
cloves
¼ teaspoon cinnamon
½ teaspoon anise
1 pound (3 medium)
tomatoes, peeled,
seeded, and chopped
1 1-ounce square
unsweetened chocolate
Salt
Freshly ground pepper
1 teaspoon sugar

Prepare the chiles as described in the Introduction.

Place the turkey and pork in a large kettle with enough salted water to cover. Bring to a boil, and cook, covered, for 1 hour. Drain, reserving the stock. Dry the turkey and pork pieces thoroughly with paper towels. Heat the lard in a large, heavy skillet. Brown the turkey and pork pieces, a few at a time; then transfer to a flameproof casserole. In the electric blender, blend the almonds, peanuts, tortilla, *2 tablespoons of the sesame seeds*, cloves, cinnamon, anise, tomatoes, and the prepared chiles, and reduce to a coarse puree.

Heat the lard remaining in the skillet, adding a little more if necessary, and cook the mixture for 5 minutes, stirring constantly. Add 2 cups of the reserved stock, the chocolate, salt and pepper to taste, and sugar. Stir until the chocolate has melted. Pour the sauce over the turkey and pork in the casserole; cover; and cook over very low heat for about 1 hour, taking care not to let it burn. Sauce should be the consistency of heavy cream, so, if necessary, thin with more stock. Sprinkle with remaining sesame seeds just before serving. Serves 8 to 10.

# *Mole Castellano*

## *MOLE* IN THE CASTILIAN FASHION

.6 *ancho* chiles
1 4- to 5-pound turkey,
    ready to cook, cut into
    serving pieces
2 cups chicken stock
Bouquet garni: 2 sprigs of
    parsley, ½ bay leaf,
    ⅛ teaspoon thyme
Salt
Freshly ground pepper
¼ cup almonds
¼ cup pine nuts
    (piñones, pignolias)

¼ cup filberts
¼ cup walnuts
2 tablespoons sesame seeds
1 clove garlic, chopped
1 small tomato, peeled,
    seeded, and chopped
½ teaspoon ground
    coriander seed
2 tablespoons lard or
    olive oil
½ teaspoon sugar

Prepare the chiles as described in the Introduction.

Place the turkey pieces in a flameproof casserole with a cover; add the stock and bouquet garni. Season to taste with salt and pepper, and cook for 1 hour, or until almost tender. Remove from heat, and cool the turkey in the stock.

Place all the nuts, the sesame seeds, garlic, tomato, coriander seed, and prepared chiles in the electric blender, and reduce to a coarse puree. Heat the lard in a skillet, and cook the puree for 5 minutes, stirring constantly. Remove the turkey from the casserole, and strain the stock. Add the stock and sugar to the puree. Taste for seasoning. Rinse out the casserole; return the turkey and cover with the sauce. Cook over a very low heat until the meat is tender when pierced with a fork (about 15 minutes), and the sauce has the consistency of heavy cream. Serves 6.

# *Pipián Colorado de Pepitas*

## RED CHICKEN FRICASSEE WITH PUMPKIN SEEDS

6 *ancho* chiles
1 3½- to 4-pound chicken, cut into serving pieces
2 cups chicken stock
1 cup *pepitas*
1 large onion, chopped
1 or 2 cloves of garlic, chopped

1 sprig *epazote*
4 tomatoes, peeled, seeded, and chopped
2 tablespoons lard
Salt
Freshly ground pepper
Pinch of sugar

Prepare the chiles as described in the Introduction.

Place the chicken pieces in a flameproof, covered casserole; add the stock; cover; and poach until almost tender, about 45 minutes. Drain; reserve the stock; and keep the chicken warm. Pulverize the *pepitas* in the electric blender as finely as possible. Set aside. (It is important to pulverize the *pepitas* dry. The flavor is altered if they are pureed with a liquid.) Combine the prepared chiles, onion, garlic, *epazote*, and the tomatoes in the electric blender, and blend to a coarse puree, a small quantity at a time.

Heat the lard in a skillet; add the *pepitas* and the puree. Cook for 5 minutes, stirring constantly. Season to taste with salt and pepper and a pinch of sugar. Add enough of the reserved chicken stock to bring the sauce to the consistency of heavy cream. Pour the sauce over the chicken and cook over very low heat until the chicken is tender—another 15 minutes—taking care not to let the sauce "catch." Serves 6. Serve with *Arroz Gualdo* (Golden Rice), page 63, *Arroz Amarillo* (Yellow Rice), page 66, or plain white rice.

# *Pollo Mestizo*

## TWO CULTURES CHICKEN

2 tablespoons salad oil
2 tablespoons butter
1 3½- to 4-pound
    chicken, cut into
    serving pieces
1 cup dry white wine
1 cup pineapple juice
Bay leaf
Salt
Freshly ground pepper
2 medium tomatoes,
    peeled, seeded, and
    chopped

1 onion, chopped
2 cloves garlic, chopped
1 7-ounce can pimientos,
    chopped, with the juice
3 *chorizo* sausages,
    skinned and chopped
2 tablespoons capers, well
    drained
12 new baby potatoes,
    freshly cooked and
    peeled
3 canned *jalapeño* chiles

Heat the oil and butter in a skillet, and sauté the chicken pieces until golden. Remove to a covered, flameproof casserole, and add the wine, pineapple juice, bay leaf, and salt and pepper to taste. Cover; simmer until the chicken is almost tender, about 45 minutes.

Combine the tomatoes, onion, garlic, pimientos, and juice in an electric blender, and blend to a smooth puree. Sauté the *chorizos* in the oil and butter remaining in the skillet. Drain on paper towels; then add to the casserole. Pour the puree into the skillet, and cook in the remaining fat for 5 minutes, stirring constantly. Add to the casserole along with the capers and potatoes. Rinse the *jalapeño* chiles, remove any seeds, cut in strips and sprinkle over the casserole. Taste for seasoning. Simmer over a low heat for 15 minutes, or until the chicken is very tender and the casserole is hot throughout. Serves 6.

# Pipián Verde de Pepitas

## GREEN CHICKEN FRICASSEE WITH PUMPKIN SEEDS

1 3½- to 4-pound
  chicken, cut into
  serving pieces
2 cups chicken stock
1 cup *pepitas*
6 canned *serrano* chiles
1 10-ounce can Mexican
  green tomatoes

1 large onion, chopped
1 clove garlic, chopped
Handful of fresh coriander
2 tablespoons lard
Salt
Freshly ground pepper.

Place the chicken pieces in a flameproof, covered casserole; add the stock; cover and poach 45 minutes or until almost tender. Drain; reserve the stock and keep the chicken warm. Pulverize the *pepitas* in the electric blender as finely as possible and set aside. (It is important to pulverize the *pepitas* dry. The flavor is altered if they are pureed with a liquid.) Combine the chiles, drained green tomatoes (reserving the liquid), onion, garlic, and coriander, with a little of the green tomato liquid, in the electric blender, and blend to a coarse puree.

Heat the lard in a skillet, and cook the mixture, together with the ground *pepitas*, for 2 or 3 minutes, stirring constantly. Add the rest of the green tomato liquid and enough of the chicken stock to bring the sauce to a medium-thick consistency—like heavy cream. Taste for seasoning; pour the sauce over the chicken; cover; and cook over very low heat until the chicken is tender, about 15 minutes longer. Serves 6. Serve with hot white rice.

# *Tapado de Pollo*

## SMOTHERED CHICKEN

6 tablespoons olive oil
1 3½- to 4-pound
   chicken, cut into
   serving pieces
1 large onion, sliced
2 cloves garlic, chopped
3 large tomatoes, peeled
   and sliced
1 package frozen peas,
   thawed
1 pound zucchini or
   summer squash, sliced
2 pears, peeled, cored, and
   sliced

2 cooking apples, peeled,
   cored, and sliced
4 slices fresh pineapple,
   peeled and cut into
   chunks, or 3 cups
   canned pineapple
   chunks, drained
2 ripe plantains* (*plátanos
   machos*), or 2 large,
   underripe bananas,
   peeled and sliced
Salt
Freshly ground pepper

Heat *4 tablespoons of the oil* in a skillet, and sauté the chicken pieces until golden. Arrange half the chicken pieces on the bottom of a heavy flameproof casserole which has a lid. Add, in layers, half the onion, garlic, tomatoes, peas, zucchini, apples, pineapple, and plantains. Sprinkle with salt and pepper to taste and *1 tablespoon of the oil*. Repeat the layers with the remaining chicken, vegetables, and fruits, finishing with salt and pepper and the remaining tablespoon of the oil. Cover, and cook on top of the stove over a low heat until the chicken is tender, about 1½ hours. Or, seal the lid with aluminum foil, add the cover, place the casserole in a preheated 350°F. oven, and cook for about 2 hours. Steamed rice is nice with this. Serves 6.

*Plantains are large members of the banana family which are inedible until cooked, and are traditional in this tropical Mexican dish. They are not as readily available as bananas, which make an excellent substitute if used when slightly underripe.

# *Pollo con Ciruelas*

## CHICKEN WITH PRUNES

½ pound large prunes
½ stick (4 tablespoons) butter
2 2½-pound broiler-fryers, cut into serving pieces
1 large onion, finely chopped
1 clove garlic, chopped
½ teaspoon chile *pequín*, crumbled

1 pound (about 3 medium) tomatoes, peeled, seeded, and chopped
1 cup chicken stock, or canned condensed broth
Salt
Freshly ground pepper
½ cup dry sherry

Steep the prunes in enough boiling water to cover. Set aside.

Heat the butter in a skillet, and sauté the chicken pieces until golden. Remove to a heavy, flameproof casserole with a lid. Set aside. In the same butter, fry the onion, garlic, and chile *pequín*. Add to the casserole along with the tomatoes. Drain and pit the prunes; then chop coarsely; add to the casserole with the stock. Season to taste with salt and pepper; cover; and simmer gently until the chicken is tender when tested with a fork, or about 1 hour. Five minutes before serving, add the sherry. Serves 6.

# Pollo Frito de Aguascalientes

## FRIED CHICKEN FROM AGUASCALIENTES

The small, central state of Aguascalientes (literally "hot waters") is so named for its mineral springs. It is great farming country, noted for its grains, vegetables, and fruits, especially grapes. A yearly *Festival de la Uva* (Grape Festival) is held in the capital (which is also called Aguascalientes), since some of Mexico's best wines come from the region. The far older agricultural fair, held annually on the grounds of the Garden of San Marcos, in the capital, is famous for the foods sold from the stalls, of which the most popular is the *Pollo Frito*.

2 2½-pound broiler-
  fryers, cut into serving
  pieces
2 cups chicken stock
3 medium tomatoes,
  peeled, seeded, and
  chopped
1 onion, finely chopped
1 clove garlic, crushed
¼ teaspoon cinnamon
⅛ teaspoon powdered
  cloves
½ teaspoon oregano
Salt

Freshly ground pepper
Pinch of sugar
Lemon juice
¼ cup olive oil
½ stick (2 ounces)
  butter
6 medium-sized potatoes,
  cooked, peeled, and
  sliced
3 *chorizo* sausages,
  skinned and chopped
Canned *serrano* chile
Lettuce

Poach the chicken in the stock until almost tender, about 45 minutes. Lift out of the stock and set aside. Add the tomatoes to the stock with the onion, garlic, cinnamon, cloves, oregano, salt and pepper to taste, and a pinch of sugar. Cook, uncovered, until reduced to a fairly thick sauce. Add a good squeeze of lemon juice and set aside.

Heat the oil and butter in a skillet; dip the pieces of chicken in the sauce and cook for 3 to 4 minutes on each side in the hot fat. Arrange on a serving dish and keep warm. Fry the potatoes in the same way. In the remaining fat fry the sausages and drain on paper towels. Surround the chicken pieces with the potato slices and the sausage. Warm the remaining sauce and pour it over the chicken. Serve with a bowl of undressed lettuce and a dish of *serrano* chiles on the side. Serves 6.

# Tinga Poblana de Pollo

## CHICKEN STEW FROM PUEBLA

2 2½-pound broiler-
fryers, cut into serving
pieces
2 cups chicken stock, or
canned condensed broth
2 tablespoons lard or
salad oil
3 *chorizo* sausages,
skinned and sliced
1 onion, chopped
1 clove garlic, chopped
A small handful of parsley
sprigs, chopped

1 pound (about 3 medium)
tomatoes, peeled,
seeded, and chopped
2 canned *chipotle* chiles,
chopped
Salt
Freshly ground pepper
Pinch of sugar
1 avocado, peeled and
sliced

Place the chicken pieces in a flameproof casserole which has
a lid; add the stock; cover; and cook very gently until tender,
about 1 hour. Drain; reserve the stock; return the chicken pieces
to the casserole and keep warm.

Heat the lard in a skillet, and fry the sausages until lightly
browned. Drain on paper towels and set aside. In the remaining
fat, fry the onion and garlic until the onion is golden. Add the
parsley, tomatoes, sausage, chiles, salt and pepper to taste, and
a pinch of sugar. Cook, stirring occasionally, for about 15
minutes. The sauce should be rather thicker than heavy cream.
If it is too thick, thin it with a little of the reserved stock. Pour
over the chicken, and cook, over low heat, for about 5 minutes.
Serve the avocado garnish separately. Serves 6.

*Note*: The stock can be frozen to use some other time.

# Pollo Verde

## GREEN CHICKEN

There are probably as many versions of *Pollo Verde* in Mexico as there are cooks. This, however, is the one I like best because it is so delicate and the flavor so subtle.

Good handful of fresh coriander
1 large onion, chopped
1 clove garlic, chopped
1 10-ounce can Mexican green tomatoes

Salt
Freshly ground pepper
2 2½-pound broiler-fryers, cut into serving pieces

Combine the coriander, onion, garlic, green tomatoes, and liquid from the can in the electric blender. Blend to a coarse puree. Season to taste with salt and pepper. Place the chicken pieces in a heavy, flameproof casserole with a lid; add the puree; cover; and cook, over very low heat, until the chicken is tender—about 1 hour. Serves 6.

# Otro Pollo Verde

## ANOTHER GREEN CHICKEN

2 2½-pound broiler-fryers, cut into serving pieces
1 cup chicken stock, or canned condensed broth
1 cup dry white wine
Salt
Freshly ground pepper
Heart of 1 romaine lettuce, coarsely chopped
Handful of fresh coriander, coarsely chopped

Handful of parsley, coarsely chopped
4 canned *jalapeño* chiles, deseeded, rinsed, and chopped
1 small white onion, chopped
1 10-ounce can Mexican green tomatoes
3 tablespoons lard or salad oil.

Place the chicken pieces in a heavy, flameproof casserole with a lid. Add the stock, wine, and salt and pepper to taste. Cover and simmer gently until the chicken is tender when tested with a fork, 45 minutes to 1 hour. Set aside.

Meanwhile, combine the lettuce, coriander, parsley, chiles, onion, green tomatoes, and some of the liquid from the can in the electric blender, and reduce to a coarse puree. If the blender won't accommodate this quantity, puree it in two lots. Heat the lard in a skillet, and cook the puree for 2 or 3 minutes, stirring constantly. Add the puree to the casserole, stirring gently to mix it into the broth. Cover, and heat the chicken thoroughly over a low heat without allowing it to boil, which would change the color of the sauce. Serves 6.

## *Pollo Almendrado Verde*

### GREEN CHICKEN WITH ALMONDS

| | |
|---|---|
| 2 tablespoons olive oil | ½ cup orange juice |
| 2 tablespoons butter | ½ cup dry sherry |
| 1 3½- to 4-pound chicken, cut into serving pieces | Salt Freshly ground pepper 1 cup blanched almonds |
| 1 large onion, finely chopped | 1 10-ounce can Mexican green tomatoes |
| 1 clove garlic, chopped | A good handful of fresh coriander |
| 1 cup chicken stock, or canned condensed broth | |

Heat the oil and butter in a skillet, and sauté the chicken pieces until golden. Place the pieces in a heavy, flameproof casserole which has a lid. Sauté the onion and the garlic in the oil and butter that remain in the pan until the onion is limp. Add to the casserole with the chicken broth, orange juice, sherry, and salt and pepper to taste; and cook over a very low heat, covered, until the chicken is tender when pierced with a fork—about 1 hour.

Pulverize the almonds in the electric blender, ½ cup at a time; drain the green tomatoes, reserving the liquid from the can; blend the tomatoes and coriander in the blender for a second or two; add both the almonds and tomatoes to the casserole and simmer gently for 5 minutes. The sauce should be slightly thicker than heavy cream. If it needs thinning, use a little of the reserved liquid from the canned tomatoes. Serves 6.

# Guisado de Pollo

## CHICKEN STEW

2 tablespoons salad oil
2 tablespoons butter
2 2½-pound broiler-
fryers, cut into serving
pieces
2 tomatoes, peeled,
seeded, and chopped
2 onions, sliced
2 cloves garlic, chopped
¼ pound cooked ham,
coarsely chopped

1 bay leaf
½ teaspoon thyme
¼ teaspoon oregano
6 canned *serrano* chiles
1 tablespoon capers,
drained
1½ cups dry white
wine, about
Salt
Freshly ground pepper

In a heavy, flameproof casserole which has a lid, heat the oil
and butter, and sauté the chicken pieces until golden. Add the
tomatoes, onions, garlic, ham, bay leaf, thyme, oregano, chiles,
and capers. Add enough wine to barely cover. Season to taste
with salt and pepper. Cook, covered, over low heat, until the
chicken is tender when pierced with a fork, or about 1 hour.
Serves 6.

# Pollo con Especias

## SPICED CHICKEN

4 tablespoons olive oil
2 2½-pound broiler-
fryers, cut into serving
pieces
2 cloves garlic
1 thin slice white bread
1 onion, chopped
3 or more canned *serrano*
chiles
⅛ teaspoon ground
cloves

⅛ teaspoon cinnamon
⅛ teaspoon saffron
powder
3 large tomatoes, peeled,
seeded, and chopped
1½ cups chicken stock,
about
Salt
Freshly ground pepper
½ cup dry sherry

Heat the oil in a skillet, and sauté the chicken pieces until
golden. Set aside and keep warm. In the remaining oil, fry the

garlic and bread; then the onion, adding a little more oil, if necessary. Break up the bread, and place it, with the onion and garlic, in the electric blender along with the chiles, cloves, cinnamon, saffron, tomatoes, and a little of the chicken stock, and blend to a coarse puree. You may have to do this in two batches.

Pour the sauce into a heavy, flameproof casserole which has a lid; season to taste with salt and pepper; and simmer over a low heat for a few minutes, adding enough stock to bring the sauce to a medium-thick consistency. Then add the chicken pieces, cover, and simmer over low heat until the chicken is tender, or about 1 hour. Five minutes before serving, add the sherry. Serves 6.

## Pollo en Salsa de Nuez de Castilla

### CHICKEN IN WALNUT SAUCE

3 *ancho* chiles
1 3½- to 4-pound
    chicken, cut into
    serving pieces
2 cups chicken stock, or
    canned condensed broth
4 tablespoons salad oil
2 onions, finely chopped
2 cloves garlic, chopped

1 cup walnuts
2 or 3 sprigs of fresh
    coriander
⅛ teaspoon cinnamon
⅛ teaspoon ground
    cloves
Salt
Freshly ground pepper

Prepare the chiles as described in the Introduction.

Simmer the chicken in the broth until tender when pierced with a fork—about 1 hour. Meanwhile, heat the oil in a skillet, and sauté the onions and garlic until the onions are limp, but not brown. Combine the onion, walnuts, garlic, coriander, cinnamon, cloves, and prepared chiles with *a little of the chicken broth* in the electric blender, and reduce to a smooth puree. Season to taste with salt and pepper.

Pour the sauce into a heavy, flameproof casserole with a lid; add the remainder of the chicken stock and simmer, stirring constantly, for a few minutes. The sauce should be the consistency of heavy cream. Taste for seasoning; then add the chicken to the sauce and heat through gently. Serves 6.

# *Mancha Manteles de Pollo*

## CHICKEN TABLECLOTH STAINER

The very dark chile *pasilla* gives this dish (and *Mancha Manteles de Cerdo*, Pork Tablecloth Stainer) its name. It is almost inevitable that some of the rich, deeply colored sauce will get spilled on the tablecloth, no matter how careful one may be; and the color—a lurid red—fairly shouts at you. However, my experience has been that it washes out with no trouble at all, minimizing disaster.

2 *ancho* chiles
2 *pasilla* chiles
2 2½-pound broiler-
   fryers, cut into serving
   pieces
Salt
Freshly ground pepper
2 tablespoons lard or salad
   oil
3 *chorizo* sausages,
   skinned and chopped
1 large, firm banana,
   peeled and sliced, or 1
   ripe plantain
2 slices fresh pineapple,
   peeled and sliced

6 canned *serrano* chiles,
   chopped
1 large onion, chopped
2 cloves garlic, chopped
½ cup whole blanched
   almonds
⅛ teaspoon cinnamon
⅛ teaspoon ground
   cloves
1 pound (about 3 medium)
   tomatoes, peeled,
   seeded, and chopped
2 cups chicken stock, or
   canned condensed broth
Juice of ½ lime or
   lemon

Prepare the *ancho* and *pasilla* chiles as described in the Introduction.

Season the chicken pieces with salt and pepper, and place in a heavy, flameproof casserole with a lid. Heat the lard in a skillet, and fry the sausages until lightly browned. Drain on paper towels; then add to the casserole, reserving the fat. Arrange the fruits and *serrano* chiles over the chicken pieces and sausages.

Combine the onion, garlic, almonds, cinnamon, cloves, tomatoes, and prepared chiles with *a little of the chicken stock* in the electric blender, and blend to a coarse puree. If necessary, do it bit by bit. Heat the fat remaining in the skillet; add the puree; and cook, stirring constantly, for 5 minutes. Stir in the remaining stock, taste for seasoning, and pour into the casserole. Cover; and simmer over a very low heat for about 1 hour, or until the chicken is tender when pierced with a fork. Just before serving, stir in the lime juice. Serves 6 to 8.

# *Arroz con Pollo*

## CHICKEN WITH RICE

¼ cup olive oil, about
1 3½- to 4-pound
   chicken, cut into
   serving pieces
Salt
Freshly ground pepper
2 medium onions, sliced
   thin
1 clove garlic, chopped
6 tomatoes, peeled and
   sliced

2 or more canned *serrano*
   chiles, chopped
½ teaspoon ground
   cumin
¼ teaspoon powdered
   saffron
4 cups chicken stock
2 cups rice
2 canned pimientos, cut
   into strips

Heat the oil in a skillet. Season the chicken pieces with salt
and pepper; then sauté in the hot oil until golden. Remove to
a flameproof casserole with a lid. In the same oil, sauté the
onions and garlic, and add to the chicken, with the tomatoes,
chiles, cumin, saffron, and stock. Cover, and simmer gently
for about 30 minutes.

In the oil remaining in the skillet, adding more if necessary,
sauté the rice until it has absorbed all the oil, taking care not
to let it burn. Add the rice to the chicken; cover; and continue
cooking until the chicken is tender and the rice is cooked and
quite dry—about 30 minutes. Garnish with the pimiento strips.
Serves 6.

# *Pato en Jugo de Naranja*

## DUCK IN FRESH ORANGE JUICE

1 cup orange juice (use about 4 oranges)
2 large tomatoes, peeled, seeded, and chopped
1 onion, finely chopped
1 clove garlic, chopped
2 tablespoons toasted, slivered almonds
¼ cup seedless raisins

Handful of parsley sprigs, chopped
1 bay leaf
¼ teaspoon thyme
⅛ teaspoon oregano
Salt
Freshly ground pepper
¼ cup dry sherry
½ tablespoon flour

Cut a young duckling, 4½ to 5 pounds, into serving pieces. Roll in flour seasoned with salt and pepper, and brown in a skillet with a little hot butter. Place in a heavy, lidded casserole with all the ingredients, *except the sherry and the flour*.

Place the casserole, covered, in a preheated 325°F. oven for 1½ hours, or until the duck is tender when pierced with a fork. Remove the duck pieces to a heated serving platter and keep warm.

Skim any excess fat from the sauce, and reserve. Stir in the sherry. Mix the flour with a little of the duck fat, and add to the sauce, bit by bit, over low heat, stirring constantly until smooth. Cook for a few minutes longer, still stirring. Pass the sauce separately. Serves 6.

# *Pollos en Huerto*

## CHICKENS IN THE KITCHEN GARDEN

This very old recipe is the one from which the simpler *Tapado de Pollo* is derived. It is a good example of the exuberance of the Aztec artistic reaction to new things, and reminds one of the ornate altars in the church at Tepotzotlan—so overdone in decoration that somehow it works, as indeed does this dish. The cook may vary the ingredients, adding corn, lima beans, or other fresh garden vegetables.

1 4-pound chicken, cut into serving pieces
Salt
Freshly ground pepper
4 tablespoons lard or salad oil
2 onions, sliced
2 cloves garlic
1 pound (about 3 medium) tomatoes, peeled, seeded, and chopped
1 bay leaf
2 or 3 sprigs of parsley
12 annatto seeds, ground
⅛ teaspoon ground cloves
⅛ teaspoon cinnamon
¼ pound carrots, scraped and sliced
¼ pound sweet potatoes, peeled and thickly sliced
¼ pound white potatoes, peeled and thickly sliced
2 cups dry white wine, about

¼ pound zucchini, sliced
1 cup peas
¼ pound cut green beans
1 large firm banana, peeled and sliced, or 1 ripe plantain
2 tart cooking apples, cored, peeled, and cut into chunks
2 peaches, stoned, peeled, and sliced
2 pears, cored, peeled, and sliced
2 quinces, cored, peeled, and sliced (optional)
4 slices fresh pineapple, cut into chunks
6 large ripe olives
2 tablespoons capers, drained
¼ cup raisins
3 or more canned *jalapeño* chiles, deseeded, rinsed, and cut in strips

Season the chicken pieces with salt and pepper. Heat the lard in a skillet, and sauté the chicken until golden. Remove to a very large, flameproof casserole with a lid. In the fat remaining in the skillet, sauté the onions and garlic until the onions are transparent; and add to the casserole along with the tomatoes, bay leaf, parsley, annatto, cloves, cinnamon, carrots, both kinds of potatoes, and the wine. Cover, and simmer gently for 30 minutes. Add the remaining ingredients, and continue cooking over low heat for 30 minutes, or until the chicken is tender when pierced with a fork. Serves 6 to 8.

*Note*: Frozen vegetables should be thawed and drained before using.

## *Pollo Borracho*

### DRUNKEN CHICKEN

2 tablespoons salad oil
2 tablespoons butter
2 2½-pound broiler-
  fryers, cut into serving
  pieces
¼ pound cooked ham,
  coarsely chopped
1 cup seedless raisins
⅛ teaspoon ground
  cloves
⅛ teaspoon cinnamon
⅛ teaspoon cumin
⅛ teaspoon ground
  coriander seed
2 cloves garlic, chopped
2 cups dry white wine
Salt
Freshly ground pepper
½ cup toasted, slivered
  almonds
½ cup pimiento-stuffed
  olives, cut in two
1 tablespoon capers,
  drained

In a heavy, flameproof casserole which has a lid, heat the oil and butter, and sauté the chicken pieces until golden. Add the ham, raisins, all the spices, garlic, white wine, and salt and pepper to taste. Cover, and simmer gently, over low heat, until the chicken is tender when pierced with a fork—about 1 hour. Add the almonds, olives, and capers; and heat through, uncovered, for about 5 minutes. Serves 6.

# Pollo con Naranjas

## CHICKEN WITH ORANGES

Salt
Freshly ground pepper
¼ teaspoon cinnamon
¼ teaspoon ground
  cloves
4 cloves garlic, minced
2 2½-pound broiler-
  fryers, cut into serving
  pieces
4 tablespoons olive oil
1 onion, finely chopped
2 tablespoons slivered
  almonds

¼ cup seedless raisins
1 tablespoon capers,
  drained
¼ teaspoon saffron
  powder
Strained juice of 6 oranges
Chicken stock, about 1
  cup, or canned
  condensed broth
½ cup dry sherry

Mix the salt, pepper, cinnamon, cloves, and garlic together.
Then rub the mixture into the chicken pieces on both sides.
Heat the oil in a skillet, and sauté the chicken until golden.
Set aside. In the same oil sauté the onion and almonds, adding
a little more oil, if necessary.

Place the chicken pieces in a heavy, flameproof casserole
which has a lid, along with the onion, almonds, raisins, capers,
saffron, orange juice, and enough stock to barely cover. Bring
to a boil; then reduce heat and cook, covered, over low
heat until the chicken is tender when pierced with a fork, or
about 1 hour. Five minutes before serving, stir in the sherry.
Serves 6.

# Faisán en Pipián Verde
# de Yucatán

## PHEASANT IN GREEN *PIPIÁN* SAUCE
## FROM YUCATÁN

2 pheasants*
Salt
Freshly ground pepper
Butter
Bacon or salt pork
1 cup *pepitas*
1 tablespoon annatto

1 onion, chopped
2 cloves garlic, chopped
3 or 4 leaves of *epazote*
1 10-ounce can Mexican
green tomatoes
2 cups chicken stock, or
canned condensed broth

Season the cavities of the pheasants with salt and pepper, and add a good lump of butter. Cover the breasts with thin slices of bacon or salt pork, because they are inclined to be dry. Place in a preheated 350°F. oven and roast for 45 minutes, basting frequently. Keep warm.

Pulverize the *pepitas* and annatto in the electric blender as finely as possible. Set aside. Combine the onion, garlic, *epazote*, green tomatoes, and some of the liquid from the can in the blender, and blend until smooth. Place the ground *pepitas* and annatto, the tomato mixture, the remainder of the liquid from the can, and the stock in a saucepan. Season to taste with salt and pepper; and cook, stirring very slowly until thickened—about 15 minutes. Do not allow it to boil, or it will separate.

Carve the pheasants; add the pieces to the sauce and cook for 5 minutes longer, again taking care not to allow the sauce to boil. Serves 6.

*To make Faisán en Pipián Rojo*, omit the green tomatoes, and substitute 3 medium, red tomatoes, peeled, seeded, and chopped; and puree 1 *ancho* or *mulato* chile, prepared in the usual way, with the tomatoes, the onion, and garlic as for *Pipián Verde*.

*The pheasants on the market are frozen and weigh, ready to cook, from 2¼ to 3 pounds. Obviously, they must be thawed. It will take 12 to 24 hours in the refrigerator. Birds can be thawed in the original wrapper, under cold running water, in ½ to 1½ hours, about.

# Pavo Relleno

## STUFFED TURKEY

1 6- to 8-pound turkey,
ready to cook

*Stuffing*:

2 tablespoons lard
1 onion, finely chopped
1 clove garlic, chopped
2 pounds ground pork
1 large, firm banana,
peeled and sliced, or 1
plantain
1 tart green apple, peeled,
cored, and chopped
¼ cup raisins
¼ cup toasted, slivered
almonds

1 or 2 *jalapeño* chiles,
deseeded, rinsed, and
chopped
2 medium tomatoes,
peeled, seeded, and
chopped
Salt
Freshly ground pepper
Butter
Flour
Chicken stock
Dry white wine

Heat the lard in a very large skillet, and fry the onion and
garlic until the onion is transparent. Add the pork and fry until
nicely brown, stirring constantly. Add the banana, apple, raisins,
almonds, and chiles. Drain off any excess fat; then mix
in the tomatoes well. Add salt and pepper to taste. Cook for a
few more minutes. Cool mixture before stuffing the turkey with
it.

Place the stuffed turkey, breast side up, on a rack in a
roasting pan, and cover the bird with two layers of cheesecloth
soaked in butter. Roast in a preheated 325°F. oven for 2 to
2½ hours, or until turkey is cooked, basting several times
right through the cheesecloth with pan drippings or melted
butter.

Make a gravy with the pan drippings, just enough flour to
thicken slightly, and a mixture of half stock and half wine.
Season to taste with salt and pepper. Serves 6 to 8.

# *Pollos en Adobo*

## CHICKENS IN *ADOBO* SAUCE

*Adobo* means in Spanish a pickle sauce, but it is used in Mexico to mean a very thick chile sauce which usually, though not always, contains a little vinegar. The *Adobo* itself varies from recipe to recipe.

6 *ancho* chiles
4 tablespoons lard or salad oil
2 2½-pound broiler-fryers, cut into serving pieces
1 large onion, chopped
1 clove garlic, chopped
¼ teaspoon ground cloves
¼ teaspoon cinnamon

½ teaspoon ground coriander seed
1 large tomato, peeled, seeded, and chopped
Salt
Freshly ground pepper
1 teaspoon sugar
1 tablespoon white vinegar
2 cups chicken stock, or canned condensed broth

Prepare the chiles as described in the Introduction.

Heat the lard in a large skillet, and sauté the chicken pieces, a few at a time, until golden. Remove to a heavy, flameproof casserole that has a lid. Combine the onion, garlic, cloves, cinnamon, coriander, tomato, prepared chiles, salt and pepper to taste, sugar, vinegar, and a little stock in the electric blender, and blend, a small amount at a time, to a coarse puree.

Cook the mixture in the oil remaining in the skillet for 5 minutes, stirring constantly. Add the stock and pour over the chicken pieces. Cover, and simmer for about 1 hour, or until the chicken is tender when pierced with a fork. Remove the casserole lid for the final 15 minutes of cooking. The sauce should be very thick, almost coating the meat.

Serve with lettuce, olives, capers, avocado slices, and *serrano* chiles on the side. Serves 6.

# Pollo en Nogada

## CHICKEN IN NUT SAUCE

6 *ancho* chiles
2 tablespoons salad oil
2 tablespoons butter
1 3½- to 4-pound chicken, cut into serving pieces
Salt
Freshly ground pepper
2 cups chicken stock
1 large onion, chopped
1 clove garlic, chopped
⅛ teaspoon cinnamon
⅛ teaspoon ground cloves
1 teaspoon oregano
½ cup peanuts
½ cup pecans
1 slice white bread, broken up
Liver from chicken, chopped fine

Prepare the chiles as described in the Introduction.

Heat the oil and butter in a skillet, and sauté the chicken pieces until golden. Remove to a flameproof casserole which has a lid, and season with salt and pepper. Add the stock; cover; then simmer gently until tender—about 45 minutes. Meanwhile, combine the prepared chiles, onion, garlic, cinnamon, cloves, oregano, peanuts, pecans, bread, chicken liver, and a little chicken stock in the electric blender, and blend to a coarse puree. Blend it in two batches.

Heat the oil and butter remaining in the skillet in which the chicken was sautéed, adding, if necessary, enough fat to make 2 tablespoons. Cook the puree for 5 minutes, stirring constantly. Pour the stock off the chicken; add to the sauce; and cook, over a low heat, until it is the consistency of heavy cream. Pour the sauce over the chicken in the casserole and simmer gently for 5 minutes, or long enough to heat through. Serves 6.

# *Pollo con Castañas*

## CHICKEN WITH CHESTNUTS

1 tablespoon sesame seeds
2 tablespoons salad oil
2 tablespoons butter
1 3½- to 4-pound chicken, cut into serving pieces
Salt
Freshly ground pepper
2 large onions, finely chopped
1½ cups chicken stock

½ cup dry sherry
Juice of 1 lime or ½ lemon
¼ pound boiled ham, chopped coarsely
1 11-ounce can (drained weight) peeled and cooked chestnuts
½ cup whole blanched almonds

Toast the sesame seeds in a dry skillet for about 2 minutes. Set aside.

Heat the oil and butter in a skillet. Season the chicken pieces with salt and pepper, and sauté in the hot fat until golden. Remove to a heavy, flameproof casserole that has a lid. In the fat remaining in the skillet, sauté the onions until transparent, but not browned. Add to the casserole with the chicken stock, sherry, and lime juice. Cover, and simmer over very low heat for 1 hour, or until the chicken is tender. Add the ham. Place the chestnuts, with about ¼ cup of the liquid in which they are packed, in the electric blender, and blend until smooth. Stir into the casserole. Rinse out and dry the blender. Pulverize the almonds, as finely as possible, and mix into the casserole gently. Taste for seasoning, and cook for 5 minutes longer, on the lowest possible heat, being careful not to let the sauce "catch."

Just before serving, sprinkle the chicken with the sesame seeds. Serves 6.

This is especially good with *Arroz Amarillo*, page 66, or *Arroz Gualdo*, page 63, and cooked celery hearts.

# _Pollo con Hongos_

## CHICKEN WITH MUSHROOMS

3 _ancho_ chiles
2 tablespoons salad oil
2 tablespoons butter
1 3½- to 4-pound
    chicken, cut into
    serving pieces
1 pound mushrooms with
    stems, sliced
1 onion, chopped
1 clove garlic, chopped

2 medium tomatoes,
    peeled, seeded, and
    chopped
2 sprigs of _epazote_
Salt
Freshly ground pepper
Pinch of sugar
1 cup chicken stock
½ cup heavy cream

Prepare the chiles as described in the Introduction, and set aside.

Heat the oil and butter in a skillet, and sauté the chicken pieces until golden. Remove to a flameproof casserole which has a lid. Sauté the mushrooms in the remaining fat, and add to the chicken, reserving the fat. Combine the onion, garlic, tomatoes, _epazote_, and prepared chiles in the electric blender, and blend to a coarse puree.

Heat the fat remaining in the skillet; add the puree and cook for 5 minutes, stirring constantly. Season to taste with salt, pepper, and sugar. Stir in the chicken stock. Pour over the chicken pieces; cover; and cook, over a low heat, until the chicken is tender, or about 1 hour. Just before serving, stir in the cream and heat through, without allowing the sauce to boil. Serves 6.

## *Pollo con Chorizo*

### CHICKEN WITH SPANISH SAUSAGE

2 2½-pound broiler-fryers, cut into serving pieces
2 cups chicken stock
1 onion, chopped
1 clove garlic, chopped
2 or 3 sprigs of parsley
1 bay leaf
¼ teaspoon thyme
¼ teaspoon marjoram

Salt
Freshly ground pepper
1 pound (about 3 medium) tomatoes, peeled, seeded, and chopped
Lard or salad oil
3 *chorizo* sausages, skinned and chopped
3 canned *largo* chiles

Place the chicken with the stock, onion, garlic, parsley, bay leaf, thyme, marjoram, salt and pepper to taste, and the tomatoes in a flameproof casserole with a lid. Cover, and simmer gently, over a low heat, until the chicken is tender—about 1 hour. Remove the chicken pieces from the broth to a heated serving dish and keep warm.

Meanwhile, heat a little lard in a skillet, and fry the sausages until brown, pouring off the excess fat. Drain on paper towels. Skim the fat off the broth, and remove the bay leaf and parsley. Strain the broth. Place the solids from the broth in the electric blender with the sausages, chiles, and a small amount of the stock. Blend to a smooth puree. Return to the casserole, and add the remainder of the stock. Cook, over moderate heat, until the sauce is the consistency of heavy cream. Pour over the chicken and serve. Serves 6.

# Pollo con Chipotle

## CHICKEN WITH *CHIPOTLE* CHILE

4 tablespoons salad oil
1 3½- to 4-pound
    chicken, cut into
    serving pieces
1 large onion, finely
    chopped
1 clove garlic, chopped
1 pound (about 3 medium)
    tomatoes, peeled,
    seeded, and chopped

1 sprig of *epazote*
1 canned *chipotle* chile,
    chopped*
Salt
Freshly ground pepper
2 cups chicken stock,
    about

Heat the oil in a skillet, and sauté the chicken pieces until golden. Place in a heavy, flameproof casserole with a lid; then fry the onion and garlic in the skillet until the onion is limp. Add to the chicken, with the tomatoes, *epazote*, and chile. Sprinkle with salt and pepper. Add enough chicken stock barely to cover and simmer, covered, until the chicken is tender, or about 1 hour. Serves 6.

# Pichones en Salsa de Vino Jerez

## SQUABS IN SHERRY

6 squabs
¼ pound (1 stick) butter
1 large onion, finely
    chopped
1 clove garlic, chopped
1 pound (about 3 medium)
    tomatoes, peeled,
    seeded, and chopped
Salt

Freshly ground pepper
1½ cups dry white wine
½ cup toasted, slivered
    almonds
¼ pound lean boiled
    ham, coarsely chopped
½ cup dry sherry

Split each squab lengthwise, leaving it all in one piece. Heat the butter in a skillet, and sauté on both sides until golden. Arrange the birds, overlapping, in a large, flameproof casserole

*This is an extremely *picante* chile, but 1 should give the finished dish flavor without heat. Add more if you prefer a hotter dish.

with a lid. In the remaining butter, fry the onion and garlic until the onion is transparent. Add the tomatoes, and cook to a mush. Season to taste with salt and pepper, and pour over the squabs. Add the white wine. Cover, and simmer gently until the squabs are tender, or about 45 minutes.

Place the almonds and ham in the electric blender with a little liquid from the casserole, and blend to a smooth paste. Mix into the casserole with the sherry. Cook for 5 minutes longer; and serve with plain rice and young green peas. Serves 6.

## *Pollo Almendrado Rojo*

### RED CHICKEN WITH ALMONDS

| | |
|---|---|
| 2 tablespoons olive oil | Salt |
| 2 tablespoons butter | Freshly ground pepper |
| 1 3½- to 4-pound chicken, cut into serving pieces | 1 large onion, finely chopped |
| 2 cups chicken broth | 1 clove garlic, chopped |
| ¼ teaspoon thyme | 1 cup blanched almonds |
| ¼ teaspoon marjoram | 3 large tomatoes, peeled, seeded, and chopped |
| 1 sprig of *epazote* (optional) | ½ cup dry sherry |

Heat the oil and butter in a skillet, and sauté the chicken pieces until golden. Remove to a flameproof casserole which has a lid. Add *1½ cups of the chicken broth*; the thyme, marjoram, *epazote*, and salt and pepper to taste. Cover, and simmer gently until the chicken is tender, about 1 hour.

In the oil and butter remaining in the skillet, sauté the onion and garlic until the onion is tender. Pulverize the almonds in the electric blender, ½ cup at a time. Puree the onion, garlic, and tomatoes in the blender with the remaining chicken broth. Combine with the almonds and the sherry. Stir the sauce into the casserole and cook for 5 minutes over a moderate heat, or until the sauce has thickened to a medium consistency and is hot throughout. Serves 6.

# Conejo à la Criolla

## RABBIT IN THE CREOLE MANNER

2 tablespoons salad oil
2 tablespoons butter
1 4-pound rabbit, cut into
   serving pieces
1 large onion, finely
   chopped
1 clove garlic, chopped
Handful of parsley sprigs,
   chopped
1 canned *jalapeño* chile,
   cut into strips

1 pound (about 3 medium)
   tomatoes, peeled,
   seeded, and chopped
1 cup rich meat stock
1 cup dry sherry
Salt
Freshly ground pepper
Juice of ½ lemon
¼ cup filberts, finely
   ground

Heat the butter and oil in a heavy, flameproof casserole which
has a lid, and brown the pieces of rabbit all over. Set the rabbit
pieces aside, and brown the onion, garlic, and parsley in the
same fat until the onion is limp. Add the tomatoes, chile, stock,
and sherry. Season the rabbit with salt and pepper, and return
to the casserole. Cover, and cook gently for 2½ to 3 hours,
or until the meat is tender when pierced with a fork. At this
point, stir in the lemon juice and the ground nuts. Simmer for
another 5 minutes. Serves 6.

# CARNES

## MEATS

Meats play an important role in the Mexican cuisine, with pork taking first place. The Aztecs had a type of wild pig which was hunted as boars were hunted in Europe in the Middle Ages. However, when the Spaniards introduced a domestic pig, after the Conquest, it was adopted with enthusiasm and immediately supplanted the wild pig.

There are a great many very good and unusual pork dishes in Mexico; perhaps because the pork is of an excellent quality, which doubtless encourages the cooks. These three are especially distinctive: *Tapado de Cerdo* (Smothered Pork); *Mancha Manteles de Cerdo* (Pork Tablecloth Stainer); and *Puerco con Piña* (Pork with Pineapple).

Steak is probably the most popular cut of beef, especially when it is cut from the tenderloin and cooked in what might best be described as the international manner. However, there are some distinctive beef recipes using the approach of the old Mexican kitchen. One of the most interesting is *Carne de Res con Nopalitos* (Beef with Cactus Pieces).

Meat balls, using a mixture of meats, are very highly esteemed in Mexico, and rightly so. They are not sautéed, but are poached in a thin sauce subtly flavored with chile, which gives them a delicate texture and a flavor reminiscent of the sauce as well as of their own ingredients.

Veal plays a very small role in the Mexican kitchen. Understandably, since beef was not introduced into the country until early in the sixteenth century by Cortés. Still, the cooks have skillfully adopted veal, and the existing dishes are among the most delicately flavored in the whole cuisine. Veal takes extremely well to green tomatoes and fresh coriander.

Lamb, like beef, was not introduced into Mexico until after the Conquest, and, as a result, there are not a great many specifically Mexican recipes calling for it.

The Spaniards also introduced the goat; and roast kid has become a great favorite, especially in northern Mexico. *Cabrito al Horno* (Roast Kid) is always served with wheat as well as corn tortillas, guacamole, black beans, and either *Salsa Verde*, or *Salsa Cruda*. It is not a practical dish for most home cooks in the United States, but since there are several excellent northern-style restaurants in Mexico City, it is worth bearing in mind when you are next on a Mexican holiday. Roast lamb can be used instead, and served with the traditional accompaniments. However, some specialty butchers do sell kid, in which case roast it exactly as you would the equivalent cut of lamb.

Tripe, cooked in various ways, is another triumph of the kitchen. However, it is the tongue dishes that show the Mexican genius for creating a whole series of flavors around a single basic ingredient. *Lengua Ahumada con Tomatillos* (Smoked Tongue with Green Tomatoes) is one of my greatest favorites.

# Chile con Carne

## BEEF WITH CHILE

This is the authentic northern Mexican style of cooking *Chile con Carne*, as distinct from the version that developed in Texas and has spread throughout the United States. The dish permits some variations: A mixture of pork and veal may be used instead of beef; cumin may be used in place of, or with, the oregano; peeled and chopped tomatoes are sometimes added to the chile mixture, although purists, including me, frown on this (and, I think, rightly).

toasted first

| | |
|---|---|
| 6 ancho chiles | ½ teaspoon oregano |
| 2 pounds beef chuck, cut into ½-inch cubes | Salt |
| | Freshly ground pepper |
| 1 onion, chopped | 2 cups red kidney beans, cooked |
| 1 clove garlic, chopped | |
| 2 tablespoons lard or salad oil | |

– 1 Tbl. canola

Prepare the chiles as described in the Introduction.

Place the beef in a heavy kettle with a lid; add water to cover; bring to a boil; cover; and simmer gently for 1 hour. Skim off any scum that rises to the surface. Combine the onion, garlic, and prepared chiles in the electric blender, and blend to a coarse puree. Heat the lard in a skillet, add the puree and cook for 5 minutes, stirring constantly. Stir in the oregano; then salt and pepper to taste. Add to the kettle, and cook, covered, very gently for 1 hour longer. Finally, add the cooked beans, cover, and cook for another 15 minutes. Serves 6.

*Note*: Beans for *Chile con Carne* are plainly cooked. Put the beans in a large kettle with a lid; add 1 teaspoon of salt and cold water to cover; put on the lid; and simmer over moderate heat for about 2 hours, or until the beans are tender, adding a little hot water from time to time if the beans dry out.

## Caldillo Durangueño

### BEEF STEW FROM DURANGO

3 *ancho* chiles
3 *mulato* chiles*
3 tablespoons lard or
    salad oil
3 pounds lean beef, cut
    into ½-inch cubes
1 large onion, finely
    chopped
1 clove garlic, chopped

1 pound (about 3 medium)
    tomatoes, peeled,
    seeded, and chopped
2 cups beef stock, about,
    or canned broth
Salt
Freshly ground pepper
½ teaspoon oregano
Squeeze of lemon juice

Prepare the chiles, reserving ½ cup of the seeds.

Heat the lard in a skillet, and brown the beef quickly over high heat. Place the beef in a large kettle, and set aside. Cook the onion and garlic in the same fat, and add to the beef. Cook the tomatoes in the remaining fat, and add to the beef. Place the prepared chiles and the seeds in the electric blender, and blend to a smooth puree. Add to the meat, with about 2 cups of stock or enough to cover, salt and pepper to taste, and the oregano. Cover, and simmer gently until the meat is tender when tested with a fork, or about 2 hours. A few minutes

*If *mulato* chiles are not available, increase *ancho* to 6.

before serving, stir in a good squeeze of lemon juice. This stew is quite soupy with lots of good, rich sauce. Serves 6.

# Carne de Res con Nopalitos

## BEEF WITH CACTUS PIECES

4 tablespoons lard or salad oil
3 pounds beef chuck, cut into 2-inch cubes
1 large onion, finely chopped
2 cloves garlic, finely chopped
1 8-ounce can *nopalitos*, drained
6 canned *serrano* chiles, chopped
1 10-ounce can Mexican green tomatoes
4 tablespoons tomato paste
1 cup beef stock
Scant handful of fresh coriander, chopped
Salt
Freshly ground pepper

Heat the lard in a skillet, and brown the beef cubes, a few at a time. Transfer to a heavy, flameproof casserole with a lid. Fry the onion and garlic in the remaining fat until lightly browned, and add to the casserole. Rinse the *nopalitos* thoroughly in cold water; drain; and add to the beef, with the chiles, green tomatoes and their liquid, tomato paste, stock, coriander, and salt and pepper to taste. Cover, and simmer gently until the beef is tender when pierced with a fork, or about 2½ hours. Serves 6.

# Carne de Res en Salsa de Chile Pasilla

## BEEF IN CHILE *PASILLA* SAUCE

3 *pasilla* chiles
3 pounds chuck or round steak in one piece
Salt
Freshly ground pepper
1 onion stuck with 1 clove
1 bay leaf
1 clove garlic
2 or 3 sprigs of parsley
½ teaspoon thyme
½ teaspoon marjoram
1 onion, chopped
1 clove garlic, chopped
Sprig of *epazote*
2 tablespoons lard or salad oil

Prepare the chiles as described in the Introduction.

Place the beef with salt and pepper to taste, the onion, bay leaf, garlic, parsley, thyme, marjoram, and enough water almost to cover in a heavy, flameproof casserole. Bring to a boil; reduce heat; cover and simmer for 2 hours. Cool the meat in the stock. When cool enough to handle, cut into thick slices. Rinse out the casserole and return the meat; drain the stock and set aside. Combine the onion, garlic, *epazote*, and the prepared chiles in the electric blender, and blend to a coarse puree.

Heat the lard in a skillet; add the puree and cook for 5 minutes, stirring constantly. Season to taste with salt and pepper, and pour over the beef. Thin with about 1 cup of the stock, and cook gently for ½ hour, to allow the sauce to thicken and the flavors to blend. The sauce should be quite thick, but not as thick as an *Adobo* (page 147), which coats the meat. Serves 6.

## Mole de Olla para Carne de Res

### POT *MOLE* FOR BEEF

| | |
|---|---|
| 3 *ancho* chiles | 2 tablespoons lard or |
| 1 *pasilla* chile | salad oil |
| 3 pounds stewing beef cut | 1 pound zucchini or |
| in 2-inch cubes | summer squash, sliced |
| Sprig of *epazote* | and cooked |
| 2 onions, chopped | 12 new potatoes, freshly |
| 1 clove garlic, chopped | cooked and peeled |
| 1 pound (about 3 medium) | Salt |
| tomatoes, peeled, | Freshly ground pepper |
| seeded, and chopped | |

Prepare the chiles as described in the Introduction.

Place the beef in a large kettle; add the *epazote* and enough cold water almost to cover. Bring to a boil, reduce heat, cover, and simmer for 2 hours. Meanwhile, combine the prepared chiles, onions, garlic, and the tomatoes in an electric blender, and blend to a coarse puree. Heat the lard in a skillet; add the puree and cook, stirring constantly, for 5 minutes. Season to taste with salt and pepper, and add to the beef. Add the vegetables, and simmer very gently, only long enough to heat through, or about 10 minutes. Serve with fresh corn on the cob. Serves 6.

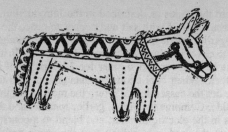

# *Carne de Res con Naranjas*

## MEXICAN BEEF WITH ORANGES

3 pounds chuck or round
    steak, in one piece
Salt
Freshly ground pepper
1 large onion, chopped
2 cloves garlic, chopped
½ teaspoon ground
    coriander
⅛ teaspoon ground
    cloves
⅛ teaspoon cinnamon

¼ teaspoon thyme
Juice of 6 oranges (about
    1½ cups), strained
Rind ½ orange
1 envelope unflavored
    gelatin
½ cup dry sherry
Garnish: Orange slices,
    capers, olives, shredded
    lettuce

Season the beef with salt and pepper; place in a heavy casserole
which has a lid; add the onion, garlic, coriander, cloves, cinnamon, and thyme. Pour in enough orange juice to cover the
beef. Cut the skin of half an orange into julienne, and stir into
casserole. Cover, and cook over a low heat until the meat is
tender when tested with a fork—about 2 to 2½ hours. Cool
the meat in the stock. Lift it out of the liquid, and cut into thin
slices. Arrange on a platter with the slices overlapping. Set
aside.

Clarify the stock, page 52. Add the sherry and enough
orange juice to bring the liquid up to 2 cups. Sprinkle the gelatin
over ¼ cup cold water to soften. Pour the stock into a
saucepan; add the gelatin and stir over low heat until dissolved.
Chill in the refrigerator until syrupy; pour over the beef, and
refrigerate until set. Decorate the platter with the orange slices,
capers, olives, and shredded lettuce. Serves 6.

# Mancha Manteles de Cerdo

## PORK TABLECLOTH STAINER

6 *mulato* chiles
4 *ancho* chiles
2 *pasilla* chiles
3 pounds boneless loin of
    pork, cut into 2-inch
    cubes
1 bay leaf
½ teaspoon thyme
¼ teaspoon oregano
1 clove
Salt
1 onion, roughly chopped
1 clove garlic, chopped
3 or 4 sprigs of fresh
    coriander
1 cup walnuts
1 10-ounce can Mexican
    green tomatoes

3 tablespoons lard or
    salad oil
Freshly ground pepper
3 tart cooking apples,
    cored, peeled, and
    sliced
3 pears, cored, peeled, and
    sliced
3 large, firm bananas,
    peeled and sliced
3 slices fresh pineapple,
    peeled and cut into
    chunks
3 zucchini, sliced
1 cup raw green peas or
    frozen peas, thawed

Prepare all the chiles as described in the Introduction, and set aside.

Place the pork in a heavy, lidded casserole with the bay leaf, thyme, oregano, clove, and enough salted, cold water almost to cover. Bring to a boil, reduce the heat, cover, and simmer for 1½ hours. Drain; strain and reserve the stock. Rinse out the casserole, and return the pork.

Combine the onion, garlic, coriander, walnuts, Mexican green tomatoes with their liquid, and prepared chiles in the electric blender. Blend, in two lots, to a smooth puree. In a large, heavy skillet, heat the lard; add the puree and cook, stirring constantly, for 5 minutes. Season to taste with salt and pepper. Then thin with 2 cups of the reserved pork stock.

Add all the fruits and vegetables to the casserole, arranging them in layers on top of the pork. Pour the puree over all, cover, and cook over low heat for 30 minutes. Serves 6 to 8.

# Carne de Res con Tomatillos

## BEEF WITH GREEN TOMATOES
## SALTILLO STYLE

2 tablespoons lard or
  salad oil
2½ pounds round steak,
  all in one piece
1 onion, sliced
1 clove garlic, chopped
1 *chorizo* sausage, skinned
  and sliced
1 10-ounce can Mexican
  green tomatoes

2 or more canned *serrano*
  chiles
Scant handful of green
  coriander sprigs,
  chopped
Salt
Freshly ground pepper
12 new, baby potatoes,
  freshly cooked and
  peeled

Heat the lard in a large, heavy skillet, and brown the steak on
both sides. Transfer the steak to a heavy, flameproof casserole
that has a lid. Set aside. In the remaining fat, sauté the onion
and garlic until limp. Add the sausage, and sauté lightly. Lift
the onion, garlic, and sausage out of the pan, with a slotted
spoon; and combine them with the steak, along with the green
tomatoes, the liquid from the can, the chiles, and coriander.
Season with salt and pepper to taste. Place over a low heat,
and simmer gently until the steak is tender when pierced with
a fork, or about 2 hours. Add the potatoes, and cook just long
enough to heat through. Serves 6

# *Picadillo*

### MINCED MEAT OR HASH

*Picadillo* is popular, in one form or another, throughout Latin America. Every country has its own favorite. The two best liked in Mexico are this *Picadillo* and *Picadillo de la Costa*.

4 tablespoons olive oil
2 pounds chopped lean beef
2 onions, finely chopped
1 clove garlic, chopped
2 apples, peeled, cored, and chopped
1 pound (about 3 medium) tomatoes, peeled, seeded, and chopped

3 canned *jalapeño* chiles, seeded and sliced
½ cup raisins
¼ cup pimiento-stuffed olives, cut in half
⅛ teaspoon cinnamon*
⅛ teaspoon cloves*
Salt
Freshly ground pepper
¼ cup slivered almonds

Heat the oil in a large, heavy skillet, and brown the meat; then add the onions and garlic. When brown, add all the other ingredients *except the almonds*, and season to taste with salt and pepper. Simmer gently, uncovered, until cooked, or about 20 minutes. Fry the almonds until golden in a little olive oil, and sprinkle over the top of the *picadillo*. Cook for a minute or two longer. Serves 6.

*⅛ teaspoon each of thyme and oregano may be substituted for the cinnamon and cloves.

# *Picadillo de la Costa*

### MINCED MEAT IN THE COASTAL STYLE

Geographically, Mexico consists of a series of high valleys ringed by mountain peaks, the largest of which is the *altiplano*, the high plateau where Mexico City is situated. The mountains run down to coasts which are lapped by the waters of the Gulf of Mexico, the Pacific Ocean, and the Caribbean. Dishes from the coastal regions, though they vary widely, are traditionally referred to simply as *de la costa*, "of the coast." This *Picadillo* is from Guerrero, home state of the famous beach resort of Acapulco.

2 tablespoons olive oil
1 pound ground pork
1 pound ground veal
2 onions, finely chopped
1 clove garlic, crushed
1 pound (about 3 medium) tomatoes, peeled, seeded, and chopped
3 canned *jalapeño* chiles, seeded and sliced
Salt
Freshly ground pepper

3 thick slices fresh pineapple, peeled and cut into chunks
3 bananas, peeled and sliced
3 pears, peeled, cored, and cut into chunks
⅛ teaspoon cinnamon
⅛ teaspoon ground cloves
¼ cup slivered almonds

Heat the oil in a large, heavy skillet, and brown the meats. Add the onions and garlic, and cook until brown. Siphon off any excess fat with a baster. Add the tomatoes, chiles, and salt and pepper to taste; and cook, uncovered, for 15 minutes. Add the fruits and spices, and simmer gently for another 15 minutes. The fruits should blend into the *picadillo* but should not disintegrate. Fry the almonds until golden in a little olive oil, and sprinkle over the top of the *picadillo*. Cook for a minute or two longer. Serves 6.

# *Puerco con Piña*

## PORK WITH PINEAPPLE

Native to Mexico and tropical America, pineapple has happily insinuated itself into everyone's cuisine the world over. It is widely used in Mexico as an ingredient in meat dishes, as well as in desserts and drinks. This, and similar dishes, comes from the Huasteca, the region embracing the coasts of Veracruz and Tamaulipas, states which border on the Gulf of Mexico. The region takes its name from the Huastecs, a Toltec Indian group. This may explain why *Puerco con Piña* is so different in its cooking point of view from the *mollis* of the high plateau, which originated with the Aztecs, the dominant tribe of the Nahuas and conquerors of the Huastecs, with a far-flung empire established before the discovery of America.

1 tablespoon of lard or salad oil

3 pounds boneless loin of pork, cut into 2-inch cubes

2 large onions, sliced thin

½ teaspoon chile *pequín*, crumbled

¼ cup dry sherry

1 medium-size pineapple, peeled and cut into chunks

1 4-ounce can pimientos, drained and coarsely chopped

6 fresh mint leaves, about, chopped,

Salt

Freshly ground pepper

1 cup meat stock

Heat the lard in a skillet. Brown the pork, drain, and place in a heavy saucepan. Brown the onions in the remaining lard; add the chile *pequín* and fry 1 minute longer; drain; and add to the pork. Pour off any lard from the skillet; rinse it out with the sherry, scraping down all the brown bits that cling to the pan; and pour over the meat. Add all the remaining ingredients. Cover and simmer gently until the pork is very tender—about 2 hours. Serves 6.

*Note*: Most good butchers and vegetable markets have fresh mint available most of the time. If you can't find it, substitute ½ teaspoon dried mint flakes.

# Tripas a la Mexicana

## MEXICAN TRIPE

3 pounds tripe
1 medium onion, sliced
1 medium onion, minced
1 tablespoon lard or salad
  oil
3 cloves garlic, chopped
6 red *pequín* chiles,
  crumbled

½ teaspoon cumin
½ teaspoon oregano
Salt
Freshly ground pepper
1 cup canned *garbanzos**

Cut the tripe into strips or squares; combine with the *sliced
onion* and enough salted water to cover; and simmer until tender
when pierced with a fork, or about 3 hours. Heat the lard or
oil in a skillet, and fry the minced onion, garlic, and chile until
the onion is lightly brown. Add to the tripe along with the
cumin, oregano, and salt and pepper to taste. Cover and simmer
gently for 30 minutes. Add the drained *garbanzos*, and just
heat through. Serves 6.

Serve the tripe in hot soup bowls, with tortillas and side
dishes of finely chopped white onion and chopped parsley or
fresh coriander.

# Tapado de Cerdo

## SMOTHERED PORK

6 *pasilla* chiles
3 pounds boneless pork
  loin, cut into 2-inch
  chunks
3 cloves garlic, chopped
4 tablespoons lard, about
1 large onion, finely
  chopped
3 large tomatoes, peeled,
  seeded, and chopped
1 10-ounce can Mexican
  green tomatoes

Salt
Freshly ground pepper
3 *chorizo* sausages,
  skinned and chopped
¼ pound boiled ham,
  chopped
¼ cup toasted, slivered
  almonds
¼ cup pimiento-stuffed
  olives, cut in two
½ cup dry sherry

*These are also known as "chick peas" or "*ceci*." To prepare chick peas, see
page 219.

Prepare the chiles as described in the Introduction.

Cook the pork in salted water until tender when pierced with a fork. About 2 hours. Drain well, discarding the stock. Puree the prepared chiles in the electric blender with the garlic, using just enough of the water in which they were soaked to make a thick paste. Heat *2 tablespoons of the lard* in a skillet, and fry the paste for 5 minutes, stirring constantly. Cool, and mix thoroughly with the pork. Pack into a heavy flameproof casserole with a lid. Heat the remaining lard in a skillet, and fry the onions until transparent but not brown; add the tomatoes and the Mexican green tomatoes with their liquid, and cook, stirring from time to time, until the sauce is smooth, about 10 to 15 minutes. Season to taste with salt and pepper, and set aside. Fry the sausages in a very little fat. Drain.

Cover the pork with the sausage, followed by the ham, and the almonds and olives. Pour the sauce over all, and finish with the sherry. Heat, covered, over a low flame until thoroughly hot through, shaking the casserole from time to time to prevent the thick sauce from "catching." Serves 6.

# *Adobo Rojo de Lomo de Cerdo*
## RED *ADOBO* OF PORK LOIN

6 *ancho* chiles
3 pounds boneless pork loin, cut into 2-inch chunks
Salt
1 whole onion stuck with 1 clove
1 onion, chopped
1 clove garlic, chopped

½ teaspoon oregano
½ teaspoon cumin
Freshly ground pepper
½ teaspoon sugar
½ pound (about 2 small) tomatoes, peeled, seeded, and chopped
2 tablespoons lard

Prepare the chiles as described in the Introduction.

Cook the pork *with the whole onion* in enough salted water to cover for 1½ hours. Pour off the stock and set aside. Discard the onion.

Combine the prepared chiles in the electric blender with the chopped onion, garlic, oregano, cumin, salt and pepper to taste, sugar, tomatoes, and ½ cup of the pork stock, and blend until smooth. Because of the quantity, it will probably be necessary to puree the mixture half at a time. Heat the lard in a skillet; add the puree and cook for 5 minutes, stirring constantly. Thin the sauce with 1 cup of the pork stock; add to the meat and cook, uncovered, over very low heat for 30 minutes. The sauce should be very thick, coating the meat. Serves 6.

# Guisado de Carne de Res con Zanahorias

## BEEFSTEAK WITH CARROTS

The miniature—only about two inches long—carrots that are sold in the San Juan Market and others in Mexico City are a deep orange, and so clean they look as if they had never associated with anything as grubby as soil. Larger ones are available for anyone silly enough to want them. The miracle is that the baby ones are a year-round phenomenon; and they give such a seemingly simple dish as beef stew a most delightful flavor. Try it when baby carrots are available in your market, or if you see some really fresh-looking medium-size ones.

½ stick (4 tablespoons) sweet butter
1½ pounds baby carrots, about 36, or medium carrots, about 12
1 large onion, sliced thin
2½ pounds round steak, all in one piece
½ cup beef stock, or canned broth
½ cup dry white wine
2 or 3 sprigs of fresh coriander
Salt
Freshly ground pepper

Heat the butter in a skillet, and sauté the carrots and the onion until the onion is transparent. Remove to a flameproof casserole with a lid. Brown the steak on both sides in the same butter, and place in the casserole, smothering it with the carrots. Add the stock, wine, coriander, and salt and pepper to taste; and simmer, covered, over very low heat, until the steak is tender when pierced with a fork, or about 2 hours. Serves 6.

# *Tinga Poblana de Cerdo*

## PORK STEW FROM PUEBLA

2 tablespoons lard or
   salad oil
3 pounds boneless pork for
   stew, cut into 2-inch
   pieces
Salt
2 *chorizo* sausages,
   skinned and sliced
1 onion, finely chopped
1 clove garlic, chopped
1 pound (about 3 medium)
   tomatoes, peeled,
   seeded, and chopped

½ teaspoon oregano
2 canned *chipotle* chiles,
   chopped
Pinch of sugar (optional)
Freshly ground pepper
12 new potatoes, freshly
   cooked and peeled
1 avocado, peeled and
   sliced

Heat the lard in a large, heavy skillet, and brown the pork. Transfer the pork to a flameproof casserole with a lid; barely cover with water; season with salt; and cook, covered, over a moderate heat until the meat is tender when pierced with a fork—about 2 hours. Strain off the stock, leaving the pork in the casserole, and set it aside.

In the fat remaining in the skillet, fry the sausages, and add to the casserole. Then fry the onion and garlic until limp. Add the tomatoes, oregano, chiles, and sugar to the pan, and cook, stirring, for about 5 minutes. Stir in about 1 cup of the reserved stock. The sauce should be quite thick. Season to taste with salt and pepper. Add the potatoes to the casserole, and pour the sauce over all. Cook, uncovered, over very low heat for about 15 minutes. Garnish with sliced avocado. Serves 6.

# *Adobo Verde de Lomo de Cerdo*

### GREEN *ADOBO* OF PORK LOIN

3 *ancho* chiles
3 pounds boneless loin of
   pork, cut in 2-inch
   cubes
1 onion, sliced
3 canned *jalapeño* chiles,
   seeded and chopped
1 onion, chopped
1 clove garlic, chopped
6 outside green leaves of
   romaine lettuce,
   chopped

½ 10-ounce can
   Mexican green tomatoes
6 sprigs of fresh coriander
2 tablespoons lard
¼ cup orange juice
Salt
Freshly ground pepper

Prepare the chiles as described in the Introduction.

Put the pork and the sliced onion in a heavy, flameproof casserole with a lid, adding water barely to cover. Bring to a boil; reduce heat; cover and simmer for 1½ hours. Drain; discard the stock, and return the pork to the casserole. Meanwhile, combine in the electric blender the prepared chiles, the *jalapeño* chiles, the chopped onion, garlic, lettuce, Mexican green tomatoes with their liquid, and the coriander. Blend in two separate lots if necessary, until smooth.

Heat the lard in a skillet, and cook the mixture, stirring constantly, for 2 or 3 minutes. Add the orange juice. Season to taste with salt and pepper, and pour over the pork in the casserole. Cook, uncovered, over the lowest possible heat for 30 minutes. The sauce will be very thick, coating the meat. Serves 6.

# *Lomo de Puerco con Manzanas*

## PORK CHOPS WITH APPLES

This recipe, obviously a Mexican adaptation of Normandy Pork Chops with Calvados, probably arrived with Maximilian and Carlotta. Many of the old recipes for this dish are so overseasoned that the flavors cancel each other out. In this version, my own, where a certain purity has been restored, it comes out very well.

| | |
|---|---|
| 2 tablespoons butter | Salt |
| 3 large, tart cooking apples, peeled, cored, and roughly chopped | Freshly ground pepper |
| | 1 teaspoon Dijon mustard |
| | 1 cup dry sherry |
| 6 thick pork loin chops, rib end | ¼ cup blanched almonds, finely ground |

Butter a heavy, flameproof casserole that has a lid, and cover the bottom with the apples. Heat the remaining butter in a skillet, and brown the chops on both sides. Arrange on top of the layer of apples. Sprinkle with salt and pepper. Mix the mustard with the sherry until smooth; then pour over the chops. Cover the casserole, and place in a preheated 350°F. oven for 1 hour, or until chops are tender when pierced with a fork. Check occasionally to see if the dish is becoming dry, since the juiciness of apples varies greatly. If dry, add a mixture of chicken stock and sherry (half and half).

When the chops are tender, remove to a heated platter and keep warm. Add the ground almonds to the liquid in the casserole; and cook, over a moderate heat, for a few minutes to thicken the sauce lightly. Serve the sauce on the side. Serves 6.

# *Puerco con Rajas*

## PORK WITH CHILE *POBLANO*

| | |
|---|---|
| 3 pounds boneless loin of pork, cut into 2-inch cubes | 2 pounds (about 6 medium) tomatoes, peeled, seeded, and chopped |
| Salt | |
| 2 tablespoons lard | 4 canned *poblano* chiles, cut into strips |
| 1 large onion, finely chopped | Freshly ground pepper |

Place the pork in a heavy, flameproof casserole with a lid; add enough water barely to cover; season with salt; and bring to a boil. Reduce heat; cover; and simmer until the meat is tender when pierced with a fork, or about 2 hours.

Heat the lard in a skillet, and sauté the onion until transparent. Stir in the tomatoes, chiles, and salt and pepper to taste; then pour the mixture over the pork. Simmer gently, uncovered, for about 15 minutes, or until the sauce has reduced somewhat and is the consistency of heavy cream. Serves 6.

## *Mole de Olla Estilo Atlixco*

### POT *MOLE* IN THE STYLE OF ATLIXCO

6 *ancho* or *mulato* chiles
2 tablespoons lard or salad oil
1 *chorizo* sausage, skinned and chopped
3 *longaniza* sausages, skinned and chopped
½ pound boneless pork for stew
1 3½- to 4-pound chicken, cut into serving pieces
1 medium onion, chopped

1 clove garlic, chopped
1 tomato, peeled, seeded, and chopped
2 tablespoons sesame seeds
¼ cup almonds
¼ cup peanuts
2 tablespoons *pepitas*
1 teaspoon oregano
Salt
Freshly ground pepper
2 cups chicken stock, or canned condensed broth

Prepare the chiles as described in the Introduction.

Heat the lard or oil in a skillet, and fry first the sausages, then the pork, and last the chicken pieces until golden. Add more fat, if necessary. Transfer to a heavy, flameproof casserole with a lid.

In the electric blender combine the chiles, onion, garlic, tomato, sesame seeds, nuts, and oregano, and blend until smooth. In the fat remaining in the skillet, cook the puree for 5 minutes, stirring constantly. Stir in the stock. Season to taste with salt and pepper. Pour over the meats in the casserole; cover; and simmer gently, over a low heat, for about 1 hour, or until the chicken is tender when pierced with a fork. Serves 6.

# Lomo de Puerco Poblano

## LOIN OF PORK PUEBLA STYLE

3 *ancho* chiles
3 *mulato* chiles
4 or 5 mint leaves, chopped
1 sprig of *epazote*, chopped
¼ teaspoon oregano
3 cloves garlic, crushed
¼ teaspoon cumin
1 bay leaf, crushed
⅛ teaspoon cinnamon
Salt
Freshly ground pepper
2 cups dry red wine
3 pounds boneless pork loin, cut into 2-inch cubes

Prepare both the chiles as described in the Introduction. Place chiles in the electric blender, and blend to a puree. Mix the puree with all the other ingredients *except the pork*. Marinade the pork in this mixture for 24 hours in the refrigerator, turning occasionally. Place the pork and the marinade in a heavy, flame-proof casserole with a lid; and cook, covered, over low heat for about 2 hours, or until the pork is tender when pierced with a fork. Serves 6.

# Guiso de Cerdo con Totopos Estilo Michoacán

## PORK STEW WITH *TOTOPOS* IN THE STYLE OF MICHOACÁN

3 pounds loin of pork, cut into 2-inch cubes
Salt
2 tablespoons lard or salad oil
2 large onions, finely chopped
2 cloves garlic, chopped
1 medium tomato, peeled, seeded, and chopped
4 canned *chipotle* chiles, sliced
1 8-ounce can *nopalitos* (cactus pieces), rinsed
1 large avocado, peeled and sliced
Grated Parmesan cheese
Freshly ground pepper

Place the pork in a heavy casserole with 2 cups of cold water; add salt; bring to a boil. Cover; then simmer until tender when pierced with a fork—about 2 hours.

Heat the lard in a skillet, and sauté the onions and garlic until tender. Add to the casserole with the tomato, chiles, and *nopalitos* (cactus pieces). Season to taste with salt and pepper; then simmer gently, uncovered, for another 15 minutes to blend the flavors and reduce the sauce slightly. Sauce should be fairly thin.

Serve with sliced avocado, cheese, and *Totopos* (below). Serves 6.

# *Totopos*

| | |
|---|---|
| 2 *ancho* chiles | 1 teaspoon salt |
| 1½ cups *masa harina* | Lard |
| ½ cup cooked red kidney beans, mashed | |

Prepare the chiles as described in the Introduction, and puree in the electric blender. Mix the *masa* and the beans together with the salt; then combine with the pureed chiles. Make into half-size tortillas on the tortilla press, page 25.

Heat the lard in a skillet, and fry the tortillas on both sides. Drain on paper towels, and keep warm until ready to serve.

# *Mole Rojo de Chile Serrano*
### RED STEW WITH MOUNTAIN CHILES

| | |
|---|---|
| 1 pound pork for stew, cut into 2-inch cubes | ½ teaspoon thyme |
| 2 cloves garlic | Sprig of *epazote* |
| 1 pound (about 3 medium) tomatoes, peeled, seeded, and chopped | Salt |
| | Freshly ground pepper |
| 12 canned *serrano* chiles* | 1 tablespoon lard or salad oil |
| ¼ teaspoon oregano | 1 3½- to 4-pound chicken |

*Anyone unfamiliar with these hot chiles may find 12 more than enough. In this case, reduce the amount.

Simmer the pork, covered, in enough salted water almost to cover, for 1 hour. Drain, reserving the stock, and set the meat aside.

Combine the garlic, tomatoes, chiles, thyme, oregano, and *epazote* in the electric blender, and blend to a smooth puree. Heat the lard in a skillet; add the puree, and cook over a moderate heat, stirring constantly, for 5 minutes. Stir in the reserved pork stock, and season to taste with salt and pepper.

Place the chicken in a large, heavy, flameproof casserole; surround with the pork, and pour the sauce over all. Cover, and cook over a low heat until the chicken is tender when pierced with a fork—about 1 hour. Serves 6.

## *Ternera con Alcaparras*

### VEAL WITH CAPERS

3 pounds boneless veal for
    stew, cut into 2-inch
    pieces
Salt
2 onions, chopped
1 clove garlic, chopped
1 bottle capers, drained

6 canned *largo* chiles
1 pound (about 3 medium)
    tomatoes, peeled,
    seeded, and chopped
Freshly ground pepper
Pinch of sugar (optional)
2 tablespoons lard

Place the veal in a heavy kettle; almost cover with water; add salt; and bring to a boil. Then simmer, covered, until tender when pierced with a fork, or about 1½ hours. Skim regularly to remove any scum that rises to the surface. Strain, and place the meat in a flameproof casserole. Reserve the stock.

Combine the onions, garlic, *all except 1 tablespoon of the capers*, chiles, tomatoes, and a little of the veal stock in an electric blender, a small quantity at a time; and blend to a smooth puree. Heat the lard in a skillet; add the puree, and cook, stirring constantly, over a moderate heat for 2 to 3 minutes. Add enough of the veal stock to the sauce to bring it to a medium-thick consistency. Season with salt and pepper. Pour over the veal; and cook, over a low heat, just long enough to blend the flavors and heat the meat.

Arrange in a hot serving dish, and sprinkle with the served capers. Serves 6.

# *Mole de Chile Pasilla de Guerrero con Puerco*

## PORK STEW WITH *PASILLA* CHILES FROM GUERRERO

6 *pasilla* chiles
3 pounds boneless pork
   loin, cut into 2-inch
   chunks
1 large onion, chopped
3 cloves garlic, chopped
¼ teaspoon cumin
⅛ teaspoon ground
   cloves
2 tablespoons sesame seeds

3 tomatoes, peeled,
   seeded, and chopped
2 tablespoons lard or
   salad oil
Salt
Freshly ground pepper
6 medium-size potatoes,
   freshly boiled and
   peeled

Prepare the chiles as described in the Introduction.

Place the pork in a heavy, flameproof casserole with a lid. Add enough water almost to cover; and cook, covered, over low heat until the meat is tender when pierced with a fork, or about 2 hours.

Combine in the electric blender the prepared chiles, the onion, garlic, cumin, cloves, sesame seeds, and tomatoes, with a little of the pork stock, if necessary, and blend until smooth. If the blender won't accommodate all ingredients at one time, puree bit by bit.

Heat the lard in a skillet, and cook the puree, over a moderate heat, for 5 minutes, stirring constantly. Season to taste with salt and pepper, and add to the pork in the casserole. Add the potatoes; cover and cook over the lowest possible heat until heated through. Serves 6.

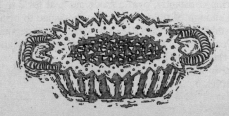

# Chile Macho de Puerco

### PORK IN HOT CHILE SAUCE

6 *pasilla* chiles
3 pounds boneless pork for
   stew, cut into 2-inch
   pieces
2 pounds (about 6
   medium) tomatoes,
   peeled, seeded, and
   chopped

1 large onion, chopped
1 clove garlic, chopped
2 tablespoons lard or
   salad oil
Salt
Freshly ground pepper

Prepare the chiles as described in the Introduction.

Place the pork in a heavy, flameproof casserole with a lid, and add enough water barely to cover. Bring to a boil, put on the lid, and cook about 2 hours, or until the pork is tender when pierced with a fork. Skim, when necessary. Combine the tomatoes, onion, garlic, and prepared chiles in the electric blender, and blend to a coarse puree. Because of the quantity, it will have to be pureed in two lots. Heat the lard in a skillet, and cook the puree for 5 minutes, stirring constantly. Drain the pork, reserving the stock. Return the pork to the casserole.

Thin the puree with enough of the stock to bring it to the consistency of heavy cream. Season to taste with salt and pepper, and pour over the pork. Cook, uncovered, over low heat for 15 minutes, or just long enough to blend the flavors and heat through. Serves 6.

# Lomo de Cerdo en Chile Verde

### LOIN OF PORK IN GREEN CHILE SAUCE

2 tablespoons lard or
   salad oil
1 large onion, finely
   chopped
2 cloves garlic, chopped
3 pounds boneless loin of
   pork, cut into 2-inch
   cubes
2 10-ounce cans Mexican
   green tomatoes

Handful of fresh coriander,
   chopped
3 canned mild *jalapeño*
   chiles, cut into strips
1 8-ounce can *nopalitos*
   (cactus pieces), rinsed
   well
Salt
Freshly ground pepper

Heat the lard or oil in a skillet, and sauté the onion and garlic until limp. Drain, and place in the bottom of a heavy, flameproof casserole that has a cover. Add the pork, the tomatoes with all their liquid, coriander, chiles, and the *nopalitos*. Sprinkle with salt and pepper. Cover; and simmer over a low heat until the pork can be pierced easily with a fork, or about 2 hours. Serves 6.

## *Mole Verde de Chile Serrano*

### GREEN STEW WITH MOUNTAIN CHILES

1 pound pork for stew, cut
   into 2-inch cubes
2 10-ounce cans Mexican
   green tomatoes
3 cloves garlic, chopped
6 sprigs of fresh coriander
12 canned *serrano* chiles*

1 tablespoon lard or salad
   oil
Salt
Freshly ground pepper
1 3½- to 4-pound
   chicken

Simmer the pork, covered, in enough salted water almost to cover, for 1 hour. Drain, reserving the stock, and set the meat aside.

Combine the green tomatoes, a little of the liquid from the can, garlic, coriander, and chiles in the electric blender, and blend to a smooth puree. Heat the lard in a skillet; add the puree, and cook, stirring constantly, over a moderate heat for 2 to 3 minutes. Stir in the remainder of tomato liquid and all the pork stock. Season to taste with salt and pepper.

Place the whole chicken in a large, heavy flameproof casserole with a lid; surround with the pork and pour the sauce over all. Cover, and cook over a low heat for about 1 hour, or until the chicken is tender when pierced with a fork. Serves 6.

*Serrano chiles are very hot. So, if 12 seem like a lot, experiment with fewer.

# Ternera en Salsa de Ciruelas Pasas

## VEAL WITH PRUNE SAUCE

1½ cups large, pitted
   prunes, chopped
1 cup dry red wine
½ stick (4 tablespoons)
   butter
6 veal cutlets
2 onions, chopped fine
1 clove garlic, chopped
   fine

1 pound (about 3 medium)
   tomatoes, peeled,
   seeded, and chopped
Salt
Freshly ground pepper
⅛ teaspoon freshly
   ground nutmeg

Soak the prunes in the wine for at least 2 hours before using.

Heat the butter in a skillet, and sauté the cutlets on both sides until nicely brown. Arrange in a flameproof casserole that has a lid. Add the onions to the butter remaining in the skillet, and sauté until limp; stir in the garlic, tomatoes, salt and pepper to taste, and the nutmeg. Pour over the cutlets; cover, and cook over a low heat until tender when pierced with a fork—from 1 to 1½ hours. When the meat is tender, add the prunes and wine; and cook, uncovered, 10 minutes longer to allow all the flavors to blend. Serves 6.

# Mole de Olla para Ternera

## VEAL STEW

3 pounds boneless veal for
   stew, cut into 2-inch
   pieces
6 small potatoes
1 cup peas
1 pound cut green beans
2 onions, chopped
1 clove garlic, chopped
6 sprigs of fresh coriander,
   chopped

6 canned *serrano* chiles or
   3 *jalapeño* chiles
1 10-ounce can Mexican
   green tomatoes
2 tablespoons lard or salad
   oil
Salt
Freshly ground pepper

Place the veal in a heavy kettle that has a lid; almost cover with cold water; add salt; and bring to a boil, skimming off any scum that rises to the surface. Reduce heat, and simmer until the meat is tender when pierced with a fork—about 1½ hours. Strain, reserving the stock. Rinse out the casserole, and return the meat. Cook the potatoes, peas, and beans separately in boiling, salted water until almost tender. They should be crisp to the bite. Drain thoroughly, and add to the veal.

Combine the onions, garlic, coriander, chiles, tomatoes, and some of the liquid from the can in the electric blender; and blend, a small amount at a time, to a smooth puree. Heat the lard in a large skillet; add the puree, and cook, over a moderate heat, stirring constantly, 5 minutes. Then stir in the remainder of the liquid from the tomatoes. The sauce should be rather thin. Season with salt and pepper to taste, and pour over the veal and vegetables. Place over a low heat and cook, uncovered, for 15 minutes—just long enough to heat through. Do not allow it to come to a boil. Serves 6.

## *Ternera en Salsa Verde*

### VEAL IN GREEN SAUCE

3 pounds boneless veal for stew, cut into 2-inch pieces
1 large onion, chopped
1 clove garlic, chopped
2 *jalapeño* chiles
6 sprigs of fresh coriander
¼ cup blanched almonds
6 medium-size leaves romaine lettuce, chopped

1 10-ounce can Mexican green tomatoes, chopped
½ stick (4 tablespoons) butter
Salt
Freshly ground pepper

Place the veal in a heavy kettle; almost cover with cold water; add salt; and bring to a boil, skimming constantly to remove any scum. Cover, reduce the heat, and simmer until meat is tender when pierced with a fork, or about 1½ to 2 hours. Drain, reserving the stock.

Combine the onion, garlic, chiles, coriander, almonds, and lettuce in an electric blender, the tomatoes and some of the liquid from the can and blend to a smooth puree. If necessary, puree part at a time. Heat the butter in a skillet; add the puree, and cook for 5 minutes, stirring constantly. Thin the sauce with the remainder of the liquid from the tomatoes and enough of the reserved stock to bring it to the consistency of heavy cream. Season with salt and pepper to taste. Pour over the veal, and heat through, but do not allow it to boil. Serves 6.

## *Ternera en Nogada*

### VEAL IN PECAN SAUCE

3 pounds veal for stew, cut into 2-inch pieces
2 onions, chopped
1 clove garlic, chopped
½ teaspoon thyme
¼ teaspoon oregano
2 cups chicken stock, or canned condensed broth

2 tablespoons butter
½ cup pecans
Salt
Freshly ground pepper
1 cup sour cream

Place the veal in a heavy saucepan that has a lid. Add *half the onions*, the garlic, thyme, oregano, and the stock. Bring to a boil, cover, and simmer gently about 1½ hours until the veal is tender when pierced with a fork. Skim off any scum that rises to the surface. Drain; set the meat aside and keep warm. Strain the stock.

Heat the butter in a skillet, and sauté the remaining onion until transparent. Add the pecans, and sauté for a minute or two. Place in the electric blender with about ½ cup of the stock, and blend until smooth. Pour into a saucepan. Add the rest of the stock, season to taste with salt and pepper, and cook for a few minutes over low heat. With a whisk, beat in the sour cream. When the sauce is well blended and hot, add the veal, and heat just long enough to warm the meat through. Serves 6.

# Pierna de Carnero Enchilada

## LEG OF LAMB WITH CHILE

6 *ancho* chiles
3 cloves garlic, slivered
½ leg of lamb, about 4 pounds
Salt
Freshly ground pepper
1 large onion, chopped

1 large tomato, peeled, seeded, and chopped
Pinch of sugar
2 tablespoons salad oil
2 cups chicken stock, or canned condensed broth

Prepare the chiles as described in the Introduction.

Insert the garlic slivers into the lamb; then rub the meat all over with a mixture of salt and pepper. Place in a heavy casserole that has a lid.

Combine the onion, tomato, and the prepared chiles in the electric blender with a pinch of sugar, and blend to a coarse puree. Heat the salad oil in a skillet; add the puree, and cook for 5 minutes, stirring constantly. Stir in the stock, and pour over the lamb. Seal the casserole with aluminum foil, and then cover with the lid. Place in a preheated 350°F. oven, and cook for about 3 hours, or until the meat is tender when pierced with a fork. Serves 6.

# Carnero Estilo Yucateco

## LAMB YUCATÁN STYLE

The Mayan kitchen of the Yucatán peninsula differs considerably from the Aztec kitchen of the high plateau. One of the characteristic differences is in the Mayan use of annatto (*achiote*), which is the seed of the tropical tree *Bixa orellana*. The seeds are surrounded by an orange-red pulp; and, when ground, give to food not only a rich golden color, but a subtle, delicate flavor.

3 pounds boneless lamb for stew, cut into 2-inch pieces
1 onion, finely chopped
1 clove garlic, chopped
Sprig of *epazote*
1 large tomato, peeled, seeded, and chopped

Salt
Freshly ground pepper
1 cup *pepitas*
1 tablespoon annatto seeds
1 tablespoon salad oil
Good squeeze of lemon juice

Place the lamb with the onion, garlic, *epazote*, tomato, salt, and pepper to taste, and enough water to cover in a flameproof casserole with a lid. Bring to a boil, cover, reduce to a simmer and cook until the lamb is tender when pierced with a fork—about 2 hours. Combine the *pepitas* and the annatto in the electric blender, and blend as finely as possible. Heat the salad oil in a skillet; add the ground seeds, and fry them for 3 or 4 minutes, stirring constantly and taking care not to let them burn. Add to the cooked lamb; taste for seasoning, and simmer, on a low heat, until the sauce is quite thick, or about 5 minutes. Just before serving, stir in a good squeeze of lemon juice. Serves 6.

## Estofado de Carnero

### LAMB STEW

This is an interesting recipe, as it demonstrates the main influences on the indigenous Mexican kitchen arising from the Conquest. From the Arabs who had dominated Spain for several centuries before Spain's conquest of Mexico come the almonds, raisins, and lamb; from Spain comes the sherry; and from Mexico the chile and tomatoes.

3 *ancho* chiles
3 pounds boneless stewing lamb in 2-inch cubes
1 pound (about 3 medium) tomatoes, peeled, seeded, and chopped
2 cloves garlic, chopped
¼ cup raisins

⅛ teaspoon ground cloves
⅛ teaspoon cinnamon
Salt
Freshly ground pepper
1 cup dry sherry
¼ cup toasted slivered almonds

Prepare the chiles as described in the Introduction.

Place the prepared chiles in the electric blender, and blend to a thick puree. Place the lamb, tomatoes, garlic, raisins, cloves, cinnamon, and salt and pepper to taste in a heavy flameproof casserole which has a lid. Add enough water to the puree to bring it to the consistency of thin cream. This should take about 1½ cups. Pour over the meat; cover the casserole; bring to a boil; lower the heat; then simmer very gently until the lamb is tender when pierced with a fork—about 2 hours. Five minutes before serving, add the sherry; and at the last minute sprinkle with the almonds. Serves 6.

# *Adobo de Carnero*

## ADOBO OF LAMB

| | |
|---|---|
| 6 *ancho chiles* | 2 or 3 sprigs of parsley |
| 3 *mulato* chiles | Salt |
| 3 pounds boneless stewing lamb in 2-inch cubes | Freshly ground pepper |
| 2 onions, chopped | ½ pound (about 2 small) tomatoes, peeled, seeded, and chopped |
| 2 cloves garlic, chopped | |
| 1 teaspoon thyme | 2 tablespoons salad oil |
| ½ teaspoon oregano | 1 teaspoon sugar |
| 1 bay leaf | 1 tablespoon white vinegar |

Prepare the chiles as described in the Introduction.

Place the lamb in a flameproof, lidded casserole with *half the chopped onions*, *1 clove garlic*, the thyme, oregano, bay leaf, parsley, salt and pepper to taste, and water barely to cover. Bring to a boil; reduce heat; then simmer gently, covered, for 1½ hours. Drain the lamb, strain the stock, and set aside. Rinse out the casserole, and return the meat to it.

Combine the *remaining onion and garlic*, tomatoes, and the prepared chiles with a little of the lamb stock, about ½ cup, in the electric blender, and blend to a smooth puree. Heat the oil in a skillet, and cook the puree for 5 minutes, stirring constantly. Thin the puree with 1 cup of the lamb stock; pour over the meat, and cook, uncovered, over very low heat for 30 minutes. The sauce will be very thick, coating the meat. Serves 6.

# *Menudo Estilo Sonora*

## SONORA-STYLE TRIPE

This northern Mexican dish, like a pot-au-feu, is both soup and meat. It is as famous a hangover cure as the onion soup which one eats at dawn at the market at Les Halles in Paris after a night on the town. After a too-late night, *Menudo* is served for breakfast and is wonderfully restorative. One is always advised to take plenty of the crumbled chile *pequín* that is customarily served with it. *Menudo* also makes a perfectly respectable lunch or dinner at any time, when no advice on the amount of chile to be taken should be offered.

2 pounds beef tripe
2 pig's feet
Salt
Fresh corn from 6 cobs
1 bunch scallions, chopped
1 handful of fresh
   coriander, chopped

Freshly ground pepper
18 lemon or lime slices
Fresh oregano, chopped
Dried *pequín* chiles,
   crumbled
1 Bermuda onion, minced

Place the tripe and the pig's feet in a kettle or deep saucepan with a lid; cover with salted water; bring to a boil; and cook, covered, until the meats are tender—about 3 hours. Cool in the stock. When cold, lift the tripe from the stock, and cut into squares or strips; remove the bones from the pig's feet, and cut into pieces. Return the meats to the stock, and set aside.

Meanwhile, strip the corn from the cobs; and add to the stock with the scallions, coriander, and salt and pepper to taste. Bring to a boil; lower the heat, and simmer gently for 5 minutes. Serve in deep soup plates, warmed, with the lime, oregano, chiles, and onion on the side. These are added to the dish according to individual taste. Serves 6.

## *Tinga de Cerdo y Ternera*

### PORK AND VEAL STEW

2 tablespoons lard or salad
   oil
1½ pounds boneless
   pork for stew, cut into
   2-inch cubes
1½ pounds veal for
   stew, cut into 2-inch
   cubes
1½ cups chicken stock
1 onion, finely chopped

1 clove garlic, chopped
½ teaspoon thyme
½ teaspoon marjoram
1 10-ounce can Mexican
   green tomatoes
2 canned *chipotle* chiles,
   chopped
Salt
Freshly ground pepper

Heat the lard in a skillet, and brown the pork and veal cubes. Drain on paper towels, and place in a flameproof casserole that has a lid. Add the stock, and cook, covered, over low heat until the meat is tender when pierced with a fork—about 2 hours. Drain; reserve the stock; return the meat to the casserole and keep warm.

Heat the lard remaining in the skillet, and fry the onion and garlic. Pour off all excess fat; add the thyme, marjoram, green tomatoes and their liquid, the chiles, and salt and pepper to taste. Simmer gently for 5 minutes; then pour over the meat in the casserole, and simmer for another 5 minutes. The sauce should be quite thick. Serves 6.

*Note*: The reserved stock can be frozen for later use.

# Albóndigas

## MEAT BALLS

1 *ancho* chile
1 slice white bread
Milk
½ pound ground lean beef
½ pound ground lamb
½ pound ground pork
¼ pound boiled ham, chopped fine
1 egg
Salt
Freshly ground pepper
2 tablespoons lard or salad oil
1 onion, finely chopped
2 cloves garlic, minced
3 medium tomatoes, peeled, seeded, and mashed
¼ teaspoon oregano
2 cups meat stock, or canned broth

Prepare the chile as described in the Introduction.

Soak the bread in milk, and squeeze dry just before using. Mix the meats and the bread thoroughly with the egg, and season to taste with salt and pepper. Form into balls about the size of a small white onion, and set aside.

Heat the lard in a skillet, and fry the onion and garlic until brown, taking care not to burn the garlic. Add the tomatoes, oregano, and the pureed chile. Taste for seasoning; then cook for a minute or two. Stir in the stock. Pour into a large saucepan, bring to a boil, and add the meat balls. Reduce the heat, cover, and poach gently for 1 hour. Serve with the sauce. Makes about 24 to 30 meat balls. Serves 6.

*Note*: Mexican cooks insert a small piece of hard-cooked egg or a piece of pimiento-stuffed olive into the center of each meat ball before poaching.

# *Albondiguítas*

## LITTLE MEAT BALLS

2 slices white bread
Milk
½ pound ground pork
½ pound ground veal
½ pound ground lamb
1 large onion, minced
2 eggs, lightly beaten

Salt
Freshly ground pepper
4 cups meat stock
2 cups tomato juice
1 canned *chipotle* chile,
    chopped

Soak the bread in milk, and squeeze dry just before using. Mix the meats, onion, bread, eggs, and seasonings together thoroughly, and form into bite-size balls. Combine the stock and tomato juice, add the chile, and heat to the boiling point. Add the meat balls to the boiling liquid, a few at a time so as not to stop the boiling. When all the meat balls have been added, reduce heat to simmer; cover; and cook gently for 45 minutes. Drain, and save the stock. Makes about 24. Serve the *albondiguítas* with toothpicks and one of Mexico's on-the-table sauces.

*Note*: The good stock in which the meat balls cooked should be saved to make soups or sauces. Freeze, if it is not going to be used within two or three days.

# *Lengua Adobada*

## TONGUE IN *ADOBO* SAUCE

3 red chiles, either *ancho*
    or *mulato*
2 veal tongues, about
    2½ pounds each
1 onion, halved
1 onion, roughly chopped
2 cloves garlic
½ teaspoon thyme
1 bay leaf

2 tomatoes, peeled,
    seeded, and roughly
    chopped
½ teaspoon cumin
2 tablespoons lard or salad
    oil
Salt
Freshly ground pepper

Prepare the chiles as described in the Introduction.

Simmer both tongues in enough boiling, salted water to cover, with 1 *halved onion, 1 clove of garlic*, the thyme, and bay leaf, until tender when pierced with a fork—about 2 hours.

In the electric blender, place the prepared chiles, 1 *roughly chopped onion*, 1 *chopped clove garlic*, the tomatoes, and cumin, and blend to a coarse puree. If the blender won't accommodate the quantity all at one time, blend the mixture piecemeal.

Heat the lard or oil in a skillet; add the puree; and cook for 5 minutes, stirring constantly. Season to taste with salt and pepper.

When the tongues are cool enough to handle, remove the skin and trim the root ends. Cut into thick slices; place in a flameproof casserole; add the sauce; and simmer gently, uncovered, until the sauce is very thick. Serves 6.

## *Lengua Almendrada*

### TONGUE IN ALMOND SAUCE

2 veal tongues, about 2½ pounds each
1 onion, stuck with 2 cloves

1 bay leaf
6 peppercorns
Salt

Place the tongues, onion, bay leaf, pepper corns, and a good tablespoon of salt in a heavy kettle; add enough cold water to cover. Bring to a boil; then reduce heat to simmer, and cook until tongues are tender when pierced with a fork—about 2 hours. Leave in their liquid until cool enough to handle. Then remove the skin, trim off the root ends, and slice rather thickly. Strain and reserve the stock.

Meanwhile, have ready the following sauce:

2 *ancho* chiles
½ cup blanched almonds
¼ cup raisins
1 slice white bread, chopped
1 large tomato, peeled, seeded, and chopped

1 tablespoon sesame seeds
2 tablespoons lard or salad oil
2 cups of the tongue stock
Salt
Freshly ground pepper

Prepare the chiles as described in the Introduction.

Combine the prepared chiles, almonds, raisins, bread, tomato, and sesame seeds in the electric blender, and blend until smooth. Heat the lard or oil in a saucepan; add the mixture, and cook, stirring constantly, for 5 minutes. Stir in the stock; bring to a boil; then simmer for another 5 minutes. Season to taste with salt and pepper. Add the sliced meat and heat through, without allowing the sauce to come to a boil. Serves 6.

## *Albondigón*

### MEAT LOAF

2 slices white bread
Milk
1 pound ground lean beef
  or veal
1 pound ground pork
1 onion, minced
½ teaspoon ground
  coriander seed
2 eggs

2 cups *Salsa de Chile
  Rojo\**
Salt
Freshly ground pepper
3 hard-cooked eggs, cut in
  half lengthwise
Pimiento-stuffed green
  olives, cut in half

Soak the bread in milk, and squeeze dry just before using. Mix the bread, meats, onion, coriander, and the 2 eggs together thoroughly. Add ½ cup of the chile sauce; then taste for seasoning.

Grease an 8 x 4 x 3-inch loaf pan, and fill with *half the meat mixture*, packing it down firmly. Arrange a row of the hard-cooked eggs down the center of the meat, cut side up, and surround with olive halves in a pattern. Cover with the remainder of the meat mixture, patting it into a compact loaf. Pour the other ½ cup of the chile sauce over the top, and bake the meat loaf, in a preheated 350°F. oven, for 1 hour. Serves 6.

*Follow the recipe on page 79, eliminating the olive oil and vinegar.

# Albóndigas con Chipotle

## MEAT BALLS WITH *CHIPOTLE* CHILE

1 slice white bread
Milk
½ pound ground veal
½ pound ground pork
½ pound ground lamb
¼ pound boiled ham, chopped fine
1 small white onion, minced
1 egg
1 onion, chopped

1 clove garlic, chopped
2 *chipotle* chiles, chopped
3 or 4 sprigs of fresh coriander
1 10-ounce can Mexican green tomatoes
1 tablespoon lard or salad oil
1 cup meat stock, or canned broth

Soak the bread in milk, and squeeze dry just before using. Mix the meats, bread, *minced onion*, and egg thoroughly, and season to taste with salt and pepper. Form the mixture into balls about the size of small white onions. Set aside.

Combine the *chopped onion*, garlic, chiles, coriander, the green tomatoes, and some of the liquid from the can in the electric blender, and blend to a smooth puree. Heat the lard in a skillet, and cook the mixture for a minute or two, stirring constantly. Pour into a large saucepan, add the remainder of the liquid from the green tomatoes and the stock. Season to taste with salt and pepper. Bring to a boil, add the meat balls, cover, and poach gently for 1 hour. Serve with the sauce. Makes about 24 to 30 meat balls. Serves 6.

*Note*: Mexican cooks insert a small piece of hard-cooked egg or a piece of pimiento-stuffed olive into the center of each meat ball before poaching.

# Sesos con Jitomate

## BRAINS WITH TOMATO

1 pair brains
2 to 3 teaspoons butter
1 onion, finely chopped
½ teaspoon Spanish
    paprika
1 large tomato, peeled,
    seeded, and chopped

6 sprigs of fresh coriander
    or parsley sprigs,
    chopped
Salt
Freshly ground pepper

Soak the brains in enough cold water to cover for 1 hour. Pull off the covering membrane and veins. Drop in boiling, salted water; reduce heat to simmer; and cook slowly for 30 minutes. Cool, drain, and slice. Heat the butter in a skillet, and sauté the onion until limp. Add the paprika, tomato, coriander, and salt and pepper to taste; and cook over a moderate heat, stirring from time to time, until the ingredients have blended into a rich sauce. Add the brains, and bring just to a boil. Serve at once. Serves 2.

*Note*: This excellent luncheon dish also makes a delicious filling for *quesadillas* and tacos.

# Menudo con Chorizo

## TRIPE WITH *CHORIZO*

3 pounds tripe
1 tablespoon lard
3 *chorizo* sausages,
    skinned and sliced
1 large onion, chopped
1 clove garlic, chopped
1 pound (about 3 medium)
    tomatoes, peeled,
    seeded, and mashed

6 sprigs of parsley,
    chopped
½ teaspoon thyme
¼ teaspoon oregano
Salt
Freshly ground pepper

Simmer the tripe in salted water to cover, covered, until tender when pierced with a fork, or about 3 hours. Drain well, and cut into squares or strips. Heat the lard in a skillet, and fry the sausages. Drain on paper towels. In the fat remaining in the skillet, fry the onion and garlic until the onion has browned lightly. Take care not to burn the garlic. Fry the tripe in the same fat, adding a little more fat, if necessary.

Combine the tripe, sausage, onion, garlic, tomatoes, parsley, thyme, oregano, and salt and pepper to taste in a deep saucepan; bring to a boil; then simmer, uncovered, for 30 minutes, or just long enough for the sauce to thicken nicely. Serves 6.

## *Otra Tripas a la Mexicana*

### ANOTHER MEXICAN TRIPE RECIPE

3 pounds tripe
4 tablespoons oil
4 large tomatoes, peeled, seeded, and chopped
1 onion, minced
3 cloves garlic, chopped
4 to 5 sprigs of parsley, chopped

¼ teaspoon oregano
½ teaspoon thyme
2 tablespoons capers, drained
Salt
Freshly ground pepper
1 teaspoon lemon juice
Canned *largo* chiles

Simmer the tripe, covered with salted water, about 3 hours until tender. Drain, reserve the stock, and cut the meat into squares or strips. Heat the oil in a skillet, and fry the tripe until golden; then place the pieces in a saucepan with the tomatoes. Set aside for the moment.

In the fat remaining in the skillet, fry the onion and garlic until transparent, and add to the tripe. Then add the parsley, oregano, thyme, capers, and salt and pepper to taste. Place over a moderate heat, and simmer gently for 30 minutes. Stir in the lemon juice just before serving.

Serve with canned *largo* chiles on the side. Serves 6.

# Lengua Ahumada con Tomatillos

## SMOKED TONGUE WITH GREEN TOMATOES

1 smoked beef tongue,
about 5 pounds
1 onion stuck with 1 clove
1 onion, chopped
2 cloves garlic
6 peppercorns
1 bay leaf
3 tablespoons lard or
vegetable shortening
18 baby new potatoes,
freshly cooked and
peeled

3 or more canned *serrano*
chiles, chopped
2 or 3 sprigs of fresh
coriander, chopped
2 10-ounce cans Mexican
green tomatoes
Salt
Freshly ground pepper

Cover the tongue with cold water; bring to a boil; then cover, and cook for 1 hour. Drain. Add fresh water, *1 onion stuck with a clove, 1 whole clove garlic*, the peppercorns, and bay leaf. Bring to a boil; then simmer for about 2 hours, or until the tongue is tender when pierced with a fork. Cool in the stock. When cool enough to handle, remove the skin and fat, and trim the root end. Slice the meat fairly thick, and place in a flameproof casserole. Strain the stock and reserve.

Heat the lard in a skillet, and fry the *chopped onion* and *1 chopped clove of garlic*. Add to the casserole. In the same fat, fry the potatoes; drain; and add to the casserole with the chiles, coriander, the Mexican green tomatoes and all their liquid. Season to taste with salt and pepper. If more liquid is needed to cover the tongue and potatoes, add a little of the reserved stock. Cover and simmer gently for 15 minutes, so that the tomatoes disintegrate and the meat and potatoes are heated through. Serves 6.

# Lengua en Nogada

## TONGUE IN WALNUT AND PEANUT SAUCE

2 veal tongues, about
2½ pounds each
Salt
1 onion, cut in two, stuck
with 2 cloves

1 bay leaf
6 peppercorns

Simmer both tongues in enough boiling, salted water to cover, along with the onion, bay leaf, and peppercorns, until tender when pierced with a fork—about 2 hours. Leave in the stock until cool enough to handle; then remove the skin and trim the root ends. Strain the broth and reserve. Slice the meat rather thickly, and set aside.

Meanwhile, have ready the following sauce:

| | |
|---|---|
| 6 *ancho* chiles | 1 slice white bread, toasted |
| ½ cup walnuts | and coarsely chopped |
| ½ cup peanuts | 3 tablespoons lard or salad |
| ⅛ teaspoon ground | oil |
| cloves | 2 cups stock from the |
| ⅛ teaspoon cinnamon | tongue |
| 1 small onion, chopped | Salt |
| 1 clove garlic, chopped | Freshly ground pepper |

Prepare the chiles as described in the Introduction.

Combine the prepared chiles, walnuts, peanuts, cloves, cinnamon, onion, garlic, and bread in the electric blender. Blend until smooth.

Heat the lard or oil in a skillet; add the pureed mixture, and cook over a moderate heat, stirring constantly, 5 minutes. Add the stock, and simmer gently for 15 minutes. Season to taste with salt and pepper. Add the tongue, and heat for about 5 minutes, or until the meat is heated through. Serves 6.

## *Fiambre Potosino*

### COLD MEATS SAN LUIS POTOSI STYLE

The central state of San Luis Potosi has a thriving cattle industry, and is a big grower of the agave (*maguey*), from which the drink *mezcal* (similar to tequila) is produced. The *Fiambre* (literally cold meat) is a great favorite for family entertaining on the cattle ranches. On Sundays, for midday dinner, tables are set outdoors, and friends and relations are invited for what is, in effect, a picnic but also a lavish meal.

*The meats*:

| | |
|---|---|
| 2 pounds boneless pork | 1 3½- to-4 pound |
| loin | chicken |
| 2 veal tongues, about 1 | 3 pig's feet, halved |
| pound each | Salt |

*Marinade*:

2 cups olive oil
⅔ cup wine vinegar
Salt
Freshly ground pepper
1 teaspoon Dijon mustard

Scant handful of parsley
    sprigs, chopped
1 clove garlic, crushed
1 tablespoon drained,
    chopped capers

*The garnish*:

1 head lettuce, shredded
3 large tomatoes, peeled
    and sliced
3 large avocados, peeled
    and sliced
5 canned *chipotle* chiles,
    stuffed with cottage
    cheese

Radishes
Ripe olives
1 white onion, finely
    chopped

Cook each of the meats separately, covered, in simmering salted water. Allow about 2 hours for the pork and the veal tongues; 1 hour for the chicken; and 3 hours for the pig's feet. Cool each of the meats in its own stock. When cool enough to handle, slice the pork and the tongue; divide the chicken into serving pieces; bone and cut up the pig's feet. Set all aside.

*Make the marinade as follows*: Mix together the oil, vinegar, salt, pepper, mustard, parsley, garlic, and capers. Sprinkle half the marinade over the various meats, and allow to stand for 1 hour.

*To serve*: Make a bed of lettuce on a large platter, and arrange the meats on top. Decorate the platter with the sliced tomatoes, avocados, the stuffed *chipotle* chiles, radishes, and olives. Sprinkle the onion on the tomatoes. Serve the remaining vinaigrette sauce in a sauceboat. Serves 8 to 10.

*Note*: Tortillas, cut into four and fried until crisp, or *Tortillas del Norte*, make a good accompaniment. Traditionally, tamales without any filling at all (*tamales blancos*) were served with the *Fiambre*.

# *Angaripola*

## A GAUDY DISH

*Angaripolas*, aside from cookery, are gaudy ornaments on clothes. The *chorizo* sausages, which contain paprika, plus the saffron and the tomatoes give this dish a gaudy color, hence its amusing name.

3 pig's feet, split, or hocks
1 onion stuck with 1 clove
1 carrot, scraped and sliced
2 or 3 sprigs of parsley
¼ teaspoon thyme
¼ teaspoon marjoram
1 bay leaf
Salt
Freshly ground pepper
2 *chorizo* sausages,
    skinned and chopped
Lard or salad oil
1 3½- to 4-pound
    chicken, cut into
    serving pieces
2 pounds boneless loin of
    pork, cut in 2-inch
    cubes

1 large onion, finely
    chopped
1 clove garlic, chopped
1 pound (about 3 medium)
    tomatoes, peeled,
    seeded, and chopped
¼ teaspoon powdered
    saffron
6 canned *largo* chiles, cut
    in strips
2 tablespoons capers,
    drained
½ cup pimiento-stuffed
    olives, chopped

Simmer the pig's feet in salted water to cover, with the onion, carrot, parsley, thyme, marjoram, bay leaf, and salt and pepper to taste, until tender—about 3 hours. Cool in the stock; then remove the bones, and cut the meat into serving pieces. Strain the stock and set aside.

Fry the sausages in a little lard or oil. When brown, drain and set aside. In the same fat, which will now be orange-red from the sausages, fry the chicken pieces until golden. Set them aside. Next, fry the pork until nicely brown. Drain. Finally, fry the chopped onion and garlic. Drain. Place the chicken, pork, sausages, and the meat from the pig's feet in a heavy, flameproof casserole that has a lid; add the tomatoes, saffron, 2 cups of the reserved stock, the chopped onion, and garlic. Bring to a boil, cover, and simmer gently until all the meats are tender when pierced with a fork—about 1 hour. Just before serving, stir in the chiles, capers, and olives. Serves 6.

## *Pozole Estilo Jalisco*

### POT-AU-FEU JALISCO STYLE

3 pig's feet
1 whole head garlic,
  separated and peeled
1 3½- to 4-pound
  chicken, cut into
  serving pieces
1 pound boneless pork
  loin, cut in 2-inch cubes
2 cups canned hominy or 2
  cups canned *garbanzos*

Salt
Freshly ground pepper
Chicken stock
*Pequín* chiles, crumbled
2 limes or lemons, cut into
  wedges
1 bunch radishes
1 head lettuce, shredded
1 Bermuda onion, minced

Simmer the pig's feet with the garlic in salted water to cover about 3 hours, until almost tender. Add the chicken and pork, and cook gently for 45 minutes; add the hominy, and continue cooking for 15 more minutes, or until the meats are tender when pierced with a fork; season to taste with salt and pepper.

Since this is a soup as well as a meat dish, there should be plenty of broth. If the stock boils away, add more. Serve the broth and meats together in deep, heated soup bowls. Hand separately the chiles, limes, radishes, lettuce, and onion, which are added to the soup according to the individual taste. Serves 6 to 8.

# Puchero

## MEXICAN POT-AU-FEU

1 cup *garbanzos* (chick
   peas)*
1 pound boneless beef
   stew, cut into 2-inch
   cubes
1 pound boneless lamb
   stew, cut into 2-inch
   cubes
½ pound ham, diced
1 3½- to 4-pound
   chicken, cut into
   serving pieces
1 marrowbone
1 large onion, sliced
1 clove garlic, chopped
1 cup kernel corn
3 medium carrots, scraped
   and sliced
3 turnips, peeled and sliced
3 zucchini or summer
   squash, sliced

1 small cabbage, cut into
   wedges
½ pound sweet
   potatoes, peeled and
   sliced
Salt
Freshly ground pepper
3 white potatoes
3 tablespoons lard or salad
   oil
2 large, firm bananas,
   peeled and sliced
   lengthwise
3 peaches, peeled and
   sliced
3 pears, cored, peeled, and
   sliced
Scant handful of fresh
   coriander, chopped
Lime or lemon wedges
1 recipe guacamole

Soak the *garbanzos* overnight. Drain. Place the *garbanzos*, all
the meats, and the marrowbone in a large kettle with the onion
and garlic. Cover with cold water; bring to a boil; lower the
heat; cover, and simmer gently for 45 minutes. Add the corn,
carrots, turnips, zucchini, cabbage, *sweet potatoes*, and salt
and pepper to taste. Cover and simmer gently until the meats
and vegetables are tender—about 20 minutes. Meanwhile, parboil the *white potatoes* for 10 minutes. Drain, peel, and cut
into slices. Heat the lard in a skillet, and sauté the potatoes.
Set aside and keep warm. In the same fat, sauté the bananas
until golden brown. Keep warm with the potatoes.

While waiting for the potatoes to parboil, put the peaches
and pears on to cook in a saucepan with a little water; and
poach, covered, for about 10 minutes. They should be tender
but still firm. Drain. At this point all the meats, vegetables,

*If using cooked, canned *garbanzos* simply rinse and drain them, and add
to the *Puchero* with the vegetables.

and fruits in the *Puchero* will be ready. Strain the soup into a large tureen. Garnish with the coriander, and serve with wedges of lime. Arrange the meats on a warm platter surrounded by the fruits and vegetables. Serve the guacamole separately. Serves 6 to 8.

# *Barbacoa*

## BARBECUE

Mexican *barbacoa* is entirely different from the charcoal grill barbeque with which we are all familiar. The English word "barbecue," taken from the Spanish "*barbacoa*," came into use in 1697. It referred to a rude framework used in America either for sleeping or for smoking or drying meat over a fire. By 1809 it had come to mean, in the United States, an open-air social entertainment at which animals were roasted whole. Today it usually means meats, fish, or fowl cooked over an open fire, basted with a barbecue sauce.

This is a far cry from the *barbacoa* of Mexico, which should probably have been called something else—but it is a little late to change names now. It has more in common with the luau of Hawaii and the clambake of New England, though Ti leaves are used for the luau, and seaweed for the clambake. In Mexico *pencas de maguey*, agave leaves, are used. In Yucatán, as a further refinement, the meat is wrapped in banana leaves. It is a very ancient method of cooking, probably going as far back as Neolithic times.

Experts say that the best barbecue comes from the Valley of Mexico, where both the state of Mexico and the Federal District, site of the capital, are located. Within this region the two best sources are the town of San Juan Teotihuacán, near the famous pyramids of the Sun and the Moon, and the village of Texcoco, which was an important center in pre-Columbian times. It can also be bought in Mexico City, a good source being the suburb of San Angel. It can be eaten in a barbecue restaurant or taken out.

It really is not practical to make yourself, unless you live on a ranch in a region where agave grows, or have both a large garden and a large number of friends, as you really can't barbecue a couple of lamb chops with any great success. It takes the entire animal.

However, if you decide to have a barbecue, the first step is to slaughter your lamb the day before. Skin and dress it and cut it into sections: backbone, legs, shoulders, ribs, and head.

The following morning dig a hole 4 feet deep and 2 feet square; and plaster the sides with mud so that they won't collapse inward. Put some light, porous stones on the bottom of the pit, volcanic rocks being the best as they hold the heat very well and don't split. There are plenty to be had in the Valley of Mexico. Fill the pit with dry wood, set it alight, and let it burn down to smokeless ashes.

Meanwhile, gather a number of agave leaves and clean them carefully with a cloth. Use the fire in the pit to roast them on both sides until they are limp. Line the sides of the pit with the overlapping leaves, with the tops laid back on the surface of the ground around the pit, so that it looks like an open flower. It is wise to hold the leaves down with stones while you proceed to the next step.

Lower a grate into the hole to rest on the stones. On this, stand a large casserole or enamel basin containing the ingredients for *Consomé de Barbacoa* (Barbecue Consommé). On top of this, place a rack (an oven rack will do splendidly). Now arrange the pieces of lamb on the rack. Do not salt them, as this toughens the meat. Fold the agave leaves down over the meat and cover them carefully with a sheet of wood or metal. Lay more agave leaves on top. Finish with a *petate*, a palm mat, and seal the whole thing with mud.

Some authorities advise building a wood fire on top of the pit and keeping it burning until the lamb is cooked, 4 to 6 hours, according to the age of the animal. Other authorities say the fire on top of the pit is quite unnecessary, as it is the sealed-in heat which does the cooking. I am inclined to agree.

When the pit is opened, the meat is taken out, placed on platters, carved, and seasoned. The juices from the agave leaves together with the meat drippings will have filled the casserole or enamel basin with a delicious consommé. This is served with the meat, pot-au-feu fashion.

Traditionally, *Salsa Borracha* (Drunken Sauce) is served with the barbecue. This cannot be made without *pulque*. If *pulque* is not available, use any of the on-the-table sauces, such as *Salsa de Chile Rojo*, or *Salsa Verde*. Gaucamole is a pleasant addition to the menu, and there should be lots of hot tortillas. *Pulque* or beer are the drinks to serve.

# *Cochinita Pibil*

## BARBECUED SUCKLING PIG YUCATÁN STYLE

This is the Mayan version of *barbacoa* and is a great favorite in Yucatán. The barbecue pit is called a *pib* in the Maya language, and *pibil* means cooked in a barbecue pit, which is prepared in exactly the same way as for the barbecued lamb. *Pollo Pibil* (Barbecued Chicken), page 204, is perhaps even more popular: it is served in all the restaurants in Merida, the capital, as well as throughout the Yucatán peninsula. It can be successfully cooked in a steamer or in a covered casserole in the oven.

| | |
|---|---|
| 1 suckling pig, about 10 pounds | ⅛ teaspoon cumin seed |
| Juice of 8 bitter oranges* (2 cups, about) | 12 cloves garlic, chopped |
| | 1 teaspoon oregano |
| Salt | 1 tablespoon annatto |
| ½ teaspoon peppercorns (24, about) | Banana leaves |

Score the prepared suckling pig all over, in a crisscross pattern, with a sharp knife. Rub thoroughly with orange juice and salt. In the electric blender, place the remaining orange juice, peppercorns, cumin seeds, garlic cloves, oregano, and annatto, and blend until smooth. Rub the pig all over, inside and out, with this marinade; and refrigerate, for 24 hours, reserving the remaining marinade. Line a very large covered utensil with banana leaves; put in the pig; pour the remaining marinade over it; and cover with banana leaves.

Place the tub with the pig in the prepared pit, and cover as for lamb. Allow the pig to cook for 3 hours. Remove from the pit, and serve with hot tortillas. Although the very good beer of Yucatán traditionally accompanies *Cochinita Pibil*, the flavor is so subtle and delicate that a dry white wine makes an excellent accompaniment. Serves 8 to 10.

*Note*: An oval metal wash tub, with a lid, is probably the most suitable utensil.

*These are the Seville oranges used for marmalade. If they are not available, use a mixture of orange juice and lemon juice in equal quantities.

# Salsa Borracha

## DRUNKEN SAUCE

6 *pasilla* chiles
3 cloves garlic
3 tablespoons olive oil

1 pint *pulque*
Salt
Freshly ground pepper

Prepare the chiles as described in the Introduction. Place them in the electric blender with the garlic and a little of the *pulque*, and blend until smooth. Add the oil, season to taste with salt and pepper, and stir in the rest of the *pulque*.

# Pollo Pibil

## BARBECUED CHICKEN YUCATÁN STYLE

½ teaspoon salt
Juice of 3 bitter oranges*
 (¾ cup, about)
12 peppercorns
4 cloves garlic
1 tablespoon annatto
½ teaspoon oregano

¼ teaspoon cumin
½ teaspoon allspice
1 3½- to 4-pound
 chicken, cut into
 serving pieces
Banana leaves

Place the salt, orange juice, peppercorns, garlic, and the herbs and spices in the electric blender, and blend until smooth. Place the chicken pieces in a shallow dish and cover with the marinade, rubbing it well into each piece. Refrigerate for 24 hours, turning once or twice during the marinating period.

Wrap each piece of chicken in a banana leaf, distributing any marinade equally. Place in a steamer, and cook for about 3 hours, or until the chicken is very tender. The chicken can be cooked successfully in the oven. Wrap each piece of banana-leaf-wrapped chicken in foil, and cook in an oven preheated to 325°F. for about 2½ hours. It should be very tender, and really fall off the bones. Serves 4 to 6.

Serve with hot tortillas. A dry white wine is an excellent accompaniment to this extremely delicate dish.

*These are the Seville oranges used to make marmalade. They grow throughout the West Indies. If they are not obtainable, use orange and lemon juice in equal quantities.

# Consomé de Barbacoa

## BARBECUE CONSOMMÉ

½ cup rice, soaked for
  15 minutes
½ cup *garbanzos*,
  soaked overnight
½ pound potatoes,
  peeled and thinly sliced
2 large carrots, scraped
  and thinly sliced

1 small cabbage, quartered
3 canned *chipotle* chiles,
  sliced
1 sprig of *epazote*
Salt
Freshly ground pepper

Place all the ingredients in the casserole or basin as directed above.

# VERDURAS
## VEGETABLES

There is a widespread and mistaken notion that Mexicans do not care for green vegetables. It would be more accurate to say that they do not care for *plain* green vegetables. The list of those for which the world must thank Mexico is impressive: wax beans, green beans, chayote (christophine), the squashes, cactus paddles (*nopalitos*), green bell and other sweet peppers. Mexico also contributed tomatoes, which aren't exactly a green vegetable but which have become indispensable almost everywhere.

In addition to these well-known vegetables, there is a large group of lesser known ones, many of them succulents. They include *verdolages* (purslane; *Portulaca oleracea*), and *romeritos*, similar in appearance to rosemary, the fine, succulent leaves of which are stripped off the coarse stem and then cooked. Probably many of them grow wild in parts of this continent.

These vegetables are collectively known in Mexico as "*quelites*," from the Nahuatl word "*quilitl*," meaning any edible green herb. *Quelites* is, in fact, the exact equivalent of our own word "greens," and applies to vegetables to be eaten both cooked and raw.

Many of the best Mexican vegetable recipes are for *quelites* we don't have in the United States, but since it is the sauce and the cooking method that are important in the recipes, I have included any I have very much enjoyed, whether or not the particular *quelites* are available. I think it is perfectly legitimate in this instance to use any of our own extensive list of greens: turnip greens, collard greens, kale, mustard greens, dandelion greens, and curly endive (chicory). Some of the recipes are for greens we have in common, such as spinach and Swiss chard.

Green vegetable dishes in Mexico, being elaborate, are often served as courses in themselves. They can, therefore, be a good basis for a light luncheon. They are excellent with plain roast or broiled meat or fish, as they provide both vegetable and sauce.

## GENERAL DIRECTIONS

Wash the vegetables thoroughly, but do not soak them. Don't drown them when cooking, but use just enough water to cover vegetables like green beans, broccoli, cabbage, and cauliflower. (Spinach needs only the water left on its leaves after washing.) Put the water into a heavy pan with a tight-fitting lid; add a small amount of salt, about half a teaspoon per pound of vegetable; bring to a boil; add prepared vegetable; cover and cook until tender. For steaming, place vegetables in steamer over boiling water; cover tightly; reduce heat so that water simmers; and cook, allowing a little more time than for boiling. Salt may be added before or after cooking, or at any point when you are checking to see if the vegetable is done. When using frozen vegetables, follow directions given on the package.

## TIMETABLE FOR COOKING
## GREEN VEGETABLES

*(with Serving Amounts for 6, Generously)*

| | | |
|---|---|---|
| Beans, green: lima or broad | 20-30 minutes | 1½ pounds |
| Beans, green (snap) or wax | 15-20 minutes | 1½ pounds |
| Beet greens | 10-15 minutes | 2 pounds |
| Broccoli | 10-15 minutes | 2 pounds |

| | | |
|---|---|---|
| Cabbage | 5 minutes shredded | |
| | 10-15 minutes quartered | 1 medium head |
| Cabbage, Chinese | 8-10 minutes | 1½ pounds |
| Cauliflower, flowerets | | |
| | 8-10 minutes | 1 medium head |
| Cauliflower, whole | 15-20 minutes | 1 medium head |
| Celery | 10-15 minutes | 1 large bunch |
| Chard, Swiss | 10-15 minutes | 1½ pounds |
| Chayote | 20 minutes | 1½ pounds |
| Collard greens | 15-25 minutes | 1½ pounds |
| Cucumbers, whole | 10-15 minutes | 2 large |
| Dandelion greens | 15-25 minutes | 1½ pounds |
| Endive, curly (chicory) | 15-20 minutes | 1½ pounds |
| Kale | 20-25 minutes | 1½ pounds |
| Mustard greens | 15-20 minutes | 1½ pounds |
| Peas | 10-15 minutes | 3 cups shelled, or 3 pounds in the pod |
| Peppers, green, whole | 5-10 minutes | 1 per person |
| Spinach | 5-10 minutes | 2 pounds or more |
| Summer squash, sliced | 10-15 minutes | 1½ pounds |
| Turnip greens | 15-25 minutes | 1½ pounds |
| Zucchini, sliced, or, if very small, left whole | 10-15 minutes | 2 pounds |

## *Acelgas con Crema*

### CREAMED SWISS CHARD

1½ pounds Swiss chard, green leaves only
2 tablespoons butter
1 small white onion, finely chopped
3 *poblano* chiles, peeled, seeded, and pureed in blender

Salt
Freshly ground pepper
1 cup sour cream or heavy cream

Cook the Swiss chard according to general instructions at the beginning of this section, drain well, and chop. Heat the butter in a skillet, and sauté the onion until tender, without allowing it to brown. Add the pureed *poblano* chiles, and cook, over low heat, stirring for 3 or 4 minutes; add the Swiss chard; season to taste with salt and pepper. Fold the cream gently into mixture, and just heat through. Do not allow it to boil. Serves 6.

# Chicharitos o Ejotes en Salsa de Almendra Roja o Verde

## YOUNG PEAS OR GREEN BEANS IN RED OR GREEN ALMOND SAUCE

Cook the peas or beans according to general directions on page 223. Meanwhile, make 2 cups of *Salsa de Almendra Roja* or *Verde*. Add the well-drained vegetables to the sauce. Heat through and serve at once.

# Chayote

This member of the squash family deserves to be better known, although it has, indeed, travelled far from its original home. Popular in Mexico, it is used widely in the southwestern United States, the West Indies, Australia, and South America, where it is variously known as chayote, christophine, chocho, choko, and chuchu. Botanically a fruit, it is, however, eaten mostly as a vegetable or salad. *Chayotes Rellenos*, an unusual dessert, is the exception.

The green or white, pear-shaped chayote, peeled, then halved or quartered, is cooked according to the general directions at the beginning of this section. It is good simply mashed with butter and salt and pepper to taste, or served with *Salsa de Jitomate*, *Salsa de Chile Rojo*, *Salsa de Almendra*, or any other of the on-the-table sauces. The single seed, called the heart, is edible; and, as is so often true of the outside cut of a fine roast, it usually goes to the cook.

## Calabacitas Picadas

### CHOPPED ZUCCHINI

1 pound zucchini* or
   summer squash
1 onion, chopped
1 clove garlic, chopped
2 medium tomatoes,
   peeled, seeded, and
   chopped
2 canned *jalapeño*
   chiles,** seeded and cut
   into strips

½ teaspoon ground
   coriander seed
Salt
Freshly ground pepper
Monterey Jack cheese

Combine all the ingredients, *except the cheese*, in a saucepan. Cover, and cook over a low heat, for 10 minutes. Be sure the zucchini is still crisp to the bite. The time depends on the age of the zucchini. Drain well, and pour into a flameproof serving dish. Garnish with thin strips of the cheese, and run under a preheated broiler just long enough for the cheese to start melting—a minute or two.

## Calabacitas con Huevos

### ZUCCHINI WITH EGGS

½ stick (4 tablespoons)
   butter
2 cups zucchini or summer
   squash, coarsely
   chopped
Salt

Freshly ground pepper
2 eggs
1 cup freshly grated
   cheese, Parmesan,
   Gruyère, or Monterey
   Jack

Heat the butter in a saucepan; add the zucchini; cover and cook for 10 minutes, or until the zucchini is tender to the bite. The time depends on the age of the zucchini. Drain, season to taste with salt and pepper, and place in a skillet.

---

*If the zucchini is small, slice about ½ inch thick; if large, slice and chop coarsely.

**Or 1 canned *poblano* chile, peeled, seeded, and cut into strips.

Beat up the eggs with 2 tablespoons of water, and combine thoroughly with the grated cheese. Pour over the zucchini, mixing it gently, and cook over a low heat until the eggs are set—3 to 4 minutes. Serve at once. A comfortable lunch for 2.

## *Acelgas con Papas y Garbanzos*

### SWISS CHARD WITH POTATOES AND CHICK PEAS

| | |
|---|---|
| 1½ pounds Swiss chard, green leaves only | Salt |
| 1 onion, finely chopped | Freshly ground pepper |
| 1 clove garlic | Pinch of sugar |
| ½ teaspoon *pequín* chiles, crumbled | 6 baby new potatoes, freshly cooked and peeled |
| 3 tomatoes, peeled, seeded, and chopped | 1 cup *garbanzos* or corn kernels, cooked |
| 3 tablespoons of oil or lard | Grated Parmesan cheese |

Cook the chard according to general directions at the beginning of this section, drain well, and chop.

Heat the oil or lard in a skillet, and sauté the onion and garlic until the onion is tender, but not brown. Add the chiles; then put in the tomatoes; and simmer gently, stirring from time to time, until the sauce is well blended and has thickened to the consistency of heavy cream. Season to taste with salt and pepper and a pinch of sugar. Add the potatoes, the *garbanzos* or corn, and the chard; mix well and heat through only. Serve with grated cheese.

## *Chiles Rellenos*

### STUFFED PEPPERS

The dark green *poblano* chile is the one used for all of the stuffed-pepper dishes, but, if it is not available, green bell peppers can, in a pinch, be substituted.

To prepare the chiles, hold them on a fork over a gas flame or electric burner until the skin blisters. Wrap in a damp cloth and leave for half an hour, when the thin, papery skin will easily peel off. *Poblanos* should be slit lengthwise, and the stem, seeds, and veins removed. With bell peppers, it is better to cut off the stem end to remove the seeds and to replace it as a sort of lid. *Poblanos* can be secured with toothpicks, though the batter in which they are fried usually seals them effectively. If the *poblanos* are very *picante*, soak them in 1 quart of water with 1 tablespoon salt for several hours before using. Cook chiles in boiling water for 5 minutes; drain and cool. They are now ready to stuff.

## *Chiles Rellenos de Frijoles*

### PEPPERS STUFFED WITH BEANS

6 *poblano* chiles, or 6 bell
    peppers
3 cups *Frijoles Refritos**
2 eggs, separated
Flour

Lard or oil for frying
½ cup heavy cream
¼ pound Monterey Jack
    or mild cheddar cheese,
    shredded

Prepare the chiles as described on page 214.

Stuff the chiles with the beans. Set aside. Beat the egg yolks until thick; then beat the whites until they stand in stiff, shiny peaks when you hold up the beater. Fold into the yolks. Dust the chiles with flour; dip into the eggs. Heat the lard in a skillet and fry the chiles until golden brown. Arrange in an ovenproof dish; cover with the cream; sprinkle with the cheese; and cook in a preheated 350°F. oven until the cheese has melted and the dish is hot throughout—about 20 minutes. Serves 6.

*Another way*: Mask the chiles, after frying, with sour cream, and decorate with pomegranate seeds. The hot chiles and the cold sour cream make an interesting contrast.

    *Either pinto or red kidney beans.

# Chiles Rellenos

### STUFFED PEPPERS

Of the stuffed-pepper dishes, this is the one served most often, and is known simply as *Chiles Rellenos*.

6 *poblano* chiles, or 6 bell peppers
½ recipe *Picadillo*, or *Picadillo de la Costa*
1 pound (about 3 medium) tomatoes, peeled, seeded, and chopped
1 onion, chopped fine
1 clove garlic, chopped fine

1 cup chicken stock, or canned condensed broth
1 tablespoon lard or salad oil
Salt
Freshly ground pepper
2 eggs, separated
Flour
Lard or salad oil for frying

Prepare the chiles as described on page 214.

Stuff the chiles with the *Picadillo*. Place the tomatoes, onion, and garlic in the electric blender with a little stock, and blend to a smooth puree. Heat the lard in a skillet; add the tomato mixture; and cook, stirring constantly, for 5 minutes. Pour the tomato mixture into a saucepan large enough to hold the chiles. Stir in the stock, and season to taste with salt and pepper.

Beat the egg yolks until thick. Beat the whites until they stand in stiff, shiny peaks. Fold the whites into the yolks. Dip the chiles in flour, then in the egg, and fry in deep fat until golden brown. Drain on paper towels. Heat the tomato sauce, add the chiles, and cook for 2 to 3 minutes. Arrange the stuffed chiles on a hot serving platter, and spoon the sauce over them. Serves 6.

# Chiles en Nogada
## CHILES IN WALNUT SAUCE

This famous dish from Puebla, where it is served on St. Augustine's Day (August 28), is also a popular dish throughout the Republic on September 15, Mexico's Independence Day—since the colors of the dish are those of the Mexican flag, red, white, and green

6 *poblano* chiles, or 6 bell        ½ recipe *Picadillo*
 peppers

*Sauce*:
1 cup walnuts,* chopped           1 cup milk, about
 very fine                        Sugar and cinnamon**
½ cup blanched                     1 pomegranate, peeled,
 almonds, chopped very             with seeds separated
 fine
1 8-ounce package cream
 cheese, softened

Prepare the chiles as described on page 214.

Stuff the chiles with the *Picadillo*, fasten with toothpicks, arrange on a serving platter. Work the walnuts and almonds into the cream cheese with enough milk to make a sauce about as thick as mayonnaise. If you want it flavored with cinnamon, stir in both sugar and cinnamon to taste, now. Pour the sauce over the chiles, and decorate with the pomegranate seeds.

If the chiles are to be served hot, separate the whites from the yolks of 2 eggs. Beat the yolks. Beat the whites until they stand in peaks, and fold into the yolks. Dust the chiles with flour, dip into the egg, and fry in deep fat until golden brown. Arrange on a serving platter, pour the nut sauce over them, and decorate with the pomegranate seeds. Serves 6.

*The classic recipe calls for fresh, peeled walnuts, which are in season in Puebla around St. Augustine's Day.

**It's traditional to sweeten the dish and flavor it with cinnamon. Personally, I like it without any sweetening.

# Adobo de Col

## CABBAGE IN *ADOBO* SAUCE

1 cabbage, finely shredded
Salt
*Adobo* Sauce*

Freshly ground pepper
3 hard-cooked eggs, sliced

Toss the cabbage into rapidly boiling, salted water, and cook quickly for 5 minutes. Drain. Return to the saucepan; add the *Adobo* Sauce, and taste for seasoning. Reheat; then place in a warm serving dish, and garnish with the sliced eggs.

# Chile con Queso

## GREEN CHILE WITH CHEESE

This dish from the north of Mexico has become very popular in the American Southwest and in California. The chile called for is the chile *güero*, a mild, pale green chile with a tapering shape. It is often available fresh in both vegetable markets and supermarkets where it is called either California green pepper or simply "green pepper," to distinguish it from the green bell pepper. *Chile con Queso* is good as a dip with *tostaditas* (tortillas cut in four and fried crisp), and makes a pleasant luncheon or Sunday breakfast dish served with *frijoles refritos*, and tortillas.

2 tablespoons butter
1 large onion, very finely
   chopped
2 medium tomatoes,
   peeled, seeded, and
   chopped
1 cup chopped, peeled
   green chiles

Salt
Freshly ground pepper
1 8-ounce package cream
   cheese, cubed**
¾ cup heavy cream

Heat the butter in a skillet, and cook the onion until transparent. Add the tomatoes, chiles, and salt and pepper to taste, and cook, uncovered, for 10 to 15 minutes. Add the cheese; when it begins to melt, stir in the cream; and cook just long enough to heat through. Serves 3 to 4.

*Make ½ recipe of *Adobo Rojo de Lomo de Cerdo*, page 169, omitting pork and substituting chicken stock for pork stock.
**In Mexico *queso fresco* (fresh cheese) is used. It is worth asking for it in cheese shops. Cream cheese is a reasonably good substitute.

# Garbanzos con Pimientos

## CHICK PEAS WITH PIMIENTOS

*Garbanzos*, which are a great favorite in Spain, are almost equally as popular in Mexico.

¼ cup olive oil
1 onion, finely chopped
2 cloves garlic, chopped
3 *chorizo* sausages,
    skinned and chopped
1 1-pound, 4-ounce can
    *garbanzos*,\* drained and
    rinsed

1 4-ounce can pimientos,
    cut into strips, with
    their liquid
¼ teaspoon oregano
Salt
Freshly ground pepper

Heat the oil in a skillet. When hot, add the onion, garlic, and sausages, and sauté until the onion is transparent. Combine with the *garbanzos*, the pimientos and their liquid, and the oregano. Mix thoroughly; then season to taste with salt and pepper. Heat through before serving with any broiled or roasted meats.

# Ejotes con Pimientos Morrones

## GREEN BEANS WITH PIMIENTOS

1 pound cut green beans
3 tablespoons salad oil
1 onion, finely chopped
3 pimientos,\*\* coarsely
    chopped

Salt
Freshly ground pepper

Cook the beans according to general directions at the beginning of this section. Drain.

Heat the oil, and sauté the onion until it is tender but not brown. Add the beans and the pimientos; season to taste with salt and pepper; and heat through, stirring constantly.

---

  \**To cook chick peas*, the English name for *garbanzos*, soak the peas overnight. Drain; rinse; then cover with fresh water, and cook, covered, ½ hour. Add salt; then continue cooking until the peas are very tender—about 1 hour. The time will vary somewhat, depending on the age of the peas. Drain.

  \*\*Canned California green peppers are also excellent for this dish.

# *Hongos con Chipotle*

## MUSHROOMS WITH *CHIPOTLE* CHILE

1 pound mushrooms*
1 medium onion, chopped
1 clove garlic
¼ teaspoon dried
   *epazote*
1 canned *chipotle* chile**
2 tablespoons tomato paste

⅔ cup chicken stock, or
   canned condensed broth
4 tablespoons olive oil
Salt
Freshly ground pepper
4 tablespoons butter
Juice of ½ lemon

Wipe the mushrooms with a damp cloth. Remove the stems, chop them coarsely, and place in the electric blender with the onion, garlic, *epazote*, chile, tomato paste, and the stock. Blend to a smooth puree.

Heat *2 tablespoons of the oil* in a skillet; add the puree, and cook, over a medium heat, for 5 minutes, stirring constantly. Taste for seasoning. Heat *the remaining oil and all the butter* in a large, heavy skillet over a high heat. Add the mushroom caps, and cook, tossing and shaking the pan, for about 5 minutes or until the mushrooms are lightly brown. Reduce the heat to very low; add the chile puree, and heat through. Do not cook further. Stir in the lemon juice, and serve at once. Serves 6.

# *Habas Verdes*

## GREEN LIMA BEANS OR GREEN BROAD BEANS

1½ pounds green lima
   or green broad beans
2 tablespoons butter
1 onion, finely chopped
1 clove garlic, chopped
2 tomatoes, peeled,
   seeded, and chopped

1 *jalapeño* chile, peeled,
   seeded, and chopped
Salt
Freshly ground pepper
3 hard-cooked eggs, sliced
6 or 8 sprigs of parsley,
   chopped

---

*Quarter large mushrooms; leave small ones whole.

**The milder *ancho* chile can be used in place of the hot *chipotle*. In this case, prepare the chiles as described in the Introduction; then puree with the mushroom stems and other ingredients.

Cook the beans according to general directions at the beginning of this section. Drain, and keep hot in a vegetable dish.

Heat the butter in a skillet, and sauté the onion and garlic until the onion is tender. Add the tomatoes and the chile; season to taste with salt and pepper; and simmer, stirring from time to time, until all the ingredients are blended into a sauce. Pour over the beans, and serve garnished with the sliced eggs and a sprinkling of parsley.

## *Nopales con Queso*
### CACTUS PIECES WITH CHEESE

2 10-ounce cans *nopalitos*
2 tablespoons butter
1 white onion, finely chopped
½ teaspoon dried *epazote*

3 canned *serrano* chiles, chopped
1 6-ounce package cream cheese, cubed
Salt
Freshly ground pepper

Thoroughly rinse and drain the cactus pieces. Heat the butter, and wilt the onion. Add the cactus pieces, *epazote*, and chiles; and cook, stirring from time to time, until the onion is transparent. Season to taste with salt and pepper. Scatter the cheese over the dish. Once the cheese begins to melt, serve at once to 3 or 4.

This makes an excellent light luncheon for ladies, accompanied by *Arroz Gualdo*.

## *Lentejas Costeñas con Puerco*
### LENTILS WITH PORK COASTAL STYLE

½ pound pork for stew, cut into 1-inch pieces
1½ cups lentils
½ cup raisins
¼ cup olive oil
1 onion, finely chopped
2 cloves garlic, chopped
1 cooking apple, peeled, cored, and chopped

1 large, firm banana, peeled and sliced
3 slices fresh pineapple, cut into chunks*
1 pound (about 3 medium) tomatoes, peeled, seeded, and chopped
Salt
Freshly ground pepper

*If fresh pineapple is not available, use 2 cups canned pineapple chunks.

Place the pork in a large, lidded saucepan with water almost to cover; bring to a boil; then simmer, covered, for 1 hour. Drain, set the pork aside, and reserve the stock. Rinse out the saucepan; return the stock; add the lentils, raisins, and enough water to cover. Simmer, covered, for 40 minutes. Drain and set aside.

Meanwhile, heat the oil in a skillet, and sauté the pork, onion, and garlic until the pork pieces are lightly browned. Lift everything out with a slotted spoon, and add to the lentils. In the same oil, sauté the apple, banana, and pineapple for a few minutes. Add the tomatoes, season to taste with salt and pepper, and cook until most of the liquid has evaporated. Add to the lentils, stirring gently to mix all the ingredients. Simmer over a very low heat, uncovered, for 10 minutes to blend all the flavors. The finished dish should be fairly dry, with the lentils creamy. Serves 6.

This makes a good luncheon dish.

## Coliflor en Adobo Rojo

### CAULIFLOWER IN RED *ADOBO* SAUCE

| | |
|---|---|
| 1 large head cauliflower, whole | 1 recipe of *Adobo* Sauce* or *Adobo Verde* Sauce** |

Cook the cauliflower according to general directions at the beginning of this section for 15 minutes only. Place in a buttered, flameproof serving dish. Heat the *Adobo* Sauce; pour over the cauliflower; and cook, uncovered, over a very gentle heat another 5 minutes, or until the cauliflower is tender.

## Nopales con Chile Pasilla

### CACTUS PIECES WITH *PASILLA* CHILE

| | |
|---|---|
| 2 dried *pasilla* chiles | ½ teaspoon dried *epazote* |
| 2 10-ounce cans *nopalitos* | |
| 2 tablespoons olive oil | Salt |
| 1 white onion, finely chopped | Freshly ground pepper |

*From *Adobo Rojo de Lomo de Cerdo*, page 169.
**From *Adobo Verde de Lomo de Cerdo*, page 172.

Prepare the chiles as described in the Introduction, and puree in the electric blender.

Thoroughly rinse and drain the cactus pieces. Set aside.

Heat the oil, and fry the onion until it is tender, but not brown. Add the chiles, and cook, stirring constantly, for 5 minutes. Add the *epazote* and the cactus pieces, season to taste with salt and pepper, and heat through.

## *Frijoles*

### BEANS

| | |
|---|---|
| 2 cups pinto, black, or red kidney beans | 3 tablespoons lard or salad oil |
| 2 onions, finely chopped | Salt |
| 2 cloves garlic, chopped | Freshly ground pepper |
| Sprig of *epazote* or 1 bay leaf | 1 tomato, peeled, seeded, and chopped |
| 2 or more *serrano* chiles, chopped* | |

Wash the beans and place in a saucepan, without soaking, with enough cold water to cover, *1 of the chopped onions, 1 of the garlic cloves*, the *epazote* or bay leaf, and the chiles. Cover; bring to a boil; reduce heat; then simmer gently, adding more boiling water as it boils away. When the beans begin to wrinkle, add *1 tablespoon of the lard or oil.* Continue cooking until the beans are soft. At this point, stir in enough salt to taste. Cook for another 30 minutes over the same heat, but *do not add water*, as there should not be a great deal of liquid when the beans are done. Heat the remaining lard in a skillet, and sauté the remaining onion and garlic until limp. Add the tomatoes, and cook for about 2 minutes. Scoop out a cup of beans and liquid and add to the skillet, mashing with a fork until the mixture makes a smooth, fairly heavy paste. Stir this back into the beans to thicken them slightly, and simmer to heat through. Serves 6.

*Or 1 teaspoon dried *pequín* chiles, crumbled.

## *Frijoles Refritos*
### FRIED BEANS

Prepare *frijoles*.

Heat 2 tablespoons of lard in a large skillet; add the beans, tablespoon by tablespoon; and mash, over low heat, adding about 6 more tablespoons of lard from time to time, until the beans are creamy and have formed a heavy, quite dry paste.

## *Hongos a la Mexicana*
### MUSHROOMS MEXICAN STYLE

1 pound mushrooms,*
   stems on
3 tablespoons salad oil
3 tablespoons butter
1 clove garlic, chopped
¼ teaspoon dried
   *epazote*

1 or 2 canned *jalapeño*
   chiles,** rinsed,
   seeded, and sliced
Salt
Freshly ground pepper

Wipe the mushrooms with a clean, damp cloth. Heat the oil and butter in a heavy skillet. When foaming, add the garlic, mushrooms, *epazote*, chiles, and salt and pepper to taste, and cook, stirring from time to time, over a medium heat until the mushrooms are lightly browned—6 to 8 minutes.

## *Papas*
### POTATOES

Potatoes, though they were eaten in pre-Columbian Mexico, grew wild; they were not cultivated until after the Conquest, when potatoes from Peru focussed attention on this extraordinarily useful vegetable. Mexican potatoes are of superb qual-

---

*Quarter large mushrooms; leave small ones whole.

**Jalapeño* chiles vary a good deal in both size and heat. It is important to season with the chiles, but it is equally important not to overwhelm the mushroom flavor.

ity, yet the country has never taken to them as enthusiastically as it has to rice, which the Spaniards introduced from Asia. Although the rice is inclined to be quite poor, Mexican cooks perform miracles with it. I have never eaten badly cooked rice in Mexico. As a result, there are few original recipes for potatoes. Oddly, Carême's recipe for *Petit Pains de Pommes de Terre* (Little Potato Cakes) turns up in Mexican cookbooks as *Torta de Papa*, the only thing Mexican about it being the tomato sauce that is supposed to be served with it. Here is Carême's recipe:

"Peel a dozen good kidney potatoes baked in the ashes. Remove all the reddish parts and use only the white flesh; weigh out 12 ounces of this and pound with 4 ounces of Isigny butter. When this mixture becomes smooth, add to it 4 ounces of castor sugar, 2 of sieved flour, 2 yolks of egg and a grain of salt. Pound everything together into a perfectly smooth paste. Take the paste out of the mortar, put on a highly floured board, roll and cut into four parts. Roll each part, making it twice its original length, then cut into little balls the size of a walnut, give them the shape of little boats, and place them one by one on a buttered baking sheet. Brush with beaten egg and bake in a moderate oven."

## *The Mexican Interpretation of Carême*

Peel 6 medium-size potatoes, and cook in boiling, salted water until tender when pierced with the point of a small, sharp knife. Drain thoroughly. Push the potatoes through a ricer; then beat in ½ cup hot milk, 1 teaspoon of baking powder, 6 whole eggs, one at a time, 1 teaspoon grated lemon rind, 3 tablespoons of butter, and 3 tablespoons of sugar. Butter a 1-quart baking dish, spoon in the potato mixture, and bake in a preheated 350°F. oven for 30 minutes or until top is lightly browned. Serve with *Salsa de Jitomate*.

# *Papas Rellenas*

## STUFFED POTATOES

This does seem to me an original recipe, and is useful as a main course for a light meal.

3 large Idaho potatoes
1 cup thick Bechamel Sauce
½ cup freshly grated Parmesan cheese
½ cup sliced, cooked young carrots
½ cup cooked baby peas

½ cup chopped cooked white chicken meat
½ cup chopped boiled ham
1 canned *chipotle* chile, chopped fine
Salt
Freshly ground pepper

Wash the potatoes; dry thoroughly; then bake in a preheated 325°F. oven until potatoes are soft when lightly squeezed—about 1½ hours. When the potatoes are cool enough to handle, cut in half lengthwise, and scoop out about three-fourths of the flesh. Set potato shells aside. Mash the potato until perfectly smooth; then beat with butter and a little cream or milk until fluffy. Set this aside, too.

Meanwhile, make the *Bechamel Sauce*:

1½ tablespoons butter
1½ tablespoons flour
1 cup milk

½ teaspoon salt
Pinch white pepper

Melt the butter in a fairly heavy saucepan over a low heat; stir in the flour, and cook, stirring constantly, for 2 minutes. Add the milk, and cook, still over a low heat, stirring constantly, until the sauce has thickened. Stir in the salt and pepper.

To the hot Bechamel, add the grated cheese, stirring until well combined. Then fold in the vegetables, chicken, ham, and chile. Taste for seasoning. Spoon the mixture into the 6 shells, dividing it evenly, and spread mashed potato on top. Place on baking sheets in a preheated 325°F. oven for 15 to 20 minutes, or until the tops are nicely browned and the potatoes hot throughout.

# Quelites con Chile Ancho

## GREENS WITH *ANCHO* CHILE

3 *ancho* chiles
1½ pounds greens
1 onion, chopped
1 clove garlic, chopped

2 tablespoons lard or salad
   oil
Salt
Freshly ground pepper

Prepare the chiles as described in the Introduction.

Cook the greens according to general instructions at the beginning of this section. Drain well and chop coarsely. Place the prepared chiles, onion, and garlic in the electric blender, and blend to a smooth puree. Heat the lard in a skillet, and cook the puree, stirring constantly, for 5 minutes. Add the sauce to the greens, taste for seasoning, and heat through before serving.

# Quelites con Chile Poblano

## GREENS WITH *POBLANO* CHILE

1½ pounds greens
2 *poblano* chiles, peeled,
   seeded, and sliced
3 tablespoons salad oil
1 onion, finely chopped
1 clove garlic, finely
   chopped

3 tomatoes, peeled,
   seeded, and chopped
Salt
Freshly ground pepper

Cook whichever greens you are using according to the general instructions at the beginning of this section. Prepare the chiles as described in the Introduction, and slice. Heat the oil in a skillet, and sauté the onion and garlic until tender without letting them brown. Add the chiles and the tomatoes, and cook, stirring from time to time, for 5 minutes. Add the cooked greens; taste for seasoning; stir well and heat through.

# Tomate Verde con Queso

## GREEN TOMATOES WITH CHEESE

2 tablespoons butter
1 medium onion, very
   finely chopped
1 clove garlic, finely
   chopped
1 10-ounce can Mexican
   green tomatoes, drained
1 cup green chiles,
   chopped and peeled

12 sprigs of fresh
   coriander, chopped
Salt
Freshly ground pepper
½ pound cream cheese,
   cubed
¾ cup heavy cream

Heat the butter in a skillet, add the onion and garlic, and sauté until the onion is tender. Add the tomatoes, chiles, coriander, and salt and pepper to taste. Simmer very gently for 10 minutes, uncovered. Add the cheese; when it begins to melt, add the cream; and cook just long enough to heat through.

# Revoltijo

## VEGETABLE FRICASSEE

This is a popular dish for the vigils before Easter and Christmas.

1 pound *romeritos*, or any
   greens, cooked and
   chopped
1 10-ounce can *nopalitos*,
   rinsed and drained
6 baby new potatoes,
   freshly cooked and
   peeled

½ pound dried shrimp
3 tablespoons breadcrumbs
2 eggs, lightly beaten
Salad oil
2 cups of *Mole Poblano*
   Sauce

Have ready all the cooked ingredients. Meanwhile, boil *half the shrimp* for about 15 minutes. Drain and set aside. Grind the other half of the shrimp, and mix with the breadcrumbs and the eggs, adding more crumbs, if necessary, to give the mixture body. Heat the oil, and fry the shrimp mixture in a skillet, dropping it a spoonful at a time, and cooking until delicately browned on both sides. Drain the fritters on paper towels and keep warm.

Heat the *Mole* Sauce in a casserole; add the greens, cactus pieces, potatoes, and the boiled shrimp. Just before serving, add the shrimp fritters.

# Verdolagas con Chile Chipotle

## PURSLANE WITH *CHIPOTLE* CHILE

1½ pounds of any
    greens
3 tablespoons salad oil
1 onion, finely chopped
2 cloves garlic, chopped
1 or more (or to taste)
    canned *chipotle* chiles,
    chopped fine

½ pound pork stew,
    cooked and cut into
    small pieces
Salt
Freshly ground pepper

Cook the greens according to the general directions at the beginning of this section. Drain and chop. Heat the oil in a skillet; add the onion, garlic, chile, and pork; and cook until the onion is tender. Add the greens, mix well, taste for seasoning, and heat through.

# Verdolagas en Verde

## PURSLANE IN GREEN SAUCE

1½ pounds any greens
1 10-ounce can Mexican
    green tomatoes
3 canned *serrano* chiles
1 clove garlic

2 or 3 sprigs of fresh
    coriander
Salt
Freshly ground pepper
3 tablespoons oil or lard

Cook the greens according to the general directions at the beginning of this section. Drain and chop. Place the drained green tomatoes, chiles, garlic, and coriander in the electric blender with a little of the liquid from the tomatoes, and blend to a puree. Heat the oil or lard in a skillet, and cook the tomato mixture, over a moderate heat, for 5 minutes, stirring constantly. Add the greens, mix well, taste for seasoning, and heat through.

# Quintoniles con Chile Mulato

## COOKED GREENS WITH *MULATO* CHILE

*Quintoniles* is a combination of two Nahuatl words: "*quilitl*," "greens," and "*tonilli*," "cooked." It also refers to the wild red amaranth. Use any of the greens listed.

| | |
|---|---|
| 3 dried *mulato* chiles | 3 tablespoons oil or lard |
| 1 onion, chopped | Salt |
| 1 clove garlic, chopped | Freshly ground pepper |
| 1½ pounds greens | 3 hard-cooked eggs, sliced |

Prepare the chiles as described in the Introduction. Place in the electric blender with the onion and garlic, and blend to a smooth puree. Cook the greens according to general directions at the beginning of this section. Drain well and chop. Keep warm.

Heat the oil or lard in a skillet; add the puree, and cook for 5 minutes over a moderate heat, stirring constantly. Mix in the greens, and taste for seasoning. Heat through, and, just before serving, garnish with the sliced eggs.

# ENSALADAS

## SALADS

Many Mexican dishes are served garnished with lettuce, olives, radishes, and chopped onion, but it is rare to serve a green salad as we understand it.

Salads tend to be hearty and are best used as luncheon dishes within the framework of American food. In Mexico the combination vegetable salads are served with the main course instead of green vegetables. The meat or seafood salads are served as courses in themselves.

The most popular salad is the *Ensalada de Noche Buena* (Christmas Eve Salad), which is traditionally eaten on Christmas Eve, when a special supper, usually including *Pavo Relleno* (Stuffed Turkey), or *Mole Poblano* (Turkey *Mole* in Puebla Style), is served and gifts are exchanged, following the custom of France and other Latin countries—rather than the customs of northern Europe, where feasting and presents come on Christmas Day.

The Christmas Eve supper served after midnight mass, or at midnight, is the culmination of a series of parties called the *Posadas* (Inns) which mark this most sustained and joyous of all the Mexican fiestas, since Christmas Day itself is not celebrated.

The *Posadas*, which begin on December 16, commemorate the search by *Los Santos Peregrinos*, the Holy Pilgrims Mary

233

and Joseph, for room at an inn in Bethlehem for the birth of the Infant Jesus. Plaster images of Mary and Joseph are carried at the head of a procession of host and guests around the garden and through the house. Or around the apartment. Each person carries a lighted candle, a litany is sung, and through special hymns there is a re-enactment of the request for shelter, the repeated refusals, and finally the offer of the manger.

Sometimes an ambitious household will have a real donkey with some small girl and boy of the family dressed to represent Mary and Joseph. I attended one such ambitious *Posada*, and it was, predictably, a disaster. The guests all came late; and poor tired little Mary kept lurching off the donkey, three parts asleep, while Joseph, worn out with the excitement of the party, whimpered alongside her. The donkey was very young, too, and not housebroken, and the long hours of waiting took their toll.

After the religious ceremony, which lasts about half an hour, comes the breaking of the *piñata*, a big clay *olla* (pot) covered with cardboard and decorated with tissue paper to represent an animal, a boat, a flower, a clown, or whatever the fancy of the maker dictates. The *olla* is filled with fruits, candies, and small, unbreakable gifts. It is strung on a rope, usually in the patio, and often from a tree; and the children, blindfolded, take turns one by one trying to break the *piñata* with a stick, while the others manipulate the rope to move it out of reach. Eventually a lucky thwack breaks the *olla*, out spill the contents, and all the children scramble for them.

Drinks of all kinds are served, and there are great plates of fruit and candies and typical holiday foods like *buñuelos*.

After the Christmas Eve party there is a pause until the *Día de los Reyes* (King's Day, Twelfth Night), January 6, which marks the end of the Christmas season and is celebrated with *Rosca de Reyes* (King's Day Ring), and gifts for the children.

There is a curious festival held in Oaxaca on Christmas Eve called *Noche de Rábanos* (Radish Night). Large radishes are in season at this time of year, and they are cut into fancy shapes, much as one makes radish roses, and used to decorate stalls and restaurants around the *plaza*. Oaxaca is a great pottery center; and all year the vendors save up imperfect dishes. On Radish Night one eats *buñuelos*, served on them, and then breaks the dishes. By midnight the square is full of smashed crockery. This is obviously a very ancient ceremony having something to do with celebrating the end of the year. Oaxaca is still full of mysteries.

# Ensalada de Noche Buena

## CHRISTMAS EVE SALAD

3 medium-sized beets,
   cooked and chopped
3 oranges, peeled and
   sectioned
2 jícamas, or 2 tart
   cooking apples, peeled,
   cored, and chopped
3 bananas, peeled and
   sliced

3 slices fresh pineapple,
   cut into cubes
Shredded lettuce
½ cup chopped peanuts
Seeds from 1 pomegranate
1 cup mayonnaise*
1 stick sugar cane
   (optional)

Mix the beets, oranges, *jícamas*, bananas, and pineapple together. Then chill thoroughly.

Line a salad bowl with the lettuce, fill the center with the salad, and garnish with peanuts and the pomegranate seeds. Pass the mayonnaise separately.

If a stick of sugar cane is available, peel, chop, and add to the salad.

# Pico de Gallo

## ROOSTER'S BEAK

6 navel oranges, peeled,
   sectioned, and chopped
1 medium-sized jícama,**
   peeled and chopped

Salt
Cayenne pepper

Mix the oranges and jícama together, and season with salt and cayenne to taste.

---

*In Mexico's colonial days, ½ cup sugar mixed with 3 to 4 tablespoons of wine vinegar was used as a dressing.

**Very tart cooking apples can be substituted for the *jícama*, although the results will be something less than perfect, since jicama has a unique flavor that is not easily duplicated.

# Ensalada de Camarón

## SHRIMP SALAD

Lettuce
½ cup mayonnaise
½ cup sour cream
3 cups cooked jumbo
   shrimp, chopped
   coarsely
1 cup chopped celery
6 baby new potatoes,
   freshly cooked and
   diced

1 cup cucumber, diced
   with the skin on
3 hard-cooked eggs,
   coarsely chopped
½ teaspoon cayenne
   pepper
Salt

Line a large salad bowl with lettuce leaves. Mix the mayonnaise and sour cream together. Combine the shrimp, celery, potatoes, cucumber, eggs, cayenne, and salt to taste. Mix well. Fold in the mayonnaise thoroughly. Taste for seasoning. Arrange in the prepared salad bowl, and serve to 6.
   This makes an excellent luncheon dish.

# Otra Ensalada de Camarón

## ANOTHER SHRIMP SALAD

Juice of 1 lemon
Salt
Freshly ground pepper
¾ cup olive oil
2 cups cooked jumbo
   shrimp, coarsely
   chopped
1 small white onion,
   minced
1 large tomato, peeled and
   cubed

1 large avocado, peeled,
   seeded, and cubed
2 tablespoons finely
   chopped fresh coriander
¼ cup pimiento-stuffed
   green olives, cut in half
3 canned *jalapeño* chiles,
   deseeded and cut into
   strips

Combine the lemon juice and salt and pepper to taste; then whisk in the olive oil. Pour the dressing over the shrimp and onion, and allow to marinate for 2 hours. Then combine with the tomato, avocado, coriander, and olives. Toss until all ingredients are lightly coated with the dressing. Arrange on lettuce leaves with the chiles as a garnish. Serves 6.

# Ensalada de Coliflor

## CAULIFLOWER SALAD

1 medium cauliflower
2 cups *Guacamole del Norte*, page 75

½ cup freshly grated Parmesan cheese

Cook the cauliflower according to directions at the beginning of this section. Drain thoroughly and cool. Place in a suitable dish, mask with the *Guacamole del Norte Sauce*, and sprinkle with the grated cheese. Serves 6.

# Ensalada de Calabacitas

## ZUCCHINI SALAD

6 medium zucchini
Salt
1 bunch scallions with tops, chopped
2 canned *poblano* chiles,* rinsed and cut into strips

2 large avocadoes, peeled and cubed
1 cup Oil and Vinegar Dressing
Lettuce

Slice the zucchini thickly; drop into boiling, salted water; and cook, covered, about 6 to 8 minutes. The zucchini should still be crisp to the bite. Drain thoroughly and chop coarsely. Cool.

Combine all the ingredients, *except the lettuce*, with the dressing, and toss until lightly coated. Chill. Line a salad bowl with lettuce leaves, and arrange the salad in the center. Serves 6.

# Ensalada de Ejotes

## GREEN BEAN SALAD

1 pound cut green beans, cooked
3 pimientos, drained and chopped
1 tablespoon white onion, minced

5 or 6 springs of parsley, finely chopped
¾ cup Oil and Vinegar Dressing
Lettuce

*Or canned *chipotle* chile, cut into strips.

Toss all the ingredients in a large bowl with the dressing. Arrange on a bed of lettuce leaves, and serve to 6.


# *Aguacate Relleno*

## STUFFED AVOCADO

Avocado (½ avocado
  per person)
Fresh lime or lemon juice
1 4-ounce can boneless
  sardines per whole
  avocado
Salt, freshly ground
  pepper, wine vinegar to
  taste

Hard boiled eggs (½ per
  avocado)
Parmesan cheese
1-2 strips pimiento (per
  avocado)
Lettuce
Olives
Tomato (sliced)
Radishes

Allow ½ avocado per person. Peel as many avocadoes as you need, cut in half, remove the seeds, and sprinkle with fresh lime or lemon juice.

Mash the contents of 1 4-ounce can boneless sardines for each whole avocado, including the oil from the can. Add salt, freshly ground pepper, and a little wine vinegar to taste. Fold in ½ hard-cooked egg, finely chopped. Stuff the avocado halves with this mixture. Sprinkle each one with grated Parmesan cheese, and decorate with 1 or 2 strips of pimiento.

Place the avocadoes on lettuce leaves; garnish with ripe olives, tomato slices, and radishes.


# *Ensalada de Jitomate y Aguacate*

## TOMATO AND AVOCADO SALAD

3 large avocadoes, peeled
3 large tomatoes, peeled
Lettuce
Scallions or chives, finely
  chopped

Oil and Lemon Juice
  Dressing or mayonnaise

Cut the avocadoes and the tomatoes into an equal number of fairly thick slices. Arrange the tomato slices on a bed of lettuce;

place the avocado slices on top. Sprinkle with the scallions or chives, and serve with dressing or with mayonnaise on the side. Serves 6.

## Otra Ensalada de Coliflor

### ANOTHER CAULIFLOWER SALAD

4 tablespoons Oil and Vinegar Dressing
Flowerets from 1 medium cauliflower, cooked

Lettuce leaves
1 recipe guacamole
Freshly grated Parmesan cheese, optional

Pour the dressing over the cauliflower, and marinade for about 1 hour. Chill. When cold, arrange the flowerets in mounds on lettuce leaves. Mask with the guacamole, and sprinkle with grated cheese. Serves 6.

## Jitomates Rellenos de Guacamole

### TOMATOES STUFFED WITH GUACAMOLE

6 medium tomatoes
Salt
3 large, ripe avocadoes
2 tablespoons white onion, finely chopped
2 tablespoons fresh coriander, finely chopped

3 or more canned *serrano* chiles, chopped
Freshly ground pepper
Lettuce leaves

Peel the tomatoes; cut a slice off the top of each; and carefully scoop out the pulp with a spoon, leaving a thick shell. Sprinkle with salt, turn upside down, and allow to drain for 15 minutes.

Peel and mash the avocadoes; combine well with the onion, coriander, and chiles. Season to taste with salt and pepper. Stuff the tomatoes with the mixture, and arrange on individual plates with a garnish of lettuce leaves. Serves 6.

# Ensalada de Chayote

## CHAYOTE SALAD

3 medium chayotes
Salt
Freshly ground pepper
Tiny pinch of sugar
½ teaspoon Dijon
  mustard
2 tablespoons wine vinegar

6 tablespoons salad oil or
  olive oil
1 onion, finely chopped
2 medium tomatoes, peeled
  and cut into eighths
Ripe olives

Peel the chayotes; cut in half; and cook in boiling, salted water until tender when pierced with the point of a small sharp knife—about 20 minutes. Drain, cool, and cut into chunks about the size of the tomato wedges.

Place the salt, pepper, sugar, mustard, and wine vinegar in a salad bowl, and whisk until well combined. Add the oil slowly, whisking constantly. Add the chayotes, tomato, and onion to the salad bowl, and toss lightly in the dressing. Garnish with ripe olives, and serve to 6.

# Ensalada de Nopalitos

## CACTUS SALAD

2 10-ounce cans *nopalitos*
3 tomatoes, peeled,
  seeded, and chopped
3 tablespoons white onion,
  finely chopped

1 tablespoon fresh
  coriander, chopped
¾ cup Oil and Vinegar
  Dressing

Carefully rinse and drain the cactus pieces. Mix with the tomatoes, onion, and coriander; then toss in the dressing. Serve chilled. Serves 6.

# *Ensalada de Carne de Res*

## COLD MEAT SALAD

1½ pounds rare roast
  beef, cut into strips
1 Bermuda onion, very
  thinly sliced
2 navel oranges, peeled
  and thinly sliced

Oil and Vinegar Dressing
Lettuce
Fresh, hot red peppers, cut
  to form flowers*
Sprigs of fresh coriander

Combine the beef, onion, and orange slices in a bowl; pour
the dressing over them; and marinade for 2 hours.

Make a bed of lettuce on a platter; arrange the beef, onion
rings, and orange slices on top; and sprinkle with the dressing
remaining in the bowl. Garnish with the peppers and sprigs of
coriander. Serves 6.

With crusty bread and sweet butter, this makes a robust
luncheon dish.


## HOW TO MAKE OIL AND VINEGAR DRESSING

Mix 3 parts oil with 1 part vinegar; add salt and freshly ground
pepper to taste. Lemon juice is used in place of vinegar in
certain recipes.

---

*Cut 4 or 5 strips from the tips down to the stem ends of the peppers, without
severing them completely.

# POSTRES

## DESSERTS

The ancient Mexicans did not have many cakes, pies, or puddings, probably because they lacked wheat flour, sugar, butter, and cream—for which corn and honey are not adequate substitutes. They did serve *tamales* stuffed with strawberries and other fruits as a dessert; but, for the most part, they relied on their enormous variety of fresh fruits.

It was the Spanish nuns, especially in Puebla, who created the desserts for which colonial Mexico is famous. It is interesting that they practically ignored vanilla and chocolate in favor of the cinnamon and cloves that Spain had introduced to the New World. Perhaps the reason is that chocolate, flavored with vanilla and sweetened with honey, and taken after meals, was a drink forbidden to women. It is ironical that the sacred chocolate of the kings, priests, and nobles has become a favorite children's drink.

## *Rosca de Reyes*

### KING'S DAY RING

January 6—Twelfth Night, Epiphany, King's Day, *Día de los Reyes*—the date on which the Three Kings came to visit the Infant Jesus with their gifts, is a traditional gift-giving holiday in Mexico. It is also traditional to serve the *Rosca de Reyes*, which has a tiny china doll, representing the Infant, baked in it. Although in many countries it is simply considered good luck to get the piece of cake with the doll in it, it is sometimes believed as well that, if a girl gets it, she will be married within a year. Mexico, however, has a further refinement. Whoever gets the doll figure is obliged to give a party on February 2, Candlemas Day, regarded as the special day of godparents.

1 package active dry yeast
   or 1 cake compressed
   yeast
¼ cup lukewarm water
2½ cups all-purpose
   flour
½ teaspoon salt
¼ cup sugar
2 eggs, well beaten
4 egg yolks
1 stick (8 tablespoons)
   butter, at room
   temperature

Grated rind of 1 lemon
1½ cups mixed,
   chopped candied fruits
   and peels
1 tiny china doll
1 cup sifted confectioner's
   sugar
2 tablespoons light cream
Maraschino cherries, cut in
   half

Sprinkle active dry yeast or crumbled compressed yeast over lukewarm water to soften.

In a large bowl, mix *half of the flour* with the salt, sugar, eggs, egg yolks, butter, grated lemon rind, yeast, and water, beating until well blended. Dust *1 cup of the fruits and peel* with flour, and combine with the yeast mixture. Add the remaining flour, and mix to a soft but not sticky dough, adding a little more flour, if necessary. Turn onto a lightly floured board, and knead until smooth and satiny—about 5 minutes. Shape into a ring, tucking the china doll into the dough. Place on a greased baking sheet, cover with a cloth, and leave in a warm place to double in bulk, 2 hours or more.

At this point, brush the ring with melted butter, place in a preheated 350°F. oven, and bake for 30 minutes. Allow to cool.

Mix the sifted confectioner's sugar with the light cream, and spread over ring. Decorate with the remaining ½ cup fruits and peel and with halved maraschino cherries.

# Pan de Muerto

## BREAD OF THE DEAD

It is traditional in Mexico for people to visit their family graves on November 2, All Souls' Day, as a mark of love and respect. They take with them a special round coffee cake, *Pan de Muerto* (Bread of the Dead), that is decorated with a cross made of pieces of baked dough in the form of alternating teardrops and bones with a knob in the center, the whole covered with pink sugar crystals. They also take bunches of *zempazuchbitl* flowers, a bright orange marigold.

These visits are not, as one might expect, full of sorrow. They are more like a picnic in which the dead symbolically participate. Candy skulls are sold, and, while you wait, your name is written on them in a contrasting color; one is supposed to nibble cheerfully away at one's own inevitable future. Everything is gay and brilliant, from the blue sky and yellow sun to the orange marigolds and bright skirts, shirts, and *rebozos* worn by the members of family parties lovingly tending graves in the family plot. Other mourning days are for weeping. All Souls' Day is a fiesta.

In Janitzio, the small island in Lake Patzcuaro, Michoacan, the ceremony is extremely elaborate, suggesting rites belonging to the pre-Christian faith of the region. Two days ahead of time the men of the village go duck hunting, using the traditional harpoon instead of guns. The women make tamales filled with duck meat cooked with chile sauce. They take these on All Souls' Eve to the cemetery, along with huge bunches of marigolds and a candle for each person in the family who has died. The women and older children keep an all-night vigil at the graves while the men keep vigil at home. The following day the family has a feast of tamales served with *atole*, coffee, *pulque*, beer, tequila, and *Pan de Muerto*.

| | |
|---|---|
| 1 package active dry yeast or 1 cake compressed yeast | 1 cup (1 stick) butter, melted |
| ½ cup lukewarm water | 6 eggs, lightly beaten |
| 3½ cups sifted all-purpose flour | 1 tablespoon orange-blossom water |
| 1 teaspoon salt | 2 tablespoons anise water* |
| ½ cup sugar | Grated rind of 1 orange |

Sprinkle the yeast over the lukewarm water to soften. Add enough flour to make a light dough. Knead, shape into a ball, and place this sponge in a warm place to double in bulk—about 1 hour.

Sift remaining flour with salt and sugar. Work in the melted butter, cooled, the eggs, orange-blossom water, anise water,

*To make anise water:* Boil 1 teaspoon of anise seeds in 3 tablespoons of water for 2 or 3 minutes. Cool and strain.

and grated orange rind. Knead well on a lightly floured board until smooth. Then add the sponge, and knead again until satiny. Cover with a cloth, and let the dough rest in a warm place about 1½ hours, until it has doubled in bulk. Shape into two round loaves, setting aside enough dough for the decorations.

Place loaves on a greased baking sheet, and decorate with a cross made of pieces of dough, alternately shaped like bones and teardrops. Roll two small pieces of dough into knobs. Allow these to rise, and attach them at the center of each loaf before baking. Cover decorated loaves, and stand in a warm place until double in bulk. Bake the loaves in a preheated 375°F. oven for about 30 minutes. When cool, frost, and sprinkle with colored sugar.

*To make frosting*: Add sifted confectioner's sugar to ¼ cup boiling water or milk until it is of the right consistency for spreading. Sprinkle with pink sugar crystals.

# Almendrado

## ALMOND PUDDING

| | |
|---|---|
| 1 envelope unflavored gelatin | ½ teaspoon almond extract |
| 1 cup boiling water | 1 5-ounce can slivered toasted almonds |
| 6 egg whites, stiffly beaten | |
| 1 cup granulated sugar | |

Sprinkle the gelatin over ¼ *cup of cold water* to soften. Add the boiling water and stir until the gelatin is dissolved. Add the sugar, and stir until it, too, has dissolved. Stir in the almond extract. Chill until the mixture begins to thicken. Then beat until frothy.

Fold the stiffly beaten egg whites into the gelatin mixture gently but thoroughly. Pour a layer of the mixture into a 6-cup mold that has been rinsed in cold water, and follow with a layer of almonds. Repeat until all the mixture is used, ending with a layer of almonds. Chill until firm.

*Note*: This looks very attractive unmolded. Finish with the gelatin mixture and save enough almonds to sprinkle over the top if you wish.

*Custard Sauce*:
2 cups milk
6 egg yolks
¼ cup sugar

Pinch of salt
½ teaspoon vanilla
    extract
½ cup heavy cream

Heat the milk in the top of a double boiler until a film shines on top. Beat the egg yolks with the sugar and salt until light, and add, very gradually, to the hot milk. Place over boiling water, and continue to cook, stirring constantly, until the mixture coats a spoon. Cool. Add vanilla extract. Beat the cream until stiff, and fold into cooled custard. Serve with the pudding.

# *Sopaipillas*

### FRITTERS

These fritters, which look like little fat pillows, are excellent served with soup, or with guacamole or any other dip. They will stay nicely puffed, if refrigerated, and can be reheated in the oven. As a dessert, with syrup or simply sprinkled with sugar and cinnamon, they are very good.

2 cups flour
2 teaspoons baking powder
1 teaspoon salt

2 tablespoons shortening
¾ cup cold water
Oil or fat for frying

Sift all the dry ingredients together; cut in the shortening with a pastry blender or 2 knives, until mealy; work in the water gradually to form a pastry-like dough. Turn onto a lightly floured board, and knead until smooth. Roll as thin as possible, cut into 2-inch or 3-inch squares, and fry one by one in the hot fat (370°F. on the thermometer). The *Sopaipillas* should puff up as they brown, and should be turned during the frying so the second side can also puff. Drain on paper towels. Makes 20 to 30 according to size.

# *Buñuelos*

### FRITTERS

1 teaspoon salt
1 teaspoon baking powder
2 tablespoons sugar
4 cups flour
2 eggs
1 cup milk

¼ cup butter, melted
Oil or fat for frying
Sugar and cinnamon
    mixture or sugar and
    ground cloves

Sift all the dry ingredients together. Set aside. Beat the eggs thoroughly; then beat in the milk. Stir the dry mixture gradually into the egg-milk mixture; then add butter. Turn on to a lightly floured board, and knead very gently until the dough is smooth and elastic.

Divide into about 40 small or 24 large balls. Roll these out to approximately 4 inches or 6 inches, respectively. Fry in very hot deep fat or oil (370°F. on the thermometer) until delicately browned on both sides. Drain on paper towels, and sprinkle with the cinnamon and sugar mixture, or with sugar and ground cloves.

Serve as a cookie; or make a light syrup as for *Capirotada*, page 251, pour over the *buñuelos*, and serve as a dessert.

# Flan

## CARAMEL PUDDING

This Spanish dessert, an immense favorite in Mexico, is made either in large caramelized mold or in individual, caramelized custard cups, so that when the dessert is unmolded it is covered with a caramel glaze.

*To caramalize the mold*: In a small sauce pan, over moderate heat, boil ½ cup granulated sugar with 2 tablespoons of water, stirring constantly until the sugar melts and turns into a rich, golden brown.

Have ready a 6-cup mold (or 6 custard cups), warmed by standing it in hot water. Pour the caramel into the mold, turning it in all directions so that the caramel covers the bottom and sides. As soon as it stops running, turn the mold upside down on a plate. Caramelize custard cups in the same way.

| | |
|---|---|
| 4 cups milk | 1 teaspoon vanilla extract |
| ¾ cup sugar | Pinch of salt |
| 8 eggs, lightly beaten | |

Heat the milk until a film shines on top. Remove from heat, and cool. Beat the sugar gradually into the eggs; add the milk, vanilla extract, and salt. Mix well, and strain into caramelized mold or custard cups. Place in a pan filled with hot water that reaches half the depth of the mold; and bake in a preheated 350°F. oven for 1 hour, or until a knife inserted in the custard comes out clean. The water in the pan should not boil. Cool the custard; then chill in the refrigerator.

To unmold, run a knife between the custard and the mold; then place a serving dish upside down over the mold and invert quickly. Serves 6.

*Variations*

Using this basic recipe, *Flan* can be varied in a number of ways:

Substitute ½ teaspoon of powdered cinnamon and ¼ teaspoon of grated lemon rind for the vanilla.

To make Coconut *Flan*, add ½ cup grated coconut.

To make Almond *Flan*, add ½ cup ground, blanched almonds.

To make Chocolate *Flan*, add 2 tablespoons of cocoa and 2 tablespoons of dark rum.

## *Capirotada*
### BREAD PUDDING

| | |
|---|---|
| 2 cups *piloncillo* or brown sugar, firmly packed | 3 apples, peeled, cored, and sliced |
| 1 2-inch piece stick cinnamon | 1 cup raisins |
| 1 clove | 1 cup chopped, blanched almonds |
| Butter | ½ pound Monterey Jack or similar cheese, cubed |
| 6 slices toast, cubed | |

Combine the sugar with *4 cups of water*, the cinnamon, and clove in a saucepan. Bring to a boil; then simmer until the mixture has cooked to a light syrup. Remove the spices, and set the syrup aside.

Butter an ovenproof casserole; cover the bottom with the cubes of toast; add a layer each of apple, raisins, almonds, and cheese. Repeat until all the ingredients are used up. Pour the syrup over all, and bake in a preheated 350°F. oven for 30 minutes. Serve hot to 6.

## *Pastelitos de Boda*
### BRIDE'S COOKIES

This recipe for Bride's Cookies (the best known of all the *Polvorones*, Mexican Sugar Cookies) was given me by my friend, Adriana Keathley

Glaze, the dancer. It comes from her mother, Mrs. Angelica Martinez Keathley. I prefer it to any other *Polvorones* recipe I have tried. The cookies are as easy to make as they are delicious.

2 cups flour
½ cup sifted
   confectioner's sugar
2 sticks (1 cup) sweet
   butter, softened

Pinch of salt
1 cup pecans, chopped fine
1 teaspoon vanilla extract

Mix the flour, sugar, salt, and nuts together. Stir in the vanilla. Work the butter into the mixture until it forms a ball. Shape the dough into 24 patties; place on a cookie sheet; and bake in a preheated 350°F. oven for 30 minutes, or until the cookies are delicately brown. Lift off the cookie sheet; cool slightly on wire racks; then dust thickly with confectioner's sugar.

*Variations*

*Polvorones de Canela* (Cinnamon Cookies). Follow directions for *Pastelitos de Boda*, replacing the pecans with ¼ cup of flour and 1 teaspoon of ground cinnamon. While still warm from the oven, roll in a mixture of 2 cups of confectioner's sugar and 2 teaspoons ground cinnamon sifted together. Cool; then roll a second time.

*Polvorones* (Sugar Cookies). Follow directions for *Pastelitos de Boda*, omitting the pecans and substituting ½ cup of flour.

*Polvorones de Cacahuate, Almendras*, etc. (Peanut, Almond, and other nut cookies). Follow exact directions for *Pastelitos de Boda*, substituting peanuts, almonds, or other nuts for the pecans.

# Conchas

## SHELLS

This is a popular sweet bread for breakfast or *merienda* (supper).

1 package active dry yeast
   or 1 cake compressed
   yeast
½ cup lukewarm water
1 teaspoon salt
½ cup sugar
¾ cup milk

1 egg, well beaten
3½ cups sifted all-
   purpose flour
2 tablespoons shortening,
   melted

*Topping*:

½ stick (4 tablespoons) butter

½ cup sugar

¼ teaspoon salt

1 teaspoon cinnamon

1 egg

½ cup sifted all-purpose flour

Sprinkle the active dry yeast or crumble the compressed yeast over the lukewarm water to soften. Stir in salt and sugar, and allow to stand for 5 minutes until dissolved. Heat the milk until a film shines on top. Cool; then combine with the yeast mixture. Stir in the egg. Gradually stir in *1¾ cups of the flour*, and beat until the dough is well mixed. Add the melted and *cooled* shortening. Beat in the remainder of the flour. Cover, and allow to stand in a warm place, away from drafts, until double in bulk—about 1 hour.

Turn onto a lightly floured board, divide into 12 equal pieces, and form into round, flat buns. Spread the topping on the buns. With a sharp knife draw lines across the topping to form a lattice pattern. Place the buns on a greased baking sheet; cover; stand in a warm place; and allow to rise until double in bulk a second time—about 1 hour. Bake in a preheated 400°F. oven for 15 to 20 minutes.

*To make topping*: Cream the butter and sugar until light and fluffy. Add the salt and cinnamon, and mix well. Add the egg, then the flour, and stir until all the ingredients are thoroughly blended.

# Molletes

## SWEET ROLLS

1 package active dry yeast or 1 cake compressed yeast

½ cup lukewarm water

1 teaspoon salt

½ cup sugar

1 teaspoon anise seed

1 cup milk

2 tablespoons shortening, melted

1 egg, well beaten

3½ cups sifted all-purpose flour

Melted butter

Sifted brown sugar

Sprinkle the yeast over the lukewarm water to soften. Stir in the salt and sugar, and allow to stand for 5 minutes. Add the anise. Heat the milk until a film shines on top; remove from heat, and cool. Mix the cooled milk, melted shortening, and the egg into the yeast mixture. Add the flour, mixing well to make a soft dough. Cover, and allow to stand in a warm place until double in bulk—about 1 hour. Turn out on a lightly floured board, and divide into 24 equal pieces. Form into balls, and place on a greased baking sheet. Cover; and allow to stand, a second time, in a warm place until double in bulk—about 1 hour. When the rolls have risen, brush with melted butter, sprinkle with brown sugar, and bake in preheated 400°F. oven for 15 minutes.

# Chongos Zamoranos

## JUNKET FROM ZAMORA, MICHOACÁN

| | |
|---|---|
| 4 cups (1 quart) milk | 1 cup sugar |
| 2 egg yolks, lightly beaten | Ground cinnamon |
| 1 rennet (junket) tablet | |

Heat the milk until *lukewarm*; then pour into a large, flame-proof skillet. Stir in the egg yolks. Dissolve the rennet tablet in a little water, and add to the milk, stirring as little as possible. Remove from heat, and allow the mixture to set in a warm place. As soon as the milk is firm, cut an "X" with a knife across the entire surface and all the way to the bottom of the skillet. Sprinkle with sugar and cinnamon.

Place over a very low heat, with an asbestos mat underneath, and cook for about 2 hours, never allowing the junket to reach a boil. At the end of two hours, the whey and sugar will have formed a syrup, and each of the pie-shaped pieces will be firm enough to lift out of the pan with a slotted spatula. Now, roll up each piece, starting at the point end. Cut the rolls into pieces about 2 to 3 inches long. Place in a glass serving bowl, and pour over the syrup. Serves 6.

# Churros

## FRIED BATTER CAKES

These are, of course, Spanish, and are named after the *churro*, a Spanish sheep with long, coarse hair. They are sold at fairs and markets from small portable cooking stalls called *churrerías* (roughly, "churro shops"), where they go straight to the customer from the frying pan. Mexico has adopted them, and you find *churrerias* in all the market areas. In Mexico a cut-up lime is heated with the cooking oil, giving the *churros* a distinctive flavor.

Oil for deep frying
1 lime or lemon, quartered
Salt
Granulated sugar

1½ cups all-purpose
   flour
1 large egg or 2 small eggs

Heat the oil, and add the lime pieces.

Combine *1 cup of water*, salt, and *1 tablespoon of sugar* in a saucepan, and heat to the boiling point. Add the flour, all at once, and beat with a wooden spoon until smooth. Remove from heat; beat in the egg until the mixture is very smooth and satiny. Remove the lime pieces from the oil, which should be very hot (390°F. on a frying thermometer). Force the mixture through a pastry tube or large funnel, and fry in long strips until golden. Remove from the oil, drain on paper towels, and cut into 3-inch pieces. Roll in granulated sugar. Makes about 1 dozen.

## *Postre de Virrey*

### VICEROY'S DESSERT

This is the Mexican version of English trifle, and very good it is, too. Puddings like this have a way of migrating. *Zuppa Inglese*, the Italian version, is said to have been introduced into Italy by Emma, Lady Hamilton, during her stay there with Lord Nelson. One wonders where the good Sisters of Mexico's colonial convents, who modified it to suit the ingredients available to them, learned the recipe. It is piously to be hoped that it was not from the wicked English pirates then infesting the coasts of New Spain, as Mexico was called at the time. But, one asks, how else? I have reduced the amount of sugar in the original recipe, as it is quite excessive for modern tastes.

1 cup sugar
16 egg yolks, lightly
   beaten
1 cup dry sherry
1 teaspoon vanilla extract
4 egg whites
Pinch of salt
1 cup heavy cream
1 tablespoon sifted
   confectioner's sugar

2 tablespoons brandy
1 pound sponge cake, cut
   into ½-inch slices
Apricot jam
Grated chocolate, or
   toasted, slivered
   almonds

Combine the sugar and *⅓ cup of water* in a saucepan, and cook to the thread stage (230°F. on the candy thermometer). Remove from heat, and place in a saucepan of cold water to cool.

Mix the yolks and the syrup together, and cook in the top of a double boiler over hot, *not boiling*, water, stirring constantly until the mixture makes a thick custard. Remove from heat, and cool; then stir in *half of the sherry* and the vanilla. Set aside. Beat the egg whites with salt until they form stiff, shiny peaks. Beat the cream with confectioner's sugar until stiff; add the brandy to the cream. Fold the egg whites into the cream mixture. Set aside.

Spread the sponge-cake slices with apricot jam, arrange a layer in a suitable serving dish, and sprinkle with some of the remaining sherry—enough to moisten but not to saturate. Follow with a layer of custard, another layer of sponge cake, sherry, and a layer of the whipped cream. Continue in this way, alternating the layer of custard with the layer of whipped cream, until all the ingredients are used, ending with a layer of cream. Grate the chocolate over the top of the pudding, or sprinkle with almonds. Chill in the refrigerator. Serves 6.

## *Budín de Piña*

### PINEAPPLE PUDDING

12 ladyfingers
Apricot jam
2 cups finely chopped
 fresh pineapple
½ cup blanched, ground
 almonds
4 egg yolks, lightly beaten
½ to 1 cup sugar,
 depending on sweetness
 of the pineapple

½ cup dry sherry
¼ teaspoon ground
 cinnamon
Sour cream
Toasted, slivered almonds

Split the ladyfingers, and spread with a thin layer of apricot jam. Combine the pineapple, ground almonds, egg yolks, sugar, *¼ cup of the sherry*, and the cinnamon in a saucepan; and cook, stirring constantly over a low heat, until sauce has thickened. Cool.

Place *half the ladyfingers* in the bottom of a serving dish.

Sprinkle with half the remaining sherry. Spread with half the pineapple mixture. Add a second layer of the ladyfingers, the remainder of the sherry, and the pineapple mixture. Chill, spread with a layer of sour cream, and decorate with slivered almonds. Serves 6.

## *Huevos Reales*

### ROYAL EGGS

| | |
|---|---|
| 2 tablespoons raisins | 2 cups sugar |
| ½ cup dry sherry | Piece of stick cinnamon |
| 12 egg yolks | 2 tablespoons pine nuts |

Soak the raisins in *¼ cup of the sherry*. Set aside.

Beat the egg yolks until they make ribbons. Pour into a shallow, greased pan, and set this in a larger ovenproof pan, partially filled with *hot* water. Place in a preheated 350°F. oven until the eggs are set—about 20 minutes. Cool, and cut into cubes.

Combine the sugar with *1 cup of water* and the cinnamon stick. Bring to a boil; then boil for 5 minutes. Remove the cinnamon. Add the egg cubes, and poach very gently over a low heat until the cubes are saturated with the syrup. Pour into a serving dish, stir in the remaining sherry, and sprinkle with the raisins and nuts. Serves 6.

## *Flan de Almendra*

### ALMOND SNOW

| | |
|---|---|
| 2 cups milk | Pinch of salt |
| ½ cup sugar | 1 tablespoon kirsch |
| ¼ cup ground, blanched almonds | Butter |
| 4 egg whites | Toasted, slivered almonds |

Bring the milk to a boil; add the sugar and almonds; and cook, over a very low heat, for about 15 minutes. Cool.

Beat the egg whites with a pinch of salt until they form firm peaks. Fold the whites into the almond-milk mixture gently but thoroughly. Then stir in the kirsch. Butter the top of a double boiler; add the mixture; cover; and cook, over *hot* water, until the mixture is firm. Chill. To serve, unmold on a suitable serving platter, and stick with the almonds. Serves 6.

## *Pastel de Avellana*

### FILBERT CAKE

¾ cup cake flour
1 teaspoon baking powder
¾ cup filberts
3 eggs, separated
⅔ cup sugar

1 stick (½ cup) butter,
   clarified
½ teaspoon vanilla
   extract
Pinch of salt

Sift the flour and baking powder together, and set aside. Place the filberts half at a time in the electric blender, and pulverize. Set aside. Lightly butter a round 9 × 1½-inch cake pan, and coat with flour, dumping out any excess.

Beat the egg yolks until very thick and creamy; then gradually beat in the sugar until the mixture forms ribbons. Stir *⅓ cup water* into the eggs; then add the ground filberts, beating constantly and steadily. Stir the flour combination into the egg mixture, a small amount at a time. Stir in the butter, taking care not to include any milky residue in the bottom of the pan. Then add the vanilla.

Beat the whites with a pinch of salt until they form stiff, shiny peaks when the beater is held straight up. Whisk about ¼ of the whites into the batter vigorously to lighten it. Dump the remaining whites on top, and fold in carefully but thoroughly.

Pour into the prepared cake pan, and bake in a preheated 350°F. oven for 30 to 35 minutes, or until a toothpick inserted in the center comes out dry. Remove the cake from the oven, and allow to stand about 10 minutes. Turn out of the cake pan onto cake rack, then invert so the top is uppermost. Cool for 1 hour, then spread with the warm Apricot Glaze.

*To make the glaze*: Force ½ cup apricot jam through a sieve. Pour into a saucepan; add 2 tablespoons of sugar, and cook for 2 or 3 minutes. Spread over the cooled cake while still warm.

*To make Pecan Cake*, substitute pecans for filberts, and omit the vanilla extract. Substitute 1 tablespoon strained lemon juice for the water when beating the egg yolks.

## HOW TO CLARIFY BUTTER

Melt the butter slowly in a saucepan. Allow the melted butter to stand for a few minutes; then pour off the clear, golden liquid, discarding the milky sediment that settles at the bottom of the pan.

Clarified butter can be frozen successfully; the practical way to freeze it is to pour it into individual plastic ice-cube containers.

*Note*: On freezing, clarified butter turns milky, but clears when defrosted.

### *Arroz Almendrado*
#### ALMOND RICE PUDDING

| | |
|---|---|
| ½ cup rice | ¼ cup blanched, ground |
| Salt | almonds |
| Good piece of orange rind | 2 egg yolks, well beaten |
| 1 cup sugar | Cinnamon |
| 4 cups milk | |

Soak the rice in enough hot water to cover for 15 minutes. Rinse in cold water; drain; and place in a saucepan with a pinch of salt, the orange rind, and *1 cup of water*. Bring to a boil, reduce heat, and cook, covered, until all the water has evaporated. Discard the rind.

Add the sugar, milk, and almonds to the rice; and cook, uncovered, over low heat until all the milk has been absorbed. Add the well-beaten yolks, and cook for a few minutes. Turn into a serving dish, and sprinkle lightly with cinnamon. Serve cold to 6.

### *Arroz con Leche*
#### RICE PUDDING

| | |
|---|---|
| ½ cup raisins | 4 cups milk |
| ¼ cup sherry | 1 cup sugar |
| ½ cup rice | Cinnamon |
| Good piece of lemon rind | 2 egg yolks, well beaten |
| Pinch of salt | Toasted, slivered almonds |

Cover the raisins with the sherry, and set aside.

Soak the rice in enough hot water to cover for 15 minutes. Rinse in cold water; drain; place in a saucepan with the lemon rind; add a pinch of salt and *1 cup of water*. Bring to a boil; reduce heat; cover; and cook, over a low heat, until all the water has evaporated. Remove the rind; add the milk, sugar, cinnamon to taste; and cook uncovered over low heat until all the milk has been absorbed. When the rice is cooked, stir in the egg yolks and raisins, and cook a few minutes longer. Turn into a serving dish, and sprinkle with the almonds. Serve cold. Serves 6.

# Ates

### FRUIT PASTES

A wide range of *ates*, fruit pastes, is made in Mexico. The *ates* of Morelia, capital of the state of Michoacán, are the most famous of all. Quince, guava, mango, and papaya with pineapple are the most popular. The pastes can be bought in Latin American and Spanish groceries, as well as in some shops specializing in fine imported foods, in the United States. Fruit pastes of excellent quality are also made in Florida and Puerto Rico. Served with cream cheese and saltine crackers they make an excellent dessert.

However, *ates* are easy enough to make at home. Some cooks insist that the paste should be dried in the sun for a couple of days. Others dispense with this. If they are to keep, unrefrigerated, for a long time, perhaps the sun drying is essential, but how anyone can keep them uneaten at home is something of a mystery. The recipe for *Guayabate* (Guava Paste) can be used with very slight variations for all the other *ates*.

# Guayabate

### GUAVA PASTE

2 pounds guavas                    2 pounds sugar, about

Cut the guavas in half, and scoop out the seeds. Soak the seeds in 1 cup of cold water. Place the guavas in a saucepan with ½ cup of water, bring to a boil, reduce heat to simmer, and cook until they are really soft. Take care they don't scorch.

Strain the water from the seeds (it will be slightly mucilaginous), and add to the cooked guavas. Discard the seeds.

Grind the guavas through the fine blade of a food chopper. Measure the pulp, and add an equal amount of sugar. Mix well; place in a large, heavy kettle over very low heat; and cook, stirring constantly with a wooden spoon, until the mixture is thick and a little jelly tested on a cube of ice can be lifted off, in one piece, when cold. Remove from heat, and beat with a wooden spoon for 10 minutes, or until it forms a heavy paste. Have ready a loaf pan, lined with wax paper. Turn the paste into the pan, and set aside, in a cool place, for 24 hours. To store, turn out of the pan, and wrap securely in foil.

*Note*: If possible, place the paste on wax paper on a wooden board, cover with cheesecloth, and set in the sun for 2 days, turning the board from time to time to make sure all the surfaces are exposed to the sun.

*Other fruit pastes*

*To make Membrillate* (Quince Paste), follow the same procedure as for *Guayabate*, soaking the cores of the fruit and using the water.

*To make Ate de Mango*, choose fruit that is not completely ripe; peel, remove the seed, and grind the pulp. Measure, and cook with an equal quantity of sugar, weight for weight.

*To make Papaya y Piña*, peel the papaya, remove the seeds and grind the pulp; peel and core the pineapple, grind, and mix with the papaya pulp. Combine the two, and mix with an equal quantity of sugar, weight for weight.

For those who don't wish to go to the effort of making their own pastes, delicious as they are, the commercial *ates* are really of homemade quality.

# *Chayote Relleno*

## STUFFED CHAYOTE

| | |
|---|---|
| 3 large chayotes | 1 cup dry sherry |
| Salt | 6 slices pound cake or |
| 3 eggs, well beaten | sponge cake, crumbled |
| 1 cup raisins | Cracker meal |
| 1 cup sugar | Whole or toasted, slivered |
| 1½ teaspoons freshly | almonds |
| grated nutmeg | |

Cut the chayotes in half, and place in a saucepan that has a lid. Cover with boiling water; add some salt, and cook, covered, over a moderate heat until the chayotes are tender when pierced with the point of a small, sharp knife—about 20 minutes. The time will depend on the size and age of the vegetable. When cool enough to handle, remove the seed and scoop out the pulp carefully, leaving the shell intact.

Mash the pulp, and combine with the eggs, raisins, sugar, nutmeg, sherry, and cake, mixing well. If the mixture seems too liquid, add enough cracker meal to give it body. Stuff the chayote shells; stud with the almonds; arrange in a greased baking dish; and bake in a preheated 350°F. oven until golden—about 15 minutes. Serves 6.

## Leche Quemada Sin Trabajo

### EASY MILK CANDY

This is a shortcut that is really worthwhile. The taste and texture of the candy is very like the original, perhaps a trifle blander, with a somewhat softer consistency.

Place 1, 2, or more 14-ounce cans of sweetened, condensed milk in a deep saucepan; add enough water to cover the cans completely. Bring the water to a boil; reduce heat, then simmer, uncovered, for 2½ to 3 hours. If the water evaporates below the tops of the cans, add more *boiling* water to keep the cans well covered. Lift out of the water and cool. When cold, open the cans, and spoon the candy into a serving dish. Chill in the refrigerator before serving.

*Variation with wine*: The candy can be turned into a saucepan with ¼ cup sweet sherry, Madeira, or muscatel, and cooked over low heat, stirring constantly, until the wine has been absorbed. It is then poured into a serving dish and chilled before serving.

## Tamales de Dulce

### SWEET TAMALES

Make the tamal dough as in the recipe for plain tamales (page 44) adding ½ to 1 cup of sugar, according to taste, to 2 cups of *masa harina*. Prepare corn husks. Spread the dough on corn husks. Add 1 tablespoon of combined raisins, slivered almonds, and chopped citron for each tamal, placing mixture in center of dough. Roll up and steam. Eat hot.

*Tamales de Dulce* can also be filled with candied fruits, such as pineapple, apricots, cherries, or peaches, or with preserves.

# Cocada

## COCONUT CUSTARD

| | |
|---|---|
| 1 cup sugar | 4 whole eggs |
| 1 4½-ounce can flaked coconut | 2 teaspoons vanilla* |
| | ½ cup sherry |
| Pinch of salt | Whipped cream |
| 4¼ cups milk | Toasted, slivered almonds |

Combine the sugar and *1 cup of water* in a saucepan, and bring to a boil. Reduce heat, add the coconut, and cook over extremely low heat until all the syrup has been absorbed. Add a pinch of salt and *4 cups of the milk*. Cook, stirring constantly, until the milk has reduced and the mixture has the consistency of a light custard. Beat the eggs lightly with the remaining *¼ cup of cold milk* and the vanilla. Add 3 or 4 tablespoons of the hot coconut mixture to the beaten eggs, one at a time, mixing them in well. Then combine with the remainder of the coconut mixture. Add the sherry, and cook, over a low heat, stirring constantly with a wooden spoon, until the mixture thickens into a heavy custard. Pour into a serving dish. Cool; then refrigerate. Just before serving, spread a thick layer of whipped cream over the entire surface, and stick with the almonds. Serves 6.

# Empanadas

## TURNOVERS

Wheat was introduced into Mexico by Spain, and these turnovers are, of course, Spanish in origin. More popular in the North than in the corn

---

*Though I prefer vanilla, cinnamon is the traditional flavoring for this custard. To flavor with cinnamon, add 1 whole stick to the sugar and water. Boil together 5 minutes. Remove cinnamon and follow directions.

country of the central and southern regions, large *empanadas* are good for luncheon, the half-size for cocktails.

| | |
|---|---|
| 2 cups all-purpose flour | ⅓ cup ice water |
| ½ teaspoon salt | Salad oil for deep-fat |
| 1 teaspoon baking powder | frying |
| ½ cup shortening | |

Sift the flour, salt, and baking powder together. Cut in the shortening with a pastry blender or 2 knives until the mixture is mealy. Add the water, and work into a firm dough. Roll out on a lightly floured board, and cut with a cookie cutter into 12 4-inch or 24 2-inch circles. Place 1 tablespoon of the filling (see below) in the middle of each, wet edges of pastry with water, fold over, and press together. Deep fry in hot oil until golden brown, or bake in a preheated 450°F. oven for 15 minutes.

*Note*: *Empanadas* can be filled either with sweets or savories. A favorite Mexican filling consists of cold boiled potatoes, diced, fried in butter with a little chopped onion, and moistened with a little *Salsa de Chile Rojo*, page 79. Any leftover meat or fish with a little onion, cheese, hard-cooked egg, or green olives, moistened with a little sauce, is fine. *Picadillo*, page 165, and *Picadillo de la Costa*, page 166, are both excellent fillings. Leftover *Adobo* or *Mole* are also good; in fact, any of the *Antojito* fillings may be used. Candied fruits, jams, coconut mixed with raisins, crushed pineapple and chopped almonds, and fruit preserves make delicious sweet *empanadas*.

## *Calabaza Enmielada*

### PUMPKIN IN BROWN SUGAR

This dessert is rather a heavy one at the end of a meal, and so is more often taken as a breakfast dish or at *merienda*, the light supper that is eaten in Mexico by people who have their principal meal in the middle of the day. *Cafe con Leche*, *atole*, or *Chocolate en Leche*, with sweet breads, are served at this meal, which in the feudal past, when appetites were apparently sturdier, was a collation taken between dinner (midday) and supper.

1 pumpkin, about 3 pounds
2 cups *piloncillo* or dark
    brown sugar, firmly
    packed

Wipe the pumpkin with a damp cloth, and cut into wedges. Remove the seeds. Arrange the pumpkin pieces, shell side down, in a heavy saucepan. Take *1½ cups of the sugar*, and sprinkle it over the pieces, dividing it evenly. Add ½ cup of water to the saucepan, cover, and cook over very low heat until the pumpkin is tender when pierced with the point of a sharp knife. Meanwhile, combine the remaining sugar and *¼ cup of water*, and cook over a very low heat until slightly thickened. Serve this sauce on the side with the cooked pumpkin. Serves 6.

Milk is sometimes poured over the pumpkin; or a glass of milk may be served with it.

## *Cajeta*

### CARAMEL CANDY

This is also called *Leche Quemada* (Burnt Milk), though, in fact, the milk is not burned, but cooked to a soft caramel with sugar. There is a small history behind the name *Cajeta*, literally "box," which demonstrates how things get names that make no sense at all.

It begins in the town of Celaya, in the rich farming and mining state of Guanajuato. The milk candy of Celaya, made from half cow's and half goat's milk, became famous for its excellence; and the people began packaging it in little, thin-walled wooden boxes which, in Spanish, are called *cajetas*. Travelers began to bring back the candy for friends and relations; and, as its fame grew, it was sent to shops all over the Republic. Very soon, in order to distinguish it from other milk candy, which was packaged differently and which they felt to be inferior, people started to call it *Cajeta de Leche Quemada*, meaning Boxed Burnt Milk Candy; and, as you might expect, that was soon shortened simply to *Cajeta*.

So, people in Mexico buy a "box" nowadays, making this a good example of synecdoche, the literary term which describes the human habit of naming the part for the whole. If you are in Mexico, ask for *Cajeta*, and you'll get milk candy. Or stay home and make it for yourself. Eat it with a spoon, or spread it on bread or biscuits, or serve it over ice cream.

| | |
|---|---|
| 2 quarts milk | ¼ teaspoon soda |
| 3 cups sugar | Small piece stick cinnamon |

Combine *1 quart of the milk* in a saucepan with the sugar, and cook over a low heat, stirring from time to time, until the mixture turns golden. Meanwhile, stir the soda into the remaining quart of milk in a saucepan. Add the cinnamon stick, and bring to a boil. Discard the cinnamon. Add the hot milk to the caramel mixture very gradually, stirring constantly. When all the milk is incorporated, place over a low heat, and cook very slowly until the mixture is thick. Cool slightly; then pour into a glass serving bowl, and chill.

*Variations*

*Cajeta Envinada* (Milk Candy with Wine): Follow the directions for *Cajeta de Leche*, omitting the cinnamon. When it is just about cooked, stir in 1 cup of sweet sherry, Madeira, or muscatel, and continue cooking until the wine has been absorbed.

*Cajeta de Almendra Envinada* (Milk Candy with Wine and Almonds): Pulverize ¼ cup whole, blanched almonds in an electric blender. Combine with the milk and soda, omit the cinnamon, and bring to a boil. Then add to the caramel mixture as directed in the recipe for *Cajeta de Leche*. When almost cooked, stir in 1 cup of sweet sherry, Madeira, or muscatel, and continue cooking until the wine has all been absorbed.

# BEBIDAS

## DRINKS

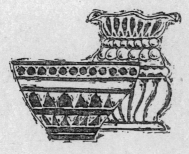

The best known of all Mexican alcoholic drinks is undoubtedly tequila, yet it did not exist before the arrival of the Spaniards. The Aztecs made *pulque*, which is the fermented sap of the *maguey*, the American agave or century plant. This milky drink, about as alcoholic as beer, still enjoys some popularity. It is "cured" with various fruits, such as strawberry and pineapple, to give it a more attractive flavor, although little can be done to disguise its sour and acrid odor. The *pulquerías*, small bars where it is sold, are mainly distinguished for their names: "The End of the World," "My Love," "My Second Wife," and so on. The many and excellent Mexican beers have overtaken *pulque* in popularity.

There is, however, a charming story concerning its origin. Legend has it that, when pressure from the Nahuatl tribes in the North drove the Toltecs out of Tula, their capital in the present-day state of Hidalgo, starting them on their long migrations to the West and South, a woman invented the "wine of the earth." She punched holes in the *maguey* plant (probably *Agave atrovirens*), drew off the sap, and fermented it, making *pulque*. Other women joined her in this noble work, and they then gave a party for the elders, both men and women. Four cups were served to each person; but the leader of one of the tribes, a man called Cuexteco, drank a fifth cup against all advice, became drunk, and took off all his clothes. In shame he fled with his people to the coastal region known as the Huasteca, on the Gulf of Mexico; to this day the inhabitants are said to be a hard-drinking people.

After the Conquest, distilling was introduced into Mexico, and in no time at all tequila, made from the blue agave, or *tequilana*, which grows principally in the state of Jalisco, made its appearance, acquiring its name from the small township there. Not quite so well known is a similar drink, *mezcal*, made from another species of agave from the Oaxaca region and also in northern Mexico. It has a somewhat stronger flavor.

It is a common misunderstanding that tequila and *mezcal* are made from cactus. Agaves are succulents belonging to the Amaryllidaceae. The cacti, also succulents, are in a group of their own.

In the past, both tequila and *mezcal* were made in small stills, and the product was often raw, and the source of impressive hangovers. Nowadays, production in large distilleries is properly controlled, and the end product ranks with any good brand of distilled spirits.

Most tequila is colorless, though some of the liqueur tequilas, the *añejos* (aged), which are left for a time in charred casks, are a light golden color. These are best taken by themselves, or with the addition of a little lemon or lime juice, always well chilled. The white or colorless tequilas are excellent in mixed drinks; but the classic way of drinking tequila is with salt and lime. One takes a lick of salt, a sip of tequila, and then a suck of lime. Nowadays, the more usual serving method is to have the traditional straight-sided 4-ounce tequila glass rimmed with salt and served with small wedges of lime on the side. For those who dislike a salt-rimmed glass, as I do, a pleasant alternative is to squeeze the lime into the glass, adding more lime as one drinks.

Sugar cane was introduced very early into the New World, and, as a result, Mexico produces many excellent rums. Its wine industry is not so successful, but its coffee-flavored liqueur, Kahlua, is widely exported.

The list of non-alcoholic drinks, the *refrescos*, is almost endless. It includes chocolate, the royal drink of the past, coffee, the *atoles* (gruel-like drinks made with corn), an immense list of herbal teas which are supposed to cure every ill known to man, all sorts of fruit punches, and *tepache*, a fermented pineapple drink, quite tart and refreshing, which Mexicans use in cooking as one might use wine or beer.

# *Atole*

This is a very ancient Mexican drink. Father Sahagún mentions women being given *atole* to drink at a banquet of merchants when the men were drinking chocolate. Many different flavorings are added to the basic *Atole de Leche*. One of them, *Champurrado*, is flavored with chocolate, so it is probably a colonial invention, and is never referred to as *atole*, but always by its name. I personally do not care for the *atoles*, but then neither do I look forward to a nourishing cup of cocoa at the end of a meal. It is a matter of taste; and I should imagine that both old people and young children might well enjoy these drinks.

## *Atole de Leche*

### BASIC MILK *ATOLE*

½ cup *masa harina*              1 cup sugar or to taste
3 cups water                    3 cups milk
Small piece of cinnamon
   stick, or 1 vanilla bean

Place the *masa* in a large saucepan, and stir in the water. Add the cinnamon stick or vanilla bean, and cook over a low heat, stirring constantly, until it has thickened. Remove from heat, and add the sugar and the milk. Return to the heat, and bring to a simmer. Discard the cinnamon stick. Serve hot in cups.

*Note*: This basic recipe for *atole* can be varied by using 2 cups of water to 4 cups of milk, or, for a richer version, 2 cups of water to 3 cups of milk and 1 of cream.

*Variations*

*Atole de Almendra* (Almond *Atole*): Add ½ cup of blanched, ground almonds with the sugar. When the *atole* has thickened, remove from heat, and add 3 well-beaten egg yolks. Reheat, stirring all the while, but do not allow it to boil.

*Atole de Fresa, Frambuesa, Zarzamora* (Fruit *Atoles*): To make strawberry, raspberry, blackberry, or guava *atoles*, add 1½ cups of the crushed fruit when adding the sugar. If the *atole* lacks color, add a few drops of red food coloring. To make a pineapple *atole*, add 1½ cups crushed pineapple. For prune, add 1 cup prunes, soaked, pitted, and pureed.

# *Champurrado*
## CHOCOLATE *ATOLE*

Replace the white sugar with 1 cup of brown sugar and add 3 1-ounce squares unsweetened chocolate, grated. Beat with a *molinillo* as in making Mexican chocolate, or beat well with a wire whisk.

# *Agua de Jamaica*
## JAMAICA FLOWER WATER

½ pound Jamaica          Sugar to taste
  flowers
3 quarts water

Heat 1 pint of water, and pour it over the Jamaica flowers in a large jug. Allow to stand for about 15 minutes. Strain; add the remainder of the water and sugar to taste. Chill in the refrigerator, and serve in tumblers with ice.

*Note*: Jamaica flowers are also known as rosella, roselle, and sorrel.

# *Agua de Tamarindo*
## TAMARIND WATER

½ pound ripe tamarinds          Sugar to taste
3 quarts water

Remove the rind from the tamarind pods, and place them in a large jug with enough cold water to cover. Soak the pods for about 4 hours until the pulp has softened. Strain through a fine sieve, add the remaining water, and sweeten to taste with sugar.

# *Horchata*

## MELON SEED DRINK

1 cup melon seeds*                  Grated rind of 1 lime or
1 cup sugar                                    lemon

Place the melon seeds in an electric blender, and pulverize as
finely as possible. Combine the melon seeds, *6 cups of water*,
the sugar, and the lemon rind in a large jug, and allow to stand
at least 4 hours. Strain through a damp cloth, squeezing it hard
to extract all the milk from the seeds. Serve on the rocks.

# *Aperitivo Chapala*

## APERITIF FROM LAKE CHAPALA

1 cup strained orange juice       Salt to taste
3 tablespoons grenadine
    syrup
1 teaspoon cayenne pepper
    or ground hot red chile
    *pequín*

Mix the ingredients thoroughly, and chill. Serve in liquor glasses
as chasers to tequila or as an aperitif before luncheon or dinner.
Delicious with the tiny fried fish that in Mexico are known as
*charalitos fritos*. These are available in many Mexican, Puerto
Rican, or Chinese markets, and also in the markets where
Indian foods are sold, since they are often served in the East
as an accompaniment to curry. The exact species of these tiny
fish from India may be different, but the taste is the same.

# *Chocolate*

Chocolate was a royal drink in pre-Columbian Mexico, taken
only by the king, the merchant nobility, and the upper ranks
of the priesthood and military. Its name is derived from two
Nahuatl words, *"xoco,"* meaning "bitter," and *"atl,"* meaning

---

*Or ½ cup of melon seeds and ½ cup of blanched almonds.

"water." It was served in a great many ways, sometimes sweetened with honey and flavored with vanilla, always beaten until it foamed with a *molinillo* (a small wooden beater you twirl between your palms—it is used to this day).

Perhaps the most interesting of all the Aztec chocolate drinks is chocolate made with *cold* water. Use 1 1-ounce square of unsweetened chocolate per cup of cold water; add honey and vanilla to taste; and beat with a *molinillo* until the chocolate dissolves and the drink is foamy. (The electric blender can, of course, be used.) It makes a stimulating and refreshing drink.

Mexican chocolate, available in Mexican, Spanish, and Puerto Rican grocery stores, is packaged already sweetened, flavored with cinnamon and cloves, and mixed with ground almonds. It comes to us from Mexico's colonial past. The Spanish contribution to the drink can clearly be seen. It was wildly popular, so much so that at one time the Church forbade worshippers' bringing their cups of chocolate to Sunday mass.

# Café con Leche

## COFFEE WITH MILK

Make drip coffee about four times as strong as usual. In other words, allow 4 tablespoons of coffee to 1 cup of water. Dilute it to taste with hot milk.

# Café de Olla

## POT COFFEE

Coffee made in this style is, customarily, served after meals in the handle-less earthenware pots in which it is traditionally made. However, a large quantity can be made in a saucepan or an enamel coffee pot, and poured into individual cups.

| | |
|---|---|
| 4 cups water | 4 whole cloves |
| ½ cup *piloncillo** | 4 tablespoons regular- |
| 2-inch piece of stick | grind, dark-roasted |
|    cinnamon | coffee |

**Piloncillo*, Mexican brown sugar, can be bought in Latin groceries and specialty stores; but American dark brown sugar is a very acceptable substitute.

Heat the water, sugar, cinnamon, and cloves in a saucepan or a heatproof coffee pot, stirring until the sugar is dissolved. Add the coffee, bring to a boil, and simmer for a minute or two. Stir, cover, and leave on the stove in a warm place for the grounds to settle. Serves 4.

## *Chía*

½ pound *chía* seeds
3 quarts water
Sugar to taste

Lime or lemon juice to
taste, strained

Place the *chía* seeds and water in a large jug, and allow to stand long enough for the seeds to swell up and become gelatinous (a few minutes, actually). Add the lemon or lime juice and sugar to taste. Don't strain. Chill before drinking.

## *Té*

### TEA

Mexico, though it drinks tea as we do, really is more interested in the *tisanes*, herbal teas. Here are some of the better known ones:

*Anise*—antispasmodic for the stomach
*Artichoke*—for the liver
*Asafetida*—for bad temper
*Boldo*—for the gall bladder
*Borage*—for fever
*Camomile*—for the stomach and as an inhalation for colds, bronchitis
*Cedar*—for the stomach
*Clove*—for toothache
*Corn silk*—for kidneys
*Hawthorn-cinnamon*—for coughs

*Jasmine*—for the nerves
*Manzanita seed*—for the kidneys
*Marnital flower*—for the heart
*Muicle*—for anemia
*Oak (bark and root)*—to strengthen the teeth
*Orange leaf*—for the nerves
*Tlalchichinole*—for the kidneys

## *Margarita*

2 ounces tequila
½ ounce Triple Sec or
    Cointreau

Juice of ½ lime

Rub the rim of a cocktail glass with the rind of the lime, and spin it in salt. Pour the ingredients over ice in a bar glass, and stir until thoroughly chilled. Strain into the prepared cocktail glass.

## *Coco Loco*

### CRAZY COCONUT

This is a worthy addition to the coconut-water drinks, the only surprising thing being that it didn't become popular sooner. It seems to have originated in Acapulco.

Proceed by slicing off the top of a green coconut with a machete or other suitable instrument, and pour in 1 jigger of white tequila. Taste; add more tequila if the coconut has abundant water. Sip through a straw.

## *Tequila Sour*

3 ounces tequila
1 teaspoon sugar
Juice of ½ lemon

Dash Angostura bitters
Sparkling water

Shake the tequila, sugar, and lemon juice and bitters with cracked ice, and strain into a sour glass. Add a splash of sparkling water.

## *Tequila Daisy*

2 ounces tequila
½ ounce lemon juice
½ ounce grenadine
    syrup

Splash of sparkling water

Combine all ingredients in a cocktail shaker with cracked ice, and shake well. Strain into a cocktail glass.

# Bertita's Special

2 ounces tequila
Juice of 1 lime
1 teaspoon sugar

2 dashes of orange bitters
Sparkling water

Combine all the ingredients in a shaker with cracked ice, and shake vigorously. Strain into a Tom Collins glass. Fill with chilled sparkling water.

*Variation*

*Taxco Fizz:* Add the white of an egg to 1 Bertita's Special. Shake very vigorously.

# Isabella

1½ ounces tequila
4½ ounces freshly
   squeezed orange juice

Combine the tequila and the orange juice. Strain over ice cubes into an old-fashioned glass.

# Tequila Cocktail

1 jigger tequila
Juice of 1 lime, strained

½ ounce grenadine or to
   taste

Mix all the ingredients, pour over crushed ice in a saucer-shaped champagne glass, and serve with a straw.

# Submarino

## SUBMARINE

Pour a well-chilled bottle of any good Mexican beer into a chilled tankard. Add a jigger of chilled tequila, pouring it right into the center. Some follow the tequila with a pinch of salt. *Do not stir.* Serve at once.

Never drink more than two. Perhaps a better name for this lethal drink might be "Torpedo."

# Tequila Sunrise

2 ounces tequila
3 dashes grenadine
Juice and rind of ½
    lime

½ teaspoon *crème de
    cassis*
Sparkling water

Place the lime juice and the rind in a tall glass, add the tequila, grenadine, *crème de cassis*, and several ice cubes. Fill with sparkling water, and stir.

# Kahlúa Kiss

Fill a liqueur glass a little more than ¾ full with Kahlúa; then top with heavy cream.

# Por mi Amante

## FOR MY LOVE

2 pint boxes or 4 cups
    strawberries

2 cups tequila

Wash the strawberries; drain thoroughly; then hull. Cut in half, and place in an air-tight jar. Add the tequila, which should cover the fruit, and seal the jar. Refrigerate for a minimum of 3 weeks. Strain. This pink and fragrant liqueur should be served straight and very cold.

*Note*: Although this is probably the most delicate of all the *Por mi Amantes*, the same method may be followed for other berries and fruits. With raspberries, follow the same directions. With larger fruit, such as peaches, peel and cut into very small chunks; then follow the same procedure.

## *Coctel Manzanillo*

### MANZANILLO COCKTAIL

The papayas served in Manzanillo, the beach resort of the tiny state of Colima on Mexico's Pacific coast, are a beautiful deep, reddish-orange color. Sweet and flavorful, the juice makes a splendid mix for Collinses and other long drinks of this type. The Manzanillo Cocktail has a most subtle flavor.

| | |
|---|---|
| 1 jigger light rum | ½ teaspoon grenadine |
| 2 jiggers papaya juice | syrup |

Shake ingredients well with cracked ice, and strain into a chilled cocktail glass, or pour over ice cubes in an old-fashioned glass.

## *Sangrita*

| | |
|---|---|
| 2 pounds (about 6 medium) tomatoes, peeled and seeded | 1 teaspoon sugar |
| | Salt |
| Juice of 3 oranges | 4 to 6 fresh green *serrano* |
| Juice of 2 limes | chiles* |
| 1 small white onion, chopped | Tequila |

Place all the ingredients, *except the tequila*, in an electric blender, and blend until smooth. If the ingredients exceed the capacity of the container, do a small quantity at a time. Chill well; then pour into tequila glasses. Customarily, *Sangritas* are drunk by sipping alternately with a glass of tequila. They are served with halved limes and salt on the side.

Many people add a little lime juice to either the *Sangrita* or the tequila, or take a little suck of lime between sips.

*Or ground dried chile *pequín*, *tepin*, or *cascabel* or cayenne pepper. A proper *Sangrita* is quite fiery.

# Rum and Coconut Water

The green coconut is the unripe nut as it is found on the tree before its outer green husk has been removed. The meat has not set, and the coconut is filled with a refreshingly tart, slightly milky-looking liquid. There is often a thin layer of a creamy substance, the immature coconut meat, which is scooped out and eaten when the drink is finished. It is delicious.

Green coconuts can quite often be found in markets selling tropical fruits and vegetables. The coconut does double duty, as it provides both the mix for your drink and the container out of which you drink it. The top is struck off with a machete (the special knife used for cutting sugar cane), a sharp ax, or a really enormous knife. Pour in 1 jigger of light rum. Taste; add more rum if the coconut has abundant water. Sip through a straw.

Gin and coconut water is also highly esteemed.

# Dorado Cocktail

| | |
|---|---|
| Juice of ½ lime or lemon | 2 ounces tequila |
| | 1 tablespoon honey |

Combine all the ingredients with cracked ice in a shaker. Shake well, and strain into a cocktail glass, or into an old-fashioned glass with ice cubes.

# Sangría

This is the famous Spanish wine drink which Mexico has adopted and altered to its own taste.

| | |
|---|---|
| 1 bottle (⅘ quart) dry red wine | Juice 2 oranges, strained |
| Juice 3 limes, strained | ½ cup sugar, about, or to taste |

Fill a very large pitcher half full of ice cubes. Pour in the juices and the wine. Add the sugar, and stir until the sugar has dissolved. Serve in tall glasses.

So the ice cubes will not dilute the *Sangría* too much, it's a good idea to remove some of them once the drink is well chilled.

## Rompope

This cooked eggnog can perhaps best be described as a Mexican version of the Dutch eggnog called Advocaat. It keeps indefinitely if refrigerated. Nowadays few people bother to make *Rompope*, since it is bottled commercially and sold widely. It can be made with brandy, although I prefer a light rum; and cinnamon may be used instead of the vanilla. Some cooks add ¼ cup finely ground almonds when adding the egg yolks, which helps to thicken the mixture and adds a delicate flavor.

| | |
|---|---|
| 1 quart milk | 12 egg yolks |
| 1 cup sugar | 2 cups light rum |
| 1 vanilla bean | |

Bring the milk, sugar, and vanilla bean to a boil; and simmer very gently, stirring all the time, for 15 minutes. Cool to room temperature, stirring from time to time to prevent a skin forming. Remove the vanilla bean. Beat the egg yolks until very thick and light in color. Then gradually beat them into the milk mixture. Return to the heat, and cook slowly until the mixture coats a spoon. Cool. Add the rum, bottle, cork tightly, and refrigerate for a day or two. Serve in liqueur glasses either as an aperitif or a liqueur.

## Tequila Sling

| | |
|---|---|
| 2 ounces tequila | Sparkling water |
| Twist of lime peel | |

Fill a tall glass half full of cracked ice; add the tequila, lime peel, and sparkling water.

## Piña Borracha

### DRUNKEN PINEAPPLE

2 cups fresh, very ripe            2 cups tequila
    pineapple, chopped

Place the pineapple and tequila in a large jar, cover securely, and refrigerate for at least 24 hours. Strain, and drink as a liqueur.

## Mexican Grasshopper

Philip S. Brown, bon vivant, cookbook writer, and food authority, gave me these excellent drinks.

1 part Kahlúa                     1 part heavy cream
1 part green *crème de*
    *menthe*

Whirl in a blender with crushed ice, and serve in a chilled cocktail glass.

## Tequila Rickey

Juice and shell of ½              Sparkling water
    lime
1½ ounces tequila

Fill a highball glass half full of ice; add the lime juice, the shell of the lime, and the tequila. Fill the glass with sparkling water, and stir.

## Mérida

1 ounce honey                     2 ounces rum
1 ounce lime juice                Sparkling water

Mix the honey, lime juice, and rum thoroughly. Pour over ice cubes in an old-fashioned glass. Serve plain; or add a dash of sparkling water.

## *Acapulco Cooler*

2 ounces rum
Juice of ½ lime

Pineapple juice

Fill a tall glass with ice cubes. Add the rum and lime juice, and fill the glass with pineapple juice. Stir.

## *Tepache*

### PINEAPPLE BEER

1 large fresh pineapple
8 cloves
2-inch stick cinnamon

4 cups brown sugar, firmly
    packed
2 cups barley

Grind up the pineapple, peel and all. Place in a large earthen-ware crock with *3 quarts of water*, the cloves, and cinnamon. Cover with a clean cloth, and allow to stand for 2 days.

Cook the barley in 1 quart of water, in a very large kettle, until the grains burst. Add the sugar; then add to the pineapple mixture. Cover again, and allow to stand another 2 days, by which time the mixture will have fermented. Line a sieve with a damp linen napkin or a double layer of dampened cheesecloth, and strain the fermented mixture. Twice, if necessary. Makes about 3 quarts.

For cooking, *Tepache* should be made with only *2 cups of brown sugar*. In Mexico, it is used in place of stock in some of the colonial dishes.

*Note*: The speed with which the beer ferments depends on the weather. If winter, it will certainly take longer than in the summer.

# Rompope Macho

## HE-MAN *ROMPOPE*

Place a couple of ice cubes in a large, stemmed wine glass. Pour in 1 ounce of light rum and 2 ounces of *Rompope*, page 281. Add a splash of sparkling water, and stir.

# Kahlúa Toreador

Another contribution from Philip Brown.

1 part Kahlúa                  1 egg white
2 parts brandy

Combine all the ingredients in a shaker with cracked ice, and shake vigorously; or blend in an electric blender with ice. Strain into a chilled cocktail glass.

# Black Russian

1 part Kahlúa                  2 parts vodka

Pour over ice cubes in an old-fashioned glass, and stir. Or stir with ice until well chilled, and strain into a chilled cocktail glass.

# Popo y Ixta

This after-dinner drink, named for the two volcanoes that overlook Mexico City, is usually made in one of two ways: A liqueur glass is filled ¾ full with Kahlúa; then enough tequila is added to bring it almost to the brim. Or the glass is filled with equal quantities of Kahlúa and tequila.

# INDEX

285

# ABOUT THE AUTHOR

Elisabeth Lambert Ortiz is the author of THE COMPLETE
BOOK OF CARIBBEAN COOKING, THE COMPLETE
BOOK OF JAPANESE COOKING, and THE BOOK OF LATIN
AMERICAN COOKING. She has traveled extensively in the
American South, Central America, the Caribbean, and the Far
East and has studied the foods and dishes unique to each area.
As a journalist, she has worked in Australia, England, Mexico,
and the United States and has written for *Gourmet* and *House
and Garden* about travel and food. She is married to a retired
United Nations official and lives in England.